THE SCIENCE OF LOVE AND ATTRACTION

The Science of Love and Attraction

The long-hidden neurobiological secrets to improve your social and romantic life

ISBN: 979-857-657-658-6

First paperback and ebook edition 2020

This book is designed to provide accurate and authoritative information regarding the subject matter covered. It is sold with the understanding that neither the publisher nor the author is engaged in rendering professional advice or services to the individual reader. The ideas, procedures, and suggestions contained in this book are not intended as a substitute for consulting with your physician. All matters regarding your health require medical supervision. Neither the author nor the publisher shall be liable or responsible for any loss or damage allegedly arising from any information or suggestion in this book.

www.love-and-attraction.com

To those seeking true love

Table of Contents

PREFACE

Love is an extraordinary feeling we have all experienced or want to experience at least once. However, we learn most things about love through our friends, movies, social media, or nondescript people who market themselves as relationship coaches. Thus, we usually have the wrong beliefs. This book presents a comprehensible synthesis of thousands of scientific studies from different fields to understand love and attraction better. It aims to convey the critical knowledge that has so far been only available to scientists to everyone. Although not all scientific papers used while writing this book are listed, there is also a very comprehensive bibliography. I am sure it will guide those who may want to have more detailed information on the science of love and attraction.

The thing that bothers me the most when I read a book is that most of them contain little useful information between pages of redundancy and unnecessary information. Unfortunately, this applies to many popular science books written about love too. It would not be appropriate for me to do something that I condemn. Yet, I also did not want this book to be like a boring textbook that only provides theoretical knowledge line by line and appeals to a limited audience. That is why I aimed to provide the most accurate and satisfying information in a balanced way that everyone would enjoy reading. Although this is a popular science book, I have also discussed some misinterpreted information in the scientific literature, such as the involvement of serotonin and phenylethylamine in love.

This book conveys the most important, interesting, and accurate scientific studies on all stages of love, from attraction to breakup. As far as I know, this is also the first work that contains all these stages in a respectable and fulfilling way. In the following pages, you will find crucial science-based information on many topics. You will discover ways to understand the unconscious flirt signals of the opposite sex. You will identify behaviors that you should avoid while flirting for a healthy relationship. You will also learn methods that will help you overcome the breakup pain easily.

The information in this book is told as if constructing a building on a foundation by putting together interconnected bricks. Thus, I tried to avoid repetition as much as possible. I either included no repetitions at all, or mentioned them briefly, or referred to what I had mentioned before. If you have not read the relevant section in places where such information is required, those topics may remain up in the air. You can read the sections that interest you separately. However, it would be most beneficial to read the book in a concentrated way from the beginning to the end, so you can truly absorb and understand the concepts better. Thus, reading the book comprehendingly will also enable you to discover many hints between the lines that I could not address in detail.

There were also times when I could not find any scientific studies on some details related to the topics I wanted to discuss in the book. At those times, I tried to guide the reader by interpreting those missing details as much as possible with my scientific knowledge and analysis. These missing details in the scientific literature will become useful hints to the neurobiologist readers of this book for their future research projects.

Unfortunately, some information in this book stands in contrast to some cultural values and idealized social norms. Although they mostly do not reflect my social standing, I gave place to these sets of information so that the book would be the most objective. Additionally, the scientific aspect of love could be conveyed most accurately because such a book would be much more beneficial to people than one that tells everyone what they want to hear or simply reflects my personal views.

The most loved books usually have happy endings. They are better remembered with the euphoria they give in the end. So, they get recommended more, get more positive reviews, and sell more. Therefore, I hesitated a lot while adding the most darksome part of love, the breakup chapter, in the book. I have questioned whether I prefer people to finish the book with a smile on their faces or finish it after seeing the bitter sides of love. However, as a scientist, I finally left aside popular concerns. I have decided that this chapter needs to be in the book to give tips to those who suffer from breakups to overcome their pain more easily. It also shows what awaits those who have not experienced a major breakup pain if they do not choose the right person.

I hope I have been able to create a work, each page of which is filled with information that will add a lot to your life. I wish you a pleasant reading. Stay with love and science.

9

M. Oktar Guloglu, Ph.D.

December 2020

INTRODUCTION

ORIGIN OF LOVE

Love... The intense feeling that caused wars, murders, and suicides... The divine feeling on which countless novels have been written, millions of songs have been sung, hundreds of thousands of movies have been made, but still, a feeling that nobody can give a consensus definition for.

What is this thing we call love? Is it this complicated? Or do we just not want to understand? To find the answers to these questions and understand love in the most accurate way, we should start by asking the most basic questions.

Is romantic love unique to humans only? Do other species fall in love as well?

There is a lot of scientific research on how some species experience love-like sentiments. However, it is impossible to touch upon every single one of them in this book. Thus, let us discuss an experiment with a simple organism: *Drosophila melanogaster*, mostly known as the fruit fly or vinegar fly.

Ulrike Heberlein and colleagues from the University of California conducted a study in 2012, which was published in Science, one of the most prestigious scientific journals in the world. According to their research, when fruit flies are sexually rejected, they behave quite similarly to humans.

In their experiment, Ulrike Heberlein and her colleagues put a group of male fruit flies in the same containers with recently mated female fruit flies. They also matched another group of male fruit flies with female fruit flies that have not mated before.

At first, all the male fruit flies are happy because there are many females in those containers. They probably say, "Oh, we fell into heaven!" However, there is something they do not take into account. Due to their nature, female fruit flies do not mate with another male if they have mated before. Thus, previously mated females reject the males no matter how much they make advances. As a result, the male fruit flies in that container cannot mate.

On the other hand, the males who are placed in the same containers with the unmated females get a response to their advances and mate with them one by one.

In the second stage of the experiment, the scientists put both groups of male fruit flies in another container. In these containers, there are two different nutrients: sugar and alcohol.

While the mated happy male flies go to the sugar in the containers, the rejected male fruit flies mostly run to the alcohol. It is impossible to know precisely what fruit flies feel as they do not have brains as advanced as ours and cannot express themselves verbally. However, do their behaviors not resemble what most people do when they are romantically rejected: drowning sorrows away!

Unfortunately, we cannot find in fruit flies more information related to the sentiment of love that we experience. However, we can deduce that love is based on the reproductive instinct in its most primitive form. Still, defining love as an advanced and sophisticated state of reproductive instinct is not enough. Because it is a feeling that not only individuals of reproductive age but also people of all ages experience.

Almost all of us had a childhood crush when we were in primary school. At that time, we were not in reproductive capacity. Similarly, people can fall in love at very advanced ages too. As in childhood, people do not have reproductive potential in their old ages. Besides, love is not just exclusive to heterosexuals. Homosexuals also fall in love. Neurobiological studies reveal that the changes in the brain and physiologies of homosexual individuals who fall in love with their same-sex partners are not different from the changes that occur to heterosexual individuals when they fall in love with someone of the opposite sex. Homosexuals feel love just like heterosexuals do. It is not possible to talk about a reproductive basis of love in this situation as well.

Besides, our behaviors when we are in love prove that it is not solely based on reproduction. When we fall in love, we concentrate on only one person. Our lives and behaviors take shape almost exclusively around them. Yet, sometimes we do not fall in love. We experience times when we have the motivation to discover life and sexuality. At those times, we can feel sexually attracted to more than one person, even on the same day. Then, what is the real motivation that lies at the foundation of love and separates it from being a purely reproductive instinct?

To find the answer to this question, we need to go beyond reproductive instincts. Why do we reproduce? Why do we feel the need to reproduce? The answer is simple: to survive!

Like all living things, we are mortal. We have a certain physiological life. This is an inevitable fact. However, reproducing allows us to transfer our genes from generation to generation, and in a sense, survive forever even if our bodies do not continue its life. Thus, reproductive motivation—in its broadest sense—is an extension of our survival instincts.

Another primitive feeling associated with our survival instinct is bonding. Except some people with certain personality disorders, we all feel committed to our loved ones, friends, parents, and children. We even observe bonding with and care for the offspring and those around them in many primitive creatures, from bees to ants. Of course, our bonding is the strongest with people who have the closest blood ties with us and those we are in love with.

In 2018, in Arizona, scientists found a fossil of an early mammal species called Kayentatherium, which lived 200 million years ago in the Jura period. The fossil displayed a mother protecting its 38 offspring and illustrates that caring for and bonding with the offspring is very strong even in very early mammals.

Recent neurobiological research also affirms that these instincts are the foundations of love. In parents' love for their children and grandparents' love for their grandchildren, not only physiologically secreted hormones but also activated brain areas show great resemblance to the activated brain areas when we fall in love with our partners. Of course, distinct from falling in love, there is no sexual drive in love for children and grandchildren.

When we transfer our genes to the next generations, we ensure their survival thanks to love and bonding. A child carries the genes not only of his parents but also of his family elders. Half of the child's genetic makeup comes from the mother and the other half from the father. It means a quarter comes from the paternal grandmother, a quarter from the paternal grandfather, a quarter from the maternal grandmother, and another quarter comes from the maternal grandfather. Thus, it is pretty normal for the family elders to have a similar love for their grandchildren, resembling parental love because the survival of the grandchild means that their genes will be passed on to the next generations safely.

The basis of love not being limited to reproduction but being an extension of our survival instinct explains the existence of this strong emotion in childhood, old age, and homosexuals. Even when there is no reproduction, establishing a bond with a partner increases our chances of survival. Because two people committed to and supported by each other are more likely to survive and live a better life than an alone individual. Just as our ancestors said, "Two heads are better than one."

Besides, reproductive instinct may still exist in homosexuals or romances at very advanced ages. With the developing medicine, individuals who have found love at a very late age can also try to have children by freezing eggs, using methods such as IVF (in vitro fertilization), surrogacy, or adoption. Similarly, homosexual couples, too, can maintain their reproductive instincts by using such methods.

The instinct of having children in homosexuals is not unique to humans. Similar to the examples observed in nature, the behavior of the gay penguin couple named Roy and Silo in the New York Central Park Zoo is also the most famous example of this instinct in other species.

In 1999, their caregivers observed that this male penguin couple also incubated during the reproductive period. With one difference: as opposed to heterosexual couples who sit on their eggs, they incubated a similarly shaped round stone that they had found instead. Watching Roy and Silo incubate a stone perfectly, the zookeepers later gave this gay couple a real egg. Having incubated this egg for 34 days, Roy and Silo eventually had a chick called "Tango." Afterward, just like other heterosexual couples, they took good care of this nestling for 2.5 months.

In the following years, other homosexual penguin couples in other zoos in different countries have been similarly recorded. They, too, successfully had offspring by incubating the eggs given to them and took care of these offspring.

Thus, for love, we can say that it is an advanced and intertwined state of reproduction and bonding, which are the two extensions of the survival instinct.

So, why and how did the two basic instincts seen even in very primitive species become this rather complex emotion we call love in humans?

EVOLUTION
LOVE

THE EVOLUTION OF LOVE

We can better understand how primeval love feeling has evolved by examining species closely related to humans. When we look at the evolutionary tree, the lifestyle of bonobo monkeys, one of our closest relatives and also known as dwarf chimpanzees, can give us a hint in this regard.

Like chimpanzees, 98% of bonobo monkeys' DNA is similar to humans. Socially, bonobo monkeys generally live in groups of 80-100. Their natural way of living is similar to small communes or tribes that our primitive ancestors lived in.

So, how are love and relationships shaped within this social group?

Bonobo monkeys are polygamous. They mate with different partners in the mating time. However, some female bonobo monkeys may also go away from the group in the breeding period with a chosen male partner from time to time. They go to nearby bushes, spend some time together and mate. Perhaps, these two individuals living together for a few days or weeks is the first version of primitive love.

Then, why and how from a few weeks of dedication to a partner observed in bonobo monkeys' love has turned into devoting oneself to a partner for months, years, and sometimes a lifetime?

When we look at humankind's evolution, our primitive ancestors, who walked on all fours 7 million years ago, rose on two legs about 3.5-4 million years ago. Studies show that compared to walking on four legs, walking on two saves around 45% of the energy we use daily.

So, even though we take the same amount of energy daily, we started using almost half of it with the influence of walking on two legs. We spent some of this remaining energy on growing our body mass. Compared to our four-legged ancestors, the body size of the human walking on his two feet increased in time.

Primitive people did not save energy only by standing on two legs. The discovery of fire around 500 thousand—1.5 million years ago and cooking food with it resulted in excess energy. Digesting food in the body is a process that requires energy. The synthesis of digestive enzymes and the breaking of chemical bonds between food molecules all require energy.

Therefore, the net calorie from food is roughly the difference between the total energy that the food has, and the energy used to digest it. Since cooking food facilitates digestion, the body uses less energy. Hence, the net energy gained from the same food is more.

In other words, when we consume raw food, the net calories we get will be less than when we eat the same food cooked[1]. Therefore, besides standing on two legs, cooking food had also provided us with excess energy during human evolution.

The human brain is an organ that weighs about 1 kilo 300 - 1 kilo 500 grams. Although it accounts for 2% of our total weight, 20-25% of the body's energy is spent on brain activities. Therefore, an important part of the extra energy gained by standing on two legs and starting to cook food was transferred to our brain's growth and development. The brain volume, which was 600 cm^3 in our primitive ancestors who walked on all fours, has increased to 1200 cm^3 in today's modern human. As our brain grew and got more complex, our cognitive power and emotions were also strengthened.

Although the growth of our brains made us smarter, it also brought some problems. One of them is the simultaneous growth of our skull that encloses and protects the brain.

Our pelvis should not be bigger than a certain size so that we can walk comfortably on two legs. However, at the same time, during human evolution, along with the growing sizes of our brain and skull, our pelvis must continuously grow to ensure the comfortable delivery of the baby. This contrasting condition is called "the obstetrical dilemma" by scientists.

---

[1] *(Author's Note):* I think those who are on a calorie restriction diet should also keep this information in mind.

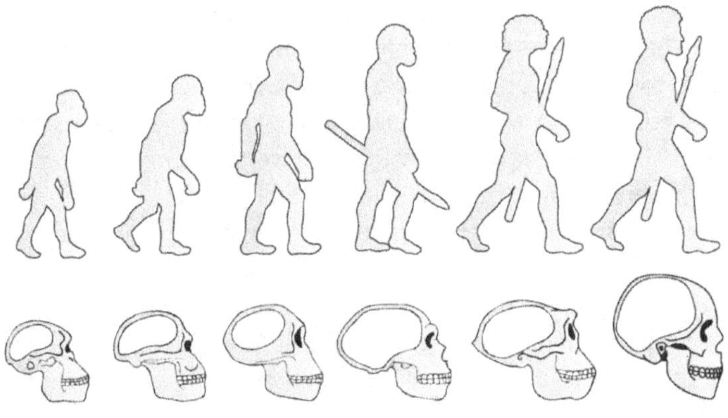

Figure 1- During human evolution, our brains have grown considerably compared to our primitive ancestors.

To cope with this dilemma, humans had begun to give birth to their babies a little earlier, before babies completed their full development. Thus, babies' heads remained at a size that would help them pass through the narrow birth canal more easily. In other words, although our nine-month and ten-day pregnancy time is accepted as a normal birth, it is a period in which the baby does not reach sufficient maturity.

Are not newborn babies too vulnerable? They are not able to grow to a maturity that would make them self-sufficient for a long time. However, when we look at other species in nature, most of them have offspring mature enough to walk and feed on their own, right after birth or within a few weeks at the latest. Thus, some obstetricians consider the first three months after birth following normal three-trimester pregnancy as the fourth trimester that should normally be spent in the womb.

As we started walking on two legs, another adaptation we had with the growth of our bodies was to reduce the number of children we had. While many other mammalian species can produce many offspring at the same time, we usually give birth to a single child. While there are occasional exceptions, such as twins, triplets, or even octuplets, each woman gives birth to a single baby in every pregnancy under normal circumstances. Because the care of more than one baby is very troublesome, especially when the baby is born in such a vulnerable state.

Let's consider how this quite troublesome situation, even in the modernized world with all the technological possibilities achieved, is in the primitive world conditions. When we look at our close relatives, the bonobo monkeys who walk on four legs, their offspring can hang on to their mothers and travel with them without being too much of a burden on their mothers while they are doing daily work. On the contrary, primitive women, who evolved to stand on two legs, had to carry their babies, who reach a considerable weight in just a few months, with their hands. Even a single baby meant that one of these hands, which these primitive women normally used to collect fruit, vegetable, and plant roots, throw stones and sticks to protect themselves when encountering wild animals, would always be occupied. If there were two babies, it meant that both hands would be occupied. This would make it difficult for primitive women to do their daily work. It would also be impossible for them to defend themselves or flee when they encountered a wild animal.

Figure 2– The offspring of bonobo monkeys, who are one of our closest relatives in the tree of evolution and walking on all fours, can easily travel by holding onto their mother's back.

In addition to our cognitive and emotional abilities that developed thanks to our growing brain when we started to walk on two legs, our babies needed more and longer care. These two brought the need for a longer duration for love in contrast to a coupling for only several days or weeks of our close relatives, bonobo monkeys, in their breeding periods.

Such a transformation has provided several advantages for men, women, and society. To better grasp these advantages, let us first draw a possible situation in which there is no love and monogamy, a situation in which polygamy prevails.

In cases where men mated with multiple females and did not establish a bond with any, women would encounter a man who was not interested in females and their children after the pregnancy and did not help in children's care. In the case where the man set up a harem with many women, almost all the burden would still be on the female since the male would have to distribute his attention and resources to many women and children.

This condition would create a disadvantage both for the good and healthy development of children and for the health of the woman who had to deal with all of this alone. Thus, the most crucial advantage of the development of love—therefore monogamy—for women was providing a relationship with a man who supports her in the child's care, helps her, and has sufficient resources to raise the child well.

The biggest advantage for the man was that he could give all his energy and resources to a single wife and child. This situation increased the chances of his children's healthy growth, as he formed a union with the number of people he could easily protect against his enemies or competitors. Thus, it increased the probability that his genes will be transferred to the next generations safely.

The advantage of love and monogamy for society is to prevent chaos and fights. In the studies on various cultures and periods in which polygamy is seen as normal and is allowed, scientists observed that polygamy gives an undue advantage to men who have better opportunities. They also observed that men above a certain level often set up a harem with 5-10, sometimes even more women.

Men having as much as women and children that they can look after may be seen as normal in terms of evolution. However, this situation's reflection on the societal order is not favorable because the number of men and women is almost equal in the world. By some men in a community having three, five, or ten wives it means that many other men will have no wives. This situation increases the competition among men for the remaining women. The studies prove that events such as thefts, lootings, and murders that damage social peace and order also increased significantly in those societies. Theft and looting made to collect the bride price prevailing in some of these communities are the best examples of this situation.

Love has evolved to overcome all these negativities. It is a feeling that will ensure that we have a long-term relationship with a single person and support them. In this way, the healthy transfer of our genes to future generations is guaranteed.

I love you!

THE STAGES OF LOVE

Because of the love at first sight scenes seen in novels and movies, many people think that love always happens like that in real life too. In fact, to fall in love with somebody, it is necessary to go through some stages.

The first of these stages is attraction. To fall in love, we first need to like particular physical, personality, or social characteristics of a person. Still, we don't usually fall in love with every person we like. Sometimes we can like a girl or a guy who comes across while walking on the street. We can appreciate their good looks. However, this attraction does not make us fall in love with that person. Similarly, no matter how much we like the actors and actresses we see on tv or in cinemas, and no matter how much platonic love we have for them, we do not fall in love with those people under normal circumstances.

The stage that we have to go through to fall in love after attraction is developed is intimacy. Thus, the accessibility of the other person is essential to fall in love. We do not have the chance to get closer to people we cannot physically reach. You have a meager chance of re-encountering someone you saw and liked while walking on the crowded streets of New York. You are also not likely to share the same social environment and get closer to the actors you see on television or cinema. So, no matter how much we like these people, it is difficult to develop a sense of love towards them.

For this reason, we do not fall in love with a charming person passing down the street. However, we can easily fall in love with someone who is in the same class or workplace as us and has more modest qualities since those people are more accessible to us. If the people we saw on that street, cinema or television were in our social circle and we could reach them, of course, we could fall in love with them too.

We call the time we spend to get intimate with the person we are attracted to flirting. If we get close enough during flirting, and if our attraction is increased as we get to know each other in terms of personal characteristics and harmony, we will start to feel attached to the other person.

Bonding is the last stage of love. If we do not sufficiently feel attached to the other person, love will not develop much, and our relationship will be short-lived. However, if we are adequately connected, love grows more intensively, and we begin to have a long-term romantic relationship.

While generally passing through all these stages for its development, love may not always follow a linear path. For example, a relationship that starts with the intention of being short-term can evolve into a long-term romantic relationship if people get more attached as they get to know each other better.

While all these stages are necessary to fall in love, there is a prerequisite that is much more critical than all. For a person to fall in love, first, they need to want to fall in love.

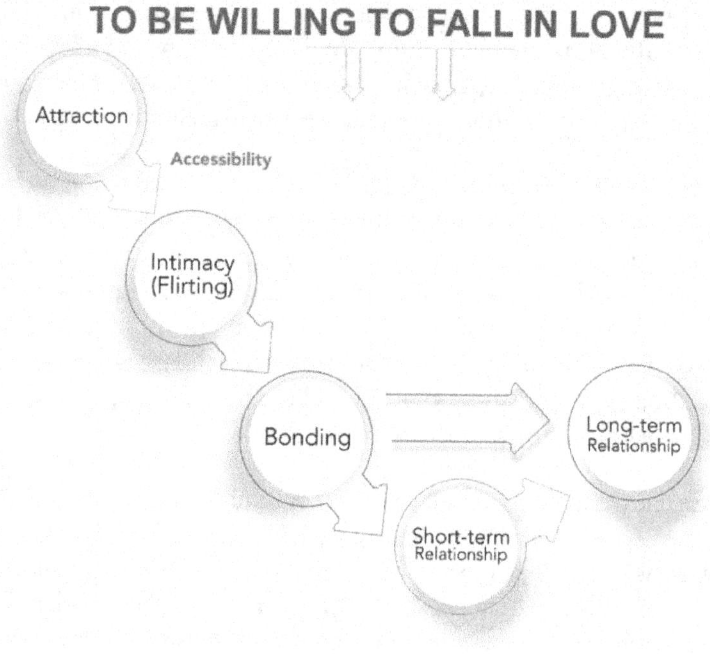

Figure 3– Love is a feeling that usually occurs after the stages of attraction, intimacy and bonding. However, the most important factor for all this to happen is wanting to fall in love and have a relationship.

Regardless of our motivation, whether we are bored of loneliness, seeking an adventure, or feeling psychologically and financially ready for marriage, we must first want to fall in love with someone and have a relationship. Without this, it is not possible to fall in love with any person.

For example, sometimes, we may not feel psychologically ready to have a new relationship due to the traumas we experienced in our previous relationships. Sometimes we can close ourselves to relationships for a while because of the workload in our business life or to concentrate on our career. Sometimes, people can also isolate themselves for a while because they think their financial status does not allow socializing for dating. In such cases, it may not be possible to fall in love no matter how much the other person is the right one or how hard they try.

ATTRACTION

While our brains grew during evolution, the most significant development occurred in the region called the prefrontal cortex. This region makes up 3.5% of the brain in cats, 11.5% in macaque monkeys, 17% in chimpanzees, and 29% in humans.

Our orbitofrontal cortex (OFC), the front-bottom part of our prefrontal cortex, is where the most development is observed during evolution. It is responsible for logical thinking, decision making, planning, value determination, personality, and intelligence. When it comes to love, OFC assumes an essential task: attraction. When we are attracted to someone, our orbitofrontal cortex is one of the primary areas activated in our brain.

Attraction is limited in primitive species whose orbitofrontal cortex is not as developed as ours. Contrary to us, they have no advanced attraction criteria. They are not attracted to the beauty of eyes, intelligence, or personality, etc. Some mate with an entirely coincidental partner, some with an individual who does the correct courtship dance or has a prominent physical feature, and some mate with the group's alpha male, as in our close relatives: chimpanzees.

With the evolution of love, our attraction criteria became more complicated than other living species. This complexity allowed us to choose more suitable partners and have healthier children to ensure the continuation of our genes.

Attraction is the first and most crucial stage of love. We do not fall in love with a person we do not like in terms of physical, personality, and social characteristics. In this chapter, we will discuss the features people get attracted to in a partner and the biological and evolutionary causes behind these choices. One of the critical tips that we will cover in this chapter is how to increase our physical attractiveness with small touches based on scientific data.

Increasing our physical attractiveness with the right touches not only enables us to be more successful in our romantic relationships but also provides us with significant advantages in many other areas, including our business and social lives. Because of this importance, I give a very detailed space to the attraction chapter of this book.

Before that, I should remind you of something about this chapter. The features that emerged from scientific studies on attractiveness reflect only the majority. Although they show similarities between cultures and communities, some people's inclinations may differ from these values.

For example, while the most desirable body mass index value in the opposite sex is between 20-22, some of us may find much slimmer people far below this value more attractive. Similarly, some also may find overweight people far above this value more attractive.

Of course, there is no such thing as a perfect person. Although our closest state to the scientifically proven ideal features increases our probability of finding a potential romantic partner, sometimes we can be very attractive to them with one of our strong qualities, though we may lack in some others. In other words, people can ignore certain deviations from these ideal features if we have other qualities to compensate.

When a potential romantic partner appears, our brain scans them within the first few seconds and decides whether we like them. Their face, body, smell, and character—as far as we can judge from their body language and facial expressions in those first moments—determine our opinion about that person.

So, what does our brain actually look for when deciding whether somebody is attractive? What do these physical and personality traits reflect?

The physical traits of the person give our brain several critical information. One of them is the general health status of that person. This is perhaps the most crucial information that our brain gets from their physical traits during the few seconds of scanning a potential partner. The answers to various questions, from the health of that person to whether they have the good genes that they can pass on to our potential child, are coded in many different physical features, from their hair to teeth, from their leg size to the distribution of fat in their body.

Another feature that our brains look for when scanning our potential partners is their reproductive potential. "Is the person at reproductive age and potential?" "If we end up together, do we have a child or children?" Our brain can find the answers to such questions just by looking at a possible romantic partner's physical traits.

Since men can maintain their reproductive potential for many years, this is a more prominent feature for women. Because the reproductive potential of women starts with menstruation and ends with menopause. With today's technology, women can have children at much later ages. They can freeze eggs, even embryos, and then, with the help of different therapies or surrogacy in certain countries, women can have babies in their 50s or 60s. However, since love is a feeling that has evolved over millions of years, we need to consider the basis of all the traits that our brains look for, according to the conditions of our primitive ancestors.

For example, raising a single child healthily is already challenging in itself, even these days. Was it possible under the primitive conditions of our ancestors? It was quite likely to lose that single child with diseases or wild animal attacks, but if we had several children, we could at least raise one of them healthy. Therefore, one of the qualities that our brains look for, especially in women, is the potential of having more than one child. The most significant indicator of this is the age of our potential partner.

Having enough resources for the health and care of the children is another feature that our brains look for in a potential partner, and this mostly applies to men. When a woman meets a potential partner, her brain questions: "Will this man help me to raise our children, or will he leave?" "Does he have enough resources to raise our children healthily?"

When the matter is to be attracted to a person's physical characteristics, the first question that comes to mind is whether our attraction criteria really have a biological foundation. Is everything primitive and instinctive in attraction, which is the first step in this feeling of love that has evolved over millions of years? Or, instead of looking for clues such as health and reproductive potential, is our brain sometimes in an illusion because of certain features that are imposed on society and idealized in the media? If that is the case, how much of these physical characteristics presented on colorful pages and screens affect our liking?

To find the answer to these questions, Langlois and his friends from Texas Austin University in the USA designed attraction experiments on a few months-old babies. There is a reason why the scientists chose a few months-old babies for these experiments. Unlike adults, babies are not affected by the concepts of beauty imposed in newspapers, magazines, and televisions. Since their brain development is not complete, they are mostly acting with their primitive impulses.

In the experiment, the scientists presented two groups of photographs to the babies: pictures of people whom adults consider attractive and photos of people whom adults find unattractive. They observed that both the 2-3-month-old babies and the 6-8-month-old babies in the study stared at the pictures of the more attractive people longer and more carefully than the photos of less-attractive people.

In the following years, many scientists showed similar results, meaning one thing: Our attraction criteria are mostly instinctive and not affected by the perception of beauty imposed by the media.

Besides, many studies in different societies and cultures reveal that the attraction criteria are mostly universal. However, sometimes some may vary slightly for various reasons.

HALO EFFECT

Attractiveness is a feature that gives us an advantage not only in our love life but also in our business and social life, leading us to reach our goals more quickly. This is due to the halo effect, known in psychology.

In 1977, Richard Nisbett and Timothy DeCamp Wilson from the University of Michigan showed the existence of the halo effect. The effect states that if we find someone physically attractive, we assume the other traits of that person as positive as well. In a word, our brain tends to categorize people as black or white, rather than including grays. In the following years, many studies showed that we perceive attractive people as smarter, more lovable, and funnier. Studies also revealed that we could create these prejudices even if we look at the person's face for just 100 milliseconds.

Because of this halo effect, attractive people earn higher salaries than their peers and climb the career ladder faster. Even when they commit a crime, jurors show leniency towards them, so they are sentenced less than unattractive people.

For example, in an experiment conducted in 2013, Busetta and her colleagues sent 11008 CVs to 1542 job advertisements published for about a year. They sent 8 CVs with the same content, but four of them did not have any photos while the other four had photographs, one of which had an attractive man's photo, the other one an attractive woman's photo, the other one an ugly male's photo, and the last one an unattractive woman's photo. Their results are quite interesting.

The CV sent with an attractive woman's photo received 54% positive response from the employers. In comparison, the positive response rate of the same CV sent with an ugly woman's picture remained at only 7%. Although this difference was less in men, it was still close to 2 times.

While the same CV sent with an attractive male's photo received 47% positive response from the employers, their positive response rate to the unattractive male's photo remained at only 26%. So, because of the halo effect, being attractive can put the person in an almost eight times more advantageous position in women and two times more advantageous in men than their peers who have the same resume and want to get the same job.

Then, what are these universal attractiveness criteria that give us an advantage not only in love but also in other areas? What we instinctively like the most in the opposite sex? What are the main reasons we like these features? How can we increase our attractiveness with some minor touches?

FACE

When we meet someone, the first and most important part we pay attention to is their face. Different regions of our face not only contain information about our health and reproductive potential but also give clues about our personality and intentions through mimics.

The contribution of each region to our physical attractiveness and the information it contains is different. And our brain has the ability to scan and evaluate all these features within a few seconds. Let us discuss these features and their meanings, which our brain instinctively scans.

FACIAL CONTRAST

One of the most important criteria when evaluating someone as attractive is facial contrast. While this contrast is higher in women, it is less in men. Therefore, as this contrast increases in women and decreases in men, they are seen as more attractive. So, what is this facial contrast?

Three areas on our face create this contrast. These are the tone difference of the eyebrows, eyes, lips, and their respective surrounding tissues.

Facial contrast generally decreases in humans as they get older. Pigmentation decreases with advancing age, which reduces the contrast on our face, making us look older. At the beginning of this chapter, we talked about how women's reproductive potential, therefore young age, is a trait that our brains scan in attraction. That is why the high facial contrast in women representing the younger age looks more attractive to men. As for men, their reproductive potential continues to much later ages. Older age is often seen as a feature in which a person begins to obtain social status and other resources. Therefore, low facial contrast is preferred in men, representing later ages.

Applying makeup is the external intervention that affects our facial contrast the most. For thousands of years, women have been increasing their facial contrast by wearing makeup, making them look younger and more attractive. According to the known written history, makeup has been in use for at least 5500 years since the ancient Egyptians and Sumerians. Since this dating is based on written sources, we can only know this much. But the real history of finding and using makeup probably goes back much earlier than that. That is to say, women have been using makeup for thousands of years to increase their facial contrast, look younger and more beautiful, and these makeup tricks have deceived men for thousands of years!

If a man has not lived in a cave for his lifetime, he can easily understand whether a woman is wearing makeup, and he is being deceived by these makeup tricks. So, why do men still find makeup attractive? The answer to this question is very simple: our primitive brain.

You remember the attraction experiment conducted with babies mentioned in the previous section. Even a few months-old babies looked longer and more attentive to people that adults find attractive. When we consider that babies' brains have not completed their development yet and have not acquired the ability to think logically, we could say that babies act mostly with their primitive brains.

When it comes to attraction, we act similarly, too. In other words, even though the part of our brain responsible for logical thinking is sure that the person in front of us is wearing makeup, the more primitive side of our brain, which is dominant when it comes to attraction, finds makeup attractive because it increases the facial contrast.

Makeup not only increases facial contrast but also, by removing skin imperfections and highlighting facial features, makes the person look healthier and more aesthetically pleasing with recently found techniques such as concealer, foundation, and contour application. Unfortunately, there is not much that men can do about this deception because our primitive brain steps in when it comes to attraction.

Do we men always get tricked by these makeup tricks because of our primitive brain's weakness? No! At least in 18th century England, a very serious law called "Swords 77" was enacted against women deceiving men with such makeup tricks.

"All women of whatever age, rank, profession, or degree, whether virgin maid or widow, that shall from and after such Act impose upon, seduce, and betray into matrimony and of His Majesty's subjects by means of scent, paints, cosmetics, washes, artificial teeth, false hair, Spanish wool, ironstays, hoops, high-heeled shoes, or bolstered hips, shall incur the penalty of the law now in force against witchcraft and like misdemeanors, and that the marriage upon conviction shall stand null and void (Swords 77)."

Women who seduced a man with makeup were on trial for charges of witchcraft under this law, at least for a certain period in medieval England. Women of today should be thankful that the politicians of that time, who regarded an innocent makeup equivalent to witchcraft, do not live today. Because we do not even want to guess what punishment would be given to those who apply techniques such as Botox, collagen fillers, contours to concealers, and aesthetic operations that almost recreate a woman.

Putting on makeup increases the attractiveness of women, but how much makeup is best? Is it a light makeup, a moderate makeup, or a heavy makeup?

In 2011, a study led by Nancy Etcoff and her colleagues from Harvard University revealed that male subjects found the woman more attractive as the makeup level in the same woman increased. However, even the highest makeup level used in this study is usually around the average amount of makeup women recently use daily or slightly below it. Therefore, you should not look at the results of this research and wear heavy makeup as if you were putting war paint. Because the same study also shows that although glamorous makeup increases women's attractiveness, their perceived trustworthiness decreases as the makeup amount increases.

In fact, it is useful to listen to your instincts about the amount of makeup you do. Even a makeup little under that may be the best according to the research done by Alex Jones and his colleagues from England. In this joint study at Aberdeen and Bangor universities, subjects were asked to apply various amounts of makeup, and photographs of these were taken. Afterward, they were asked which makeup amount they liked the most, which they thought other women would like the most, and other men would like the most. The results are interesting. All subjects thought that both other women and other men would like more than the amount of makeup they liked. The results are even more interesting when photographs of women in these different makeup amounts were shown to other subjects, both men and women, and were asked which one looks best on the person. The subjects of both sexes expressed that a makeup that is slightly below the amount that the woman normally likes in themselves looks the most attractive.

In addition to the physical effect of makeup on women's attractiveness, it has another positive contribution. The correct makeup also increases women's self-confidence. Accordingly, when a woman wears a makeup that she likes, her behavior and mood also change. In addition to facial contrast, this increase in self-confidence in women also appeals to men.

EYES

Our eyes are a contrast region, thus, an area of attraction on our face. When we look at someone's face, we mostly concentrate on the eyes of that person first.

High facial contrast in women is essential for attractiveness. Thus, highlighting the eyes and surroundings and making them appear a little larger increases women's attractiveness. With various makeup tricks, eyes are not only made more apparent but also larger. Since I am not a makeup artist, I cannot go into the details of how these makeup tricks are applied. Still, you can easily find such techniques on the internet in great detail.

So, how about men? In contrast to women, the attractiveness of men increases with slightly smaller and narrower eyes.

Pupils play a vital role in attractiveness as much as the eyes. When we like someone, our pupils dilate involuntarily under the influence of our sympathetic nervous system, even though we are not aware of it. This enlargement signals to the primitive brain of the people that our thoughts towards them are positive. Thus, enlarged pupils not only increase our appeal but also signals trustworthiness to people. Actually, in a way, not our eyes but our pupils are the windows of the soul.

Studies reveal that when someone wants to borrow money while their pupils are dilated, people are much more likely to lend money to them. So, while asking someone to lend money, asking your boss to raise your salary, or asking your dad to increase your pocket money, enlarging your pupils will increase your chances of getting a positive response. In addition to these, if you put photos of yourself with dilated pupils on Instagram, Facebook, Tinder, etc., you will get more likes. This phenomenon is also true for job applications. If you live in a country where CVs with photos are allowed, and you attach a photo of yourself with dilated pupils, your chances of positive return will improve.

Although scientific studies rediscovered the positive effect of enlarging our pupils on our attractiveness recently, this effect was known to women in medieval Italy much earlier. They used fluid from a special plant, *Atropa belladonna*, to dilate their pupils and increase their appeal.

The atropine substance in the *Atropa* plant relaxes the muscles that control the pupils, causing them to enlarge. Indeed, the plant got its Latin name according to these characteristics. *Atropa* comes from atropine that the plant secretes, and *belladonna* comes from the adjective clause that means beautiful woman in Italian.

Although atropine dilates our pupils, long-term and uncontrolled use of this substance may cause some adverse effects, including temporary blindness! Thus, using other methods than atropine to dilate our pupils is much safer for our health.

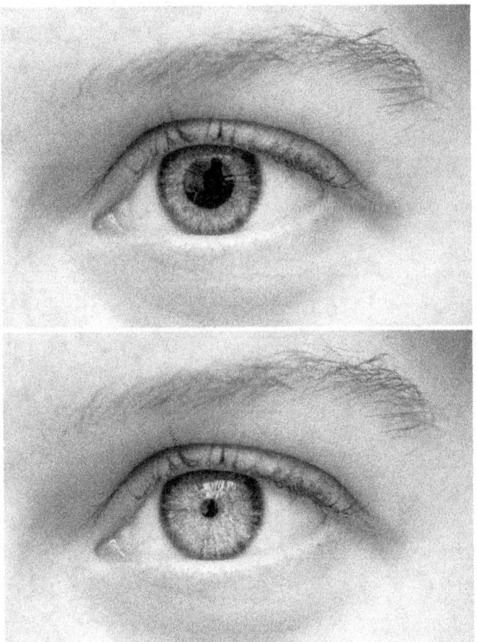

Figure 4- Dilated pupils increase our attractiveness.

One of these methods is to look away. When we speak to the person we like, if we focus our eyes not on their eyes but on a distant imaginary spot in the same direction on the back of their head, our pupils will enlarge involuntarily. Thus, we will seem more attractive to the other person. Since we focus our eyes on a distant point, we may see that person slightly blurry, but for the attraction, how they see us is more important than how we see them.

Another way to enlarge the pupils is through dim light. In a dark place where the lights are reduced, our pupils dilate. Considering that candlelight dinners lead to the dilation of both sides' pupils, the reason for such ambiances triggering romance can be better understood.

Although our brain is a highly advanced organ, our primitive brain is often incapable of distinguishing between imagination and reality. So, we do not have to be strictly in dim light to dilate our pupils. Even under normal light, if we imagine that we are in dim light and concentrate enough on it, we can fool our brain and enlarge our pupils.

In addition to these, other tricks to dilate our pupils are to think of the other person as naked, to squeeze our stomach, or to solve a hard math problem in our minds.

There is also an interesting phenomenon reflected in the study results about the effects of cognitive activities on pupil dilation. Sometimes we can tell whether someone is smart as soon as we see them. Although we do not know exactly how we guess this, we often say, "It is obvious from their eyes that they are smart." A study by Jason Tsukahara and his colleagues from the Georgia Institute of Technology in 2016 may give us a clear answer behind this instinct. According to their results on 358 subjects, the baseline pupil size is larger in smarter people than others. Therefore, we can say that a big pupil acts as a sign of not only attraction but also intelligence.

The color of our eyes is another attraction factor. Many people find light-colored eyes, especially blue and green, more attractive. Many of us think that people with light-colored eyes are more attractive because they are much less common in society. Although being rare has an influence, the underlying instinctual reason for this appeal may be very different from what we anticipated.

When someone is attracted to us, our primitive brain senses their involuntarily dilating pupils, even though we are not aware of it. So, whose pupils can be seen the most easily? People with light-colored eyes. In a sense, we can read a person with light eye colors like an open book. It is precisely for this reason that people with light-colored eyes may be more preferred by our subconscious, as we can understand them more easily.

What about dark eyes? It is challenging to distinguish the black pupil in a dark eye. Therefore, if somebody has dark eyes, it becomes difficult for our brain to understand their feelings and thoughts from the pupils. This gives the individuals with dark eyes a more mysterious aura and a mysterious charm.

EYEBROWS

Although they are especially effective in emphasizing women's youth, perhaps the most neglected and mistaken facial contrast area is the eyebrows. They should be as contrasting as possible with the tone of the surrounding tissue. However, when hairdressers dye a woman's hair in a light color, they often dye her eyebrows in the same light color to make them look more natural. This lowers a person's facial contrast. When we look at the natural blondes in the Scandinavian countries, we see that their eyebrows are mostly at least a few tones darker than their regular hair. Therefore, dying the eyebrows with the same light blond color as the hair is both unnatural and also reduces the facial contrast, making the person look older.

The contribution of eyebrows to our attractiveness is not limited only to facial contrast. Their shape and distance to the eyes are also effective in our appeal and youthful appearance.

Figure 5- Natural blondes in the Nordic countries mostly have eyebrows a few tones darker than their hair.

When we get older, collagen production in our skin decreases. The skin loses its elasticity and gradually sags with gravity. When our skin is sagging, our eyebrows go down with it, a little lower than they typically are, and the distance between our eyes and eyebrows gets shortened.

The decrease in the distance between the eyebrows and the eyes makes especially women look less attractive since it signals old age. This is why when plucking their eyebrows, perhaps instinctively, women often reduce the eyebrows near their eyes. Thus, they increase the distance between the eyebrows and the eyes. The thinning of the eyebrows and the increase of this distance also increase the attractiveness by making the eyes look a little bigger and more prominent.

So, how thin should we pluck our eyebrows? Every person should find this according to their eyebrow shape and facial structure. However, considering its effects on the facial contrast, a very thin eyebrow will not look very attractive, reducing the clarity in the facial contrast. It would be best to pluck the eyebrows in the amount that will increase the distance between the eyes and the eyebrows and make the eyes more prominent, but not in the amount that will reduce the facial ratios and contrast. One should find the right balance between the two.

LIPS

Another contrast area on our faces is our lips. It is an area of attraction in women not only due to the contrast created by its tone difference with the surrounding tissue but also by its thickness. For this reason, especially recently, most girls wear lipsticks in a way to make their lips look fuller.

So, why do men find fuller lips more attractive? There are two different biological reasons behind this. First, they emphasize facial contrast a little more, as fuller lips are more prominent. The other reason is that estrogen, known as the female hormone, thickens the lips in the person, while testosterone, known as the male hormone, thins the lips.

Contrary to popular belief, both sexes have estrogen and testosterone hormones. Only their proportions vary by gender. As women age, their estrogen hormone levels decrease, especially after menopause. When estrogen hormone levels drop, testosterone hormone shows its effects more prominently in women. As one of these effects, women's lips begin to thin with age. Thus, the fuller lips in women give this signal to the primitive brain of the opposite sex "My estrogen level is higher; I'm younger; I'm more of a female." That is why women instinctively try to make their lips look bigger than they are by various methods, such as silicone fillings or lining the lips with lipstick.

Lipsticks play two roles in the attractiveness of women. The first one is related to the fullness of their lips. When women overline their lips and apply lipstick, their lips look thicker. The second is related to the colors of lipstick because it increases facial contrast. In fact, any lipstick color that enhances the contrast appeals to men. Therefore, even the unnatural black color can stand attractive with this effect. Scientists have also researched wearing which lipstick color looks the most appealing to the opposite sex. The result of the study is not surprising. It shows that men prefer red lipsticks the most in women.

SKIN

The skin on our face is another critical factor for attractiveness. It carries information about our health, age, and even our social status. Thus, women and men worldwide spend billions of dollars every year on cosmetics and aesthetic products and interventions without any hesitation.

A smooth skin signals that we are healthy in many aspects, from our immune system to our circulatory system, the state of our internal organs, especially our liver, and our hormonal balance. If we have ever experienced a problem in one of these, even in a certain period, it is reflected in our skin in the form of an oriental sore spot, acne scars, and similar scars and irregularities in its tone and texture.

That is why, if we have different defects on our skin, we usually seek ways to get rid of or reduce these by using various methods, such as cosmetic creams, peeling, or laser treatment. The results of scientific studies support the importance of the skin on our attractiveness in both women and men. When scientists altered the skin tissues of the subjects in photographs, their attractiveness values changed significantly.

Our skin also reflects the state of our physiological health. For example, while a red skin shows a healthy metabolism that is well vascularized and filled with plenty of oxygenated blood, yellow skin may indicate hepatitis, and bluish skin may indicate a metabolism with various circulatory problems.

Estrogen hormone also takes part in vascularizing the skin on women's faces. A well-veined skin filled with oxygenated blood will appear redder, where the vessels are close to the surface. Therefore, the reddish blush that women use on their cheeks as a makeup trick actually signals to men, "I have a good vascularity on my skin; thus, my estrogen level is high, and my health is excellent."

Blush can also have another positive effect on women's appeal. When we get excited, our sympathetic nervous system causes our body to give some reactions. Some of these reactions, such as the dilation of our pupils, are perceived subconsciously by others. Some other changes caused by our sympathetic nervous system are the expansion of our veins and the increase of our heart rate, causing an increase in the blood flow.

This causes the veins on the already thin facial skin to become more pronounced and redden our faces. This redness may go to the primitive brains of the people as a positive signal that shows we value them, causing them to like us more and treat us better. For example, when someone is teasing us, the cheeks of many of us become red. However, we do not feel this sense of embarrassment from everyone. Our faces will only flush against those we value or like. When someone we care little about, like a beggar we see on the road, says the same thing, embarrassment and the blushing of our cheeks do not happen. That is why the artificial redness created by applying blush may signal to people's subconscious that we value them and make them approach us more positively.

As our skin ages, it begins to fade, wrinkle, sag, and often accumulate various spots. That is the reason why our skin is also a region that signals our age to others. People who want to look younger try to get rid of the sagging and wrinkles that occur with aging using various approaches, from cosmetic creams to surgical interventions.

So, to what degree do these methods work? Although such practices make the person look younger than they are, the effects are not significant enough to rejuvenate 10-20 years, contrary to what many believe. For example, studies on photographs of people in their 60s reveal that wrinkle removal with a laser makes the persons appear on an average of 2.5 years younger, and wrinkle removal with Photoshop software makes the persons look 3.6 years younger on average. In another study conducted with people around the age of 40, scientists found that face-lifting with cosmetic surgery makes people 4.6 years younger on average. When we evaluate these results, we can say the aesthetic operations performed on our skin make us look younger. Still, the effect of these operations on our perceived age is only limited to 3-4 years. Because when we look at somebody, our brain does not use a single criterion to estimate their age, thus, their reproductive potential. It tries to reach the most accurate estimate by evaluating many factors. So, manipulating a single factor to look younger does not dramatically change our brains' age prediction.

A comparative study carried out by Canadian and American scientists in 2012 also has results that support our brains' multi-criteria evaluation theory. According to this study, subjects who had only undergone face and neck lifting operations were perceived only 5.7 years younger than their actual age. In contrast, individuals who had undergone all the face, neck, forehead, and lower upper eyelid lifting (Blepharoplasty) operations looked 8.4 years younger.

Our skin also serves as an indicator of our social status. A smooth velvety skin hints that the person is healthy and often has the resources to protect this condition. Not only our skin structure but also our skin tone gives information to other peoples' subconscious about our social status.

Before the modernization era, common people would generally work in the fields, while the nobility or people with high status would mostly stay indoors. Someone working in a field is much more exposed to sunlight. This led to the lower class having both a much darker skin and a higher number of and deeper wrinkles due to UV light's collagen-breaking effect. On the contrary, those with higher status had a lighter skin tone, as they were not overexposed to sunlight. In fact, the variance in skin tone because of this status difference has even been the subject of some folk songs in some countries.

Today, with transportation development, people can go to very distant places and countries within a few hours whenever they want. While an average white or blue-collar has to save money for months for a week's summer vacation, people in a high status with a good income can easily go to the beaches in tropical countries in winter and get tanned. They can even have a similar sun-tan with a ski vacation in the mountains. Thus, even though our primitive brain does not, our advanced brain may perceive bronze-skinned people as having a higher status. Tanning also contributes to the person's attractiveness by making skin imperfections, tone, and color differences less apparent.

Tanning does not always contribute positively to our attractiveness. It also has some negative effects. Our facial contrast consists of the tonal difference between our lips, eyes and eyebrows, and the surrounding tissue. The tissue around these organs that affects facial contrast is our skin. When our skin gets darker with tanning, the facial contrast decreases.

Since high facial contrast is an indicator of youth, lighter skin tones increase the attractiveness of women. Research carried out in 51 different countries revealed that in 47 of these countries, men prefer women with lighter skin. Ninety-four percent (94%) is a pretty high rate!

When we compare the same woman's photos with tanned and normal skin, we see that they look older and less attractive in their tanned photos because their facial contrasts had decreased. Normally, tanning is beneficial both for attractiveness by covering skin imperfections and for health with vitamin D synthesized during sunbathing. However, considering its negative effect on facial contrast, women need to do tanning within reason.

That is also why women should prefer darker makeup to their lips and eyes to keep their facial contrasts high when they get tanned. Of course, eyebrows should not be forgotten because sunlight also breaks down the color pigments. Even though our living skin synthesizes a large amount of melanin and compensates for it, and thus, we get a tan, our hair and body hair are dead tissues. The color pigments in our eyebrows, which are fragmented by UV rays, cannot be replaced. Therefore, the hair and eyebrows of many of us turn into lighter tones in summer. Since the decrease in this eyebrow tone will affect our facial contrast, it must be compensated by various makeup methods.

In men, tanning increases attractiveness in every way. It is a social status indicator these days; it covers skin imperfections and provides low facial contrast. So, unlike women, men can comfortably get a tan.

MASSETER MUSCLE

Another point on our face that affects our attractiveness is the jaw, or the *masseter* muscle, its scientific name. Since these muscles typically grow under the influence of testosterone, it is a preferred element, especially in men's attractiveness. Although testosterone is essential for the growth of these muscles, it is not the only factor. Bruxism, known as the disease of grinding teeth, while sleeping at night, and chewing gum intensely also enlarge one's jaw muscles.

All these factors cause the growth of jaw muscles not only in men but also in women; however, unlike men, large and prominent jaw muscles are not preferred in women. Whether due to excess testosterone, or bruxism, or excessive chewing of the gum, some women's jaw muscles are prominent, thus their faces look masculine. There is a straightforward fix that turns this appearance into a more alluring feminine look: Botox!

When applied correctly by an expert, masseter Botox causes the jaw muscles to relax and weaken. They become indistinct after a few applications. If your jaw muscles are prominent for any reason, and this look bothers you as a woman, you can easily find a solution to this problem with the Botox treatment from a specialist.

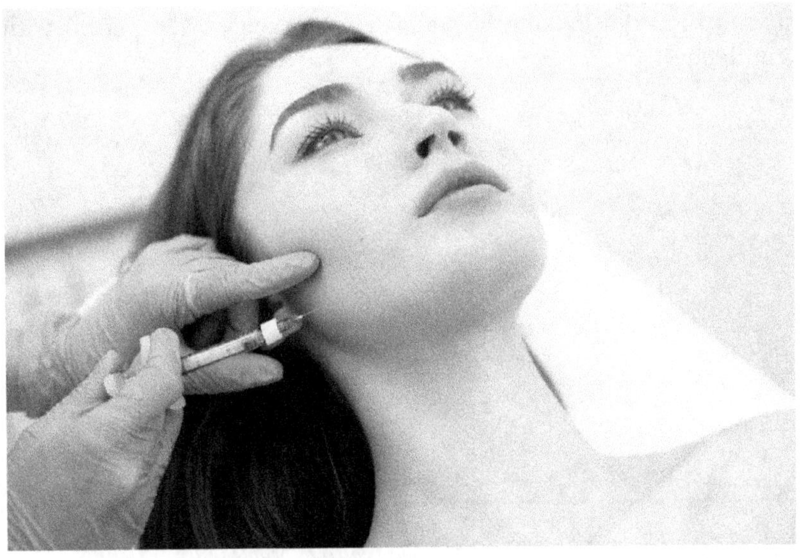

Figure 6– Botox application weakens the prominent masseter muscles in women and gives them a more feminine look.

Men whose jaw muscles are not noticeable can have these areas filled for a more masculine look. Fillings are, of course, not the only remedy. Those who do not have the financial resources or do not want an external intervention on their face can also make these muscles more prominent and have a more masculine facial structure over time by chewing plenty of gum.

HAIR

Our hair is another indicator of our health. Therefore, it is a feature of attraction, especially in women. Although today there are many cosmetic products from shampoos to hair conditioners and serums for the care and healthier look of our hair, our primitive ancestors did not have such opportunities. That is why, nutritional disorders, diseases, and infections caused by neglect or a weakened immune system would reflect on their hair as dullness, splitting, infestation with lice, dandruff, etc.

This evolutionary and biological basis is the main reason why the same person's hair will be more attractive to the subconscious of the opposite sex when it is well-kept and healthy than neglected. Besides, a woman who had her hair done at a hairdresser and is pleased with the result feels much more confident than with neglected hair. Since confidence increases attractiveness in both sexes, healthy and beautiful-looking hair adds extra appeal to the person with this extra confidence.

Figure 7- Long and well-kept hair signals good health to people's subconscious.

It is a fact that the longer our hair, the harder it is to care for. Moreover, long hair is also an indicator of a person's health status over a longer period. In this respect, longer hair appears as an additional attraction factor for women. In fact, this situation is so reflected in the subconscious of women. For example, when they go to the hairdresser and have the split ends trimmed, they mostly regret and freak out as if their hair was buzz-cut.

Not only our hair being well-groomed and healthy, but also its color and style play a part in our attractiveness. When describing a beautiful woman, most men emphasize blondness as an attraction factor.

When we examine the biological causes underlying this attraction, studies show that the average estrogen levels of blondes are slightly higher than brunettes. Therefore, the facial features of natural blondes often have more feminine lines.

Besides, light-colored hair makes the person look younger, while dark-colored hair makes them look a few years more mature. Although blondes are considered more feminine and physically preferred for all these reasons, blondness does not have a positive image in every respect. Studies show that men have various negative prejudices about blonde women. They think blonde women are less skilled and less successful.

Figure 8- Dark-colored hair makes the person look a few years more mature than blonde hair.

In contrast to blondness in women, scientific research revealed that the preferred hair color in men is dark hair, which symbolizes maturity and strength. Many women today describe a characteristic attractive man as being tall, brunette, and masculine.

But this attraction to brunettes can also be periodic and cultural. Researches show that in many cultures in the Middle Ages, from Vikings to Russians, Germans to Celts, men lightened their hair or beard with a soap made from wood ash and goat fat. Blondness and redness were privileged and preferred not only in women but also in men. On the basis of this cultural liking, the use of this natural soap also for killing lice may have a role. Men with light-colored hair may be preferred because they may be seen as people who regard their personal care and hygiene and have the resources to do so.

Like the color of the hair, its style is also an important factor in women's attractiveness. Hair can be loose and natural, or buns can be made as on special occasions, or different styles such as ponytails can be chosen as a freer and more comfortable style. So, which of them is the most appealing to the opposite sex? According to the research done by the French scientist Nicolas Gueguin, men prefer mostly loose, natural hair in women.

Unfortunately, there is not as much scientific study on the effects of hair on men's attractiveness as there are on the effects of various factors, from the hairstyle to the hair length, on the women's appeal. Studies mostly focus on the impact of hair loss on the attractiveness of men.

Baldness is a condition that affects many men. Although those men's hair loss starts in the age of twenties, it intensifies between thirties and forties. In addition to the physical change caused by the loss of hair, this transformation's stress and anxiety also cause loss of self-confidence.

Although baldness is undesirable by almost all men, studies show that it has some positive effects. Bald men are perceived as smarter, more dominant, and with more leadership potential than men with sparse or full hair. Considering that hair loss increases with age, it is normal for them to be perceived as older than they are. In addition, the experience and knowledge we gain as we age generally make us smarter. This may be the reason why bald men are subconsciously considered more intelligent by others. However, research studying hair loss's effect on physical attractiveness also reveals that men who are made bald digitally in their photos look older and physically less attractive than with their regular hair.

Men with baldness problems can have different options such as hair transplantation, wearing prosthetic hair, or shaving their heads. Of course, the methods that restore their hair will revert their attractiveness values to their normal hair state. In contrast, completely sacrificing and shaving the hair has different effects on the person's appeal.

Studies show that women perceive men who shave their hair as more dominant, stronger, a few years older, and an average of 2.5 centimeters taller than people with normal hair. Studies also revealed that women see men who shave their heads as more confident. Considering how women value their own hair, it should not be surprising that they find a man who freely gives up his hair assured. Another finding of the studies is that shaving one's hair does not decrease their physical attraction compared to natural baldness.

Considering all this, the ideal way to follow for balding men should be based entirely on their physical and social conditions. For example, for a very dominant, masculine, and tall bald man, shaving his head will strengthen these traits a little more. This may be the wrong strategy because women hesitate to choose extremely masculine-looking men for long-term relationships. On the contrary, shorter men with less masculine looks can improve these aspects by shaving their heads without losing much of their physical appeal.

Since our hair represents health, it is one of the first areas that the opposite sex instinctively looks at. So, if your head is not too symmetrical or has various deformities, shaving your head may not be the right choice. Because, just like the effect of protruding ears, a shapeless head will make it harder for the other person to focus their attention on the more important parts of your face. On the contrary, if you have a smooth head shape, shaving your head will strengthen your interaction because the time the opposite sex would typically spend to analyze your hair will now be diverted to focus on your eyes, another center of interest on your face.

BEARD

Probably we all agree that beards are not attractive in women. For men, different beard lengths can have particular attraction values for the opposite sex. While individual preferences may vary, scientific studies show that women mostly prefer short to medium-length beards in men. So, a few days or weeks old beards are the most favored beard length by women. Very long beards are not preferred much.

In fact, just like hair, the maintenance of long beards is hard and requires serious effort. Therefore, a long and well-groomed beard indicates a man's attention to his personal care. Our beards also surround our mouths. No matter how well-maintained they are, food remains, oil, and sweat accumulated here create an ideal environment for bacteria to settle and flourish. As the beard grows, the number of microorganisms accumulated here increases, and hygiene decreases. Kissing someone who has a high risk of carrying germs around his mouth is not something many women prefer. Therefore, although women prefer the beard in men since it is a masculine feature, this attraction is limited to a few days or weeks old beards, which are instinctively the most hygienic level.

Beards alter not only a person's attractiveness but also his perceived age. Studies show that bearded men are considered older than their clean-shaved state. Men's beards generally begin to come out with puberty and take their final form in youth. Therefore, a face without a beard sends a signal to people's subconscious that this individual has not reached maturity yet. In the section on skin, we have mentioned how our brain evaluates many different criteria when estimating a person's age, and the change in one of them does not affect this perception that much. This is why a clean-shaved man looks younger than his bearded state but is not perceived as a juvenile.

Beards also signal masculinity, dominance, and aggressiveness. Therefore, men instinctively grow beards to augment their masculinity. Supporting this notion, a recent study by Barnaby Dixson and Anthony Lee from the University of Queensland revealed that men are more likely to be bearded in countries where they have to compete more vigorously with each other for women.

TEETH

Have you ever thought that someone was so attractive at first glance, but then after seeing their yellow teeth, you immediately felt that you did not like them much? This situation must have happened to many of us.

Teeth are perhaps one of the most noticeable areas on our faces for attraction. According to a survey with 5500 people, 60% of men and 71% of women say that the first place they look at the opposite sex is their teeth.

If you grew up in a village or a town, you know that customers in animal markets look at the teeth of animals such as horses and donkeys to see if they are healthy. Not only animals' teeth but also our teeth are indicators of both age and health.

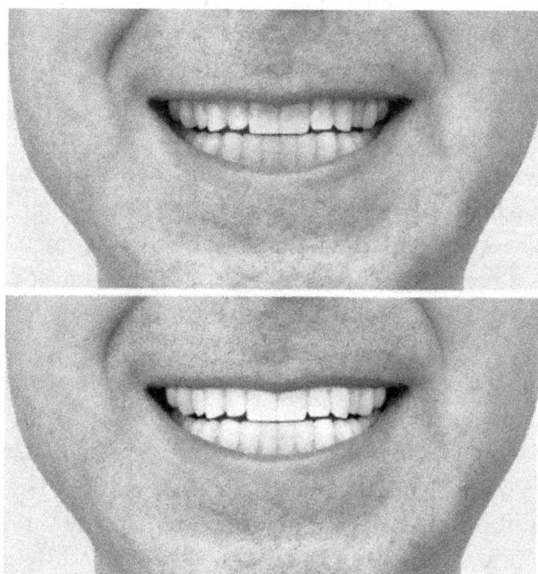

Figure 9- Neglected and distorted teeth significantly reduce our attractiveness.

For example, those who have split teeth are born with low weight. These people have a higher risk of experiencing heart problems later in life. In addition, a mouth full of decayed teeth indicates a general lack of hygiene. Both antibiotics and other drugs we use, and factors such as cigarette and coffee consumption cause our teeth to turn yellow as we age. For many such reasons, our teeth are important markers of age and health. So, they play a significant role in our attractiveness.

Recently, Yoann Lopez and his colleagues from the University of Rennes in France have designed an experiment to reveal the effects of dental health on women's attractiveness. In their study, they digitally manipulated a woman's photo by painting one of her teeth gray. They also made her one tooth slightly crooked. They uploaded both the woman's picture with proper teeth and the photo with distorted teeth on a dating site as different accounts, and over 400 people visited each account. However, while 17% of those who visited the account with the proper photo sent a message, the ratio of people who attempted to contact the account with a crooked teeth photo was only 3.5%. A difference of about five times… Decent teeth have this much importance in our attractiveness!

BODY

Our body contains a lot of information from our health to our hormonal values. In this aspect, it plays a vital role in our attractiveness. The appeal of our body's different features can also vary depending on the type of relationship that the other side wants to have. For instance, those who seek to have a short-term relationship can pay more attention to some specific body traits. However, the very same body features may be disadvantageous for long-term relationships. In this chapter, we will review the effects of all these features as well as their preferability for short and long-term relationships.

HEIGHT

One of the most crucial body criteria playing a role in attractiveness is our height. However, it is perhaps our most wrongly assessed feature, especially regarding women's heights.

When we look at social media, both men and women criticize short girls. Do the results of the scientific studies concur with this criticism? Is short stature of women really a disadvantage for their attractiveness?

Research by Daniel Nettle from the UK reveals that women who are a few inches shorter than the average of society find partners easily and in higher numbers. This rate decreases as the woman gets taller. For example, in this study conducted in England with a female height average of 162 cm, women with the highest number of partners were found to be 158 cm tall.

For men, the preference is the exact opposite. Women favor men who are taller than the society's average. If we go through the example of England again, with a male height average of 177 cm, it is revealed that men with a height of 183 cm are the most advantageous group both in finding a partner and in the number of partners in this country.

So why is that? Why is shorter height preferred for women and longer height for men? This tendency is all about our primitive brain.

A person's tall height, and in a way, his bulk, is an indicator of dominance. It makes the opponent, the enemy, and the person facing him nervous. Thus, before fighting with their enemy or in times of danger, many animals try to frighten their opponent and establish their dominance by making their bodies and bulks look bigger. This is not very different for humans. As soon as we get angry and tend to fight, if the other person's height and body are much larger than us, we often accept defeat from the beginning and go away without even fighting. Therefore, the tallness of a man is preferred in attractiveness, as it is a sign for the primitive brain of women that shows both the dominance of the man and that he can protect them physically in the event of danger.

I especially emphasize the primitive brain because today physical power occupies much less space in dominance when compared to our ancestors' times. In fact, it usually does not have much effect at all. Most of the time, intelligence and other factors can easily dominate pure physical power. When we think with our advanced brain, we are extremely conscious of this situation. However, as I have emphasized from the beginning of this book, our primitive brain mostly determines the features we find attractive in the opposite sex. Therefore, tallness, a primitive symbol of dominance, is still preferred by women as a very attractive element in men.

There may be situations when a woman chooses a man who is shorter than or equal to her height from time to time. If the man provides a dominance with his social status rather than his height, he can be preferred by women. Apart from this, if a woman feels self-confident enough, and subconsciously does not feel the need for a dominant man, the man's height is no longer an important criterion. Of course, in cases where other physical properties of men are superior, their height may also be ignored.

Short women often worry about their height in their circle of friends, and sometimes on social media. They want to be taller and think that their height is a disadvantage for them. One major reason for that concern is they misinterpret the intersexual attraction criteria. Women worry about their heights assuming, "If I get attracted to tall men, men also get attracted to tall women." Actually, this is not the case for the majority. In fact, as seen in the above-mentioned study, there is this attraction tendency for shorter women.

Men's preference for women who are shorter than average has both psychological and physiological reasons.

The psychological reason is, of course, dominance. Although today we talk about equality between women and men, men's primitive brain is programmed to be dominant against the environment. For most men, the area where he can dominate the woman most easily is his height and bulk by nature. Thus, men generally do not prefer females who are at the same height or taller than them because they would not feel psychologically dominant. Thus, they prefer women who are shorter than them. As with women, men who have reached a certain level of self-confidence can choose equally tall and sometimes taller women.

In fact, we see this instinct to be dominant for men in other areas as well. For example, since their height is not an element of dominance, short men try to compensate for this in other areas, such as career, social status, and money. Almost all workplaces have such overly ambitious short men who mostly become managers. Now you know the reason for that ambition. Sometimes, this impulse can even cause them to deviate from legal approaches. Studies show that short men are more criminalized. In other words, the real-life examples of the short chunky godfathers and gang leaders we see in the movies are also quite a lot.

The instinct of men to be the dominant side in the relationship is not limited to physicality. They also have such a desire for cultural aspects. We can find a nice example reflecting this situation and its effect on relationships in one of the Scandinavian countries. The incomes of most professions in Denmark differ little. Since most people have similar and good salaries, some men find it unnecessary to attend a university after high school and turn to simpler professions that will bring comparable earnings. As for women, they usually turn to university for better education, and often to higher education, such as masters and doctorate degrees. This creates a well-educated female group and a less-educated male group. Women do not naturally prefer men with less education than them. Men also do not turn to women who will dominate themselves with their educational and cultural levels. Therefore, even the difference in cultural dominance causes a considerable number of well-educated women in Denmark to not be able to find partners.

Women's heights also impact their physiology. We all grow taller from the moment we are born, and this increase in length continues until the early 20s. Our growth rate usually declines after adolescence because both getting taller and sexual maturation with puberty require a significant amount of energy. The body strives to do both efficiently at the same time. It must renounce one of them to a large extent. With tall women, sexual maturation is compromised. The body stops the sexual maturation for a while and directs its energy to get taller. Therefore, tall women usually enter puberty one or two years later than their peers.

Although today young girls generally begin to have menstruation at the age of 12-13, because our nutrition is mostly sufficient, in the primitive times when nutrients were insufficient, it was 17-18 when young girls enter puberty. This age was also 1-2 years ahead for tall girls.

According to the recent study of Australian scientists, the average life expectancy of our primitive ancestors was found to be about 38 years. Considering this finding, primitive women were probably entering menopause around their early 30s, in line with this genetic life expectancy. When we think that the traits preferred in the opposite sex in attraction are related to the reproductive potential, it is evident that men of the primitive times would not prefer women who have reached productivity later because of this limited reproductive age range. Therefore, the primitive brain of men does not prefer tall women physiologically as well.

Besides, tallness can bring some health risks for women. For example, studies show that the risk of developing breast cancer at later ages is higher in taller women than in short women.

If you are short, you can extend your height by an average of 6-8 centimeters with surgical interventions. In this method, the bones are cut, and an iron frame is fixed around the leg. The frame's gap is gradually increased with screws so that the broken bone is grown taller without knitting. Thus, the person's height can be extended by an average of 1 cm per month. Of course, the cost, the difficulty, and also the pain are too much. If you have a height problem, it is possible to overcome this with some small accessories and illusions without suffering.

The first thing for those who wish to appear taller is to wear heels. This is a method especially women use. Men can also extend their height by four or five centimeters with the hidden heels in their shoes. Even though classic shoes with hidden heels are produced and sold individually, you can find hidden heel accessories for very affordable prices and use them with high wrist shoes or boots comfortably.

In addition to high heels, dressing in one color is a trick that makes people look taller than they are. When we see someone, we first eye that person from head to foot. If you dress in one color, this check-out will not be interrupted by the color difference; thus, you will look taller than you actually are.

There are additional clothing tricks that contribute to the optical illusion created by this one-color outfit. The shoes being the same color as the clothes also make the person look taller than they are. Not only the color of the shoes but also the model can affect how the other person perceives our height. Square toe shoes make us appear shorter and pointed-toe shoes make us look taller.

Another accessory that affects the illusion of height perception is the belt. Since a belt will create interruption while the other person is filtering us, not using it makes us a little taller.

Turtleneck sweaters seem to increase our neck length, and V-neck t-shirts or sweaters make our chest area look taller; thus, they both increase our perceived total height. Since the hat is also added to our size, it makes us look a little taller.

In addition, the sizes of the clothes we wear are generally standard, and our eyes are used to these standards. Wearing shorter versions of some of these clothes outside these norms makes us look a little taller by breaking these routines. For example, when we wear a jacket that is shorter than normal, people are inclined to think "The jacket is short on him because he is tall," or wearing similarly short shorts, creates the deception that "The short is short on her because her legs are tall." These possible deceptions make us appear a few centimeters taller.

As for tall women, they can reduce their height disadvantages by looking a few inches shorter if they avoid these tricks or apply the exact opposites.

Legs and torso are the most basic elements that make up the height. Thus, when it comes to the influence of our height on our attractiveness, it is useful to look at the research on the effect of leg-to-body ratio. The answer to the question "Is the very long legs that tabloid magazines stretch onto forever using Photoshop, especially in women, the most attractive for men?" is actually hidden in the leg-to-body ratio investigated in these studies.

Studies on people with the same height reveal that the most attractive leg-to-body ratio for both sexes is 5% above the average ratio. This corresponds to a figure for women where the leg-to-body ratio is 0.49. When the leg-to-body ratio is less or more than this value, the person's attractiveness decreases. In other words, both the increase and the decrease in the women's leg size; thus, its proportion on the body reduces attractiveness similarly. Therefore, while men find 0.49 leg-to-body ratio in women the most attractive, they find the values of 0.46 and 0.53 the least attractive. This ratio means that if you are a woman with a 170 cm height, the most appealing leg size is 83 cm. Similarly, the length changes towards other ends, such as 90 cm or 78 cm, are the least attractive.

That is to say, tabloid magazines lengthening women's leg sizes with Photoshop to a certain level is quite attractive for our primitive brain. But much longer ones are actually a factor that reduces the appeal. Because excessively long legs can often be a sign of some genetic disorders such as Marfan and Klinefelter syndromes. In addition, a torso length that is rather short compared to the legs can point to small lungs, therefore breathing difficulties.

Although leg sizes of 5% above the average are preferred in both sexes, women's average leg length is slightly greater than men's, and this length is preferred by the opposite sex. There is an evolutionary reason why men prefer women to have slightly longer legs. Longer legs mean a wider pelvis. Therefore, women with long legs give birth more easily, and the baby has a better chance of living. In today's medicine, while many complications that may occur during childbirth can be successfully intervened, and both mother and baby's life can be saved, our primitive ancestors did not have such luxuries. That is why they preferred women with a larger pelvis, as they usually gave birth easier and more smoothly. Besides, the leg-to-body ratio in women is directly in parallel with the child's birth weight. As this value increases, the child's weight increases as well. This allows the baby to start the first days of his life a little stronger.

The leg-to-body ratio is also a marker of a person's health. Individuals with a low ratio have a high risk of having cardiovascular disease and Type II diabetes. Studies show that people with high leg-to-body ratio have a lower risk of cancer alongside lower risks of the above-mentioned disorders.

In addition, our leg size is more susceptible to environmental effects than our torso during the developmental period. Adverse conditions affect the increase in the length of our legs. If a person has a shorter leg length compared to his own height, it indicates that the individual has grown under unfavorable circumstances. This signals to our subconscious that this person may not have the right resources.

Suppose your leg-to-body ratio is apart from the ideal. In that case, you can fix this disadvantage by creating a visual illusion with some minor clothing tricks. If your legs are longer than normal, wearing low-cut pants will make your torso appear a little longer and your legs shorter. In addition, an intensive program of leg movements in the gym will make your legs more muscular. These highly muscular legs will look a little shorter than they are. In contrast, wearing high-waisted pants will make your leg length appear longer and your torso shorter. Black-colored pants will also make your legs look a little thinner, thus, longer.

BODY MASS INDEX

Body mass index (BMI) is one of the most significant indicators of attractiveness as well as health. The body mass index value, developed by the Belgian mathematician Adolphe Quetelet in 1830, has been used to determine whether individuals are overweight and obese ever since. The higher our body mass index value, the greater our risk of developing Type II diabetes, blood pressure, various cancers, and respiratory problems.

Of course, not only high BMI but also BMI lower than normal creates problems for health. When we analyze the annual mortality rates, we see that people with a BMI of around 21-22 have the lowest rate. In contrast, mortality rates increase rapidly when the BMI values are above or below this.

If our primitive brain is seeking health and reproductive potential in the physical qualities of possible romantic partners, it should not be complicated to estimate the body mass index values that look the most attractive to people in the light of these data. BMI values around 20 are the most appealing to both men and women.

However, this most attractive BMI value may differ slightly in developing countries. Researches reveal that as the stress levels of men increase, they tend to go to overweight women. Stress levels of people living in developing countries are usually higher than the people in Western countries due to reasons such as anticipatory anxiety, unemployment, and economic problems in those societies. This increased stress levels may direct a larger portion of the men in such societies to slightly overweight women.

So, how do we calculate our BMI value? It is, in fact, quite simple. When we divide our weight by the square of our height in meters, the number we get gives us our BMI value. For example, an individual who is 1.85 meters tall and weighs 80 kilos will have a BMI value of $80 / (1.85)^2 = 23.4$.

When we consider our BMI value, we should also remember that these measures are modeled upon average people. For example, an athlete's muscle mass is higher than ordinary people's. Thus, his weight and BMI value will be higher than those who look as slim as he is. There are also circumstances where the exact opposite is true. As we get older, our muscles begin to deteriorate, gradually getting replaced with fat. Therefore, an older adult's BMI value will be lower than a young person of similar size.

If we are an average person and our BMI value is above 25, we should decrease this rate to 21-22 by losing weight for both our health and attractiveness. Similarly, if our BMI value is lower than 15-16, we should increase this value to ideal levels by gaining some weight. One thing we should keep in mind is that the BMI value, ideal for attractiveness, reflects the opinion of the majority in society, but does not involve everyone. Some individuals like very slim people in the opposite sex, while others may get attracted to overweight people.

Although it is necessary for health, sometimes losing weight to bring our BMI values to the ideal level can take a long time. Until then, we can slightly change our perceived BMI value with various clothing tricks.

For example, black or vertical striped clothing makes us look skinnier than we are and reduces our perceived BMI value. Likewise, clothing with plenty of stripes parallel to the ground, and full-size clothes make the person look fatter, and increase the perceived BMI value.

WAIST TO HIP RATIO

As its name signifies, waist-to-hip ratio (WHR) is a ratio found by dividing our waist circumference to hip circumference. It refers to the distribution of fat in the body.

WHR is linked to many conditions, from health to reproductive potential, from cognitive ability to age, and from health problems to the possibility of depression.

For example, in in-vitro-fertilization (IVF), women with WHR less than 0.8 are most likely to become pregnant. Studies found that every 0.1 increase above this value decreases the probability of pregnancy by 30%. Also, in women with high WHR, the number of menstrual cycles without ovulation is higher.

Since the distribution of fat is different in men and women, the different values of WHR are attractive for each sex. While men accumulate body fat around the belly with the effect of testosterone, women accumulate more in the breast and hips due to estrogen. This fat deposition feature gives men characteristically an apple-shaped and women a pear-shaped body. Therefore, the most attractive WHR value in women is 0.7, whereas for men it is 0.9.

In scientific studies, when the women were told to alter their bodies as they liked with Photoshop software, all the subjects modified their WHRs to be 0.7. The body sizes of the models in men's magazines, such as Playboy, also have a WHR value of 0.6-0.7. The hourglass-shaped 90-60-90 measurements, which are considered ideal for models, also correspond to a 0.67 WHR. This WHR value is not only seen in today's tabloid magazines, but when we also look at the sculptures from antiquity, we see that it appears in many ancient cultures from India to Egypt and Greece.

Is this WHR value a perception of beauty imposed by the media, or does it really correspond to anything in our primitive brain? Dutch and American scientists who wanted to find the answer to this question designed an experiment in 2010 on the WHR preference of people who were blind from birth. It is impossible for people who were born blind to be influenced by female figures imposed by tabloid magazines and television. The experiment also included a control group of people with normal eyesight and another group of blindfolded people for the experiment. These three distinct groups compared women with WHRs of 0.7 and 0.84 in terms of attractiveness. Naturally, they decided on which waist and hips they prefer, just by touching women's body. All groups without exception, including those who were born blind, found the waist-hip ratio of 0.7 the most appealing for women. This experiment is another indication that most of the factors we like in the opposite sex are inherent and settled in our primitive brain.

Although a WHR value of 0.7 in women is the most attractive to people, some men may not find all the research results on women with this WHR value enjoyable. Scientific studies show that women with this WHR value experience sexuality earlier, have more sexual partners, cheat on their partners more, and have more extramarital affairs.

Since the WHR value is somewhat independent of the weight, you will be attractive to the opposite sex as long as you keep your WHR at this level, whether you be slim or overweight. A study on the attractiveness of men with different weights and various WHR values also supports this fact.

A study on slim, normal weight, and overweight men with 0.7-0.8-0.9 and 1.0 WHR values revealed that women found men with 0.9 WHR and normal weight the most attractive. When looking at slim and fat male groups with different WHRs, 0.9 WHR stands out as the most attractive ratio. So, what is the least attractive WHR value in men? As you can guess, 0.7 WHR, an indicator of the characteristic female fat deposition, is the least attractive ratio in men.

HIPS

When we analyze eye-tracking experiments, we see that one of the most frequently looked at areas by men in the female body is the hips. If we do not count the "size zero" model craze in the 90s, hips have been playing a role in women's appeal for a very long time. Women know this importance of hips in their appeal for centuries or even millennia. So much so that even in different cultures in ancient ages, the hips were often depicted quite large in most female sculptures that symbolized fertility. In the Middle Ages and later on, women wore hoop skirts to make their butts appear larger than they were, and a corset to thin their waist. A similar trend continues in some wedding dress styles even today. In daily life, too, we see that most women try to enlarge and shape their hips with Brazilian butt lift surgeries or squat movements. So why are butts so important in women's appeal? Is the reason for this men's affection for hips a visual pleasure only because of the hourglass look?

Increasing estrogen production with adolescence prevents fat accumulation around the waist in women, causing it to accumulate in buttocks, hips, and thighs-collectively called the gluteofemoral region- and the breasts. The regional fat deposition that occurs with the increase in estrogen is different from that of men and gives the female body an hourglass shape.

These fat, which accumulate in the gluteofemoral region, especially in the hips, are different from those stored in other parts of the female body and are the primary source of long-chain unsaturated fatty acids, especially omega-3 Docosahexaenoic acid known as DHA. These long-chain unsaturated fatty acids, which are extremely rare to be taken on a regular diet, make up about 20% of the human brain's dry weight. With this feature, fats in this region are essential for the fetus and the baby's healthy brain development. Therefore, it is crucial that women accumulate these fats in these regions before pregnancy. Also, 80% of the long-chain unsaturated fatty acids in breast milk come from the fats in this region. In fact, even if these long-chain unsaturated fatty acids are taken as supplementary food during breastfeeding, these supplements are less effective than those accumulated in the fats in the hips.

Studies show that children of women with large hips are, therefore, more intelligent. When I talked about this in a seminar I gave at a university a few years ago, the Rector, who was among the audience, asked whether Einstein's mother had big hips as well. Frankly, I had never thought of and searched it before, but I said that I guess it would be quite big in the light of this data. Among the laughter, some people from the audience found a picture of Einstein's mother on Google using their smartphones. I was right.

The fats in the mother's hips are so vital for the baby's brain development that the body uses these in other periods only after consuming others. Women who are on a diet with calorie restrictions generally lose weight from anywhere. Their bellies dwindle, cheeks collapse, breasts begin to shrink, but the fat on their hips are stubborn; it does not budge! This is the reason why. Since our body knows the specialty and importance of the fat accumulated here, it does not use this fat unless necessary and stores them until the end. Therefore, during the diet, the fat in the other parts of the women's body is lost first, and the fat in the hips begins to burn in the very last.

Although we can easily access almost any food we want in developed societies, this is not the case for third-world nations and poor regions. Thus, in women living in such disadvantaged communities, long-chain unsaturated fatty acids, which accumulate gradually over the years in the gluteofemoral area, are consumed with giving birth and breastfeeding. Since these women cannot replace these fats quickly due to malnutrition, they begin to thin out from the hips and buttocks with each delivery. As a result of this condition, called maternal depletion, these women usually have long-chain unsaturated fatty acids in their hips and buttocks only enough for the proper brain development and intelligence of their first child. Thus, their later children are usually less intelligent than the first child since they have a limited amount of long-chain unsaturated fatty acids accumulated on their hips because of malnutrition. The same condition is also observed in twins compared to singletons. That is to say, while the long-chain unsaturated fatty acids accumulated in the woman's hips are sufficient for the brain development and intelligence of a single child in pregnancy and breastfeeding, these fats may be insufficient for a similar rate of neural development of twins.

Women generally have a lower WHR value than men. Estrogen prevents fat from being accumulated around the waist, and therefore it is mostly collected in the hips and buttocks. However, as they get older, women's estrogen levels decrease, and testosterone begins to prevail. Consequently, as women grow old, they start to accumulate fat in their bellies, which increases their WHR. After menopause, women's WHR begins to reach the male level. If you look at the older women around you, you can see that the fat deposition becomes evident in their bellies. The reason for this is the hormonal structures that change with age. That is why our primitive brain evaluates low WHR due to high estrogen levels in women as indicators of femininity, reproduction, and age. Thus, wide hips that cause low WHR in women are instinctively preferred by men since they are both an indicator for youth and femininity and also with their effects on the brain development of the baby.

None of us have to be of ideal size. The kind of body we would like to have is completely our personal preference. Some of us may prefer to be extremely thin and not to accumulate fat in the hip and buttocks area. However, if we are planning to have a child, it is essential to accumulate fat in these areas, at least before pregnancy, to ensure the proper development of our baby's brain. Moreover, considering the possibility of maternal depletion, instead of close subsequent pregnancies, it would be wiser to make the other child after accumulating enough long-chain unsaturated fatty acids into the gluteofemoral region with a few years' interval after the breastfeeding period.

Some women desire to have bigger hips, but they have trouble doing so. The problem may be rooted in their hormonal levels and diets. If we regard that only a particular type of fat is accumulated in the hips under the influence of estrogen, we should consider adding these two factors in our diet if we are having trouble getting fat in our hips. In other words, both eating long-chain unsaturated fat-rich food and food that will increase our estrogen levels may help us get bigger hips.

Although we cannot get estrogen directly with our diet, we can get phytoestrogens from plants. Phytoestrogens have similar effects to estrogen in our bodies. They are mostly found in pistachios, soy, walnuts, dates, thyme, and parsley. Therefore, eating these types of foods as much as possible will increase our estrogen level.

As for the food rich in DHA are eggs and fatty fish such as mackerel, tuna, salmon, sardine, and anchovy. Algae are the primary source of DHA. Vegan people can get these essential fats with algae added to their diets. Foods such as flaxseed are rich in alpha-Linolenic acid (ALA), the precursor of DHA. But our body does not convert ALA to DHA very effectively. Only 1% of the ALA taken to our body is converted to DHA. Therefore, it would be a more accurate and scientific approach for us to consume DHA-rich foods instead of ALA without being fooled by some companies' marketing claims.

BREASTS

Women's breasts begin to grow with the effect of increased estrogen during adolescence. So, they are a symbol of femininity. Usually, women with large breasts are considered to be more attractive. But when we look at the results of scientific studies, we see that the effect of breast size on attractiveness is exaggerated in public.

In their study, Barnaby Dixson and his colleagues from Australia compared very small, small, medium, and large breasts in terms of attractiveness. Male subjects did not see any difference between the attractiveness of large breasts and medium breasts. For small breasts, except for those with very dark areolar pigmentation, the difference in attractiveness was also negligible.

Besides, studies show that contrary to popular belief, small-breasted women have no problem feeding their babies. So, there is no biological basis for the breast size preference myth.

The only exception to these findings is males with low socioeconomic status or who live in disadvantaged countries. Research shows that such men prefer larger breasts in general. On the contrary, studies show that educated individuals in high socioeconomic countries mostly prefer smaller breasts.

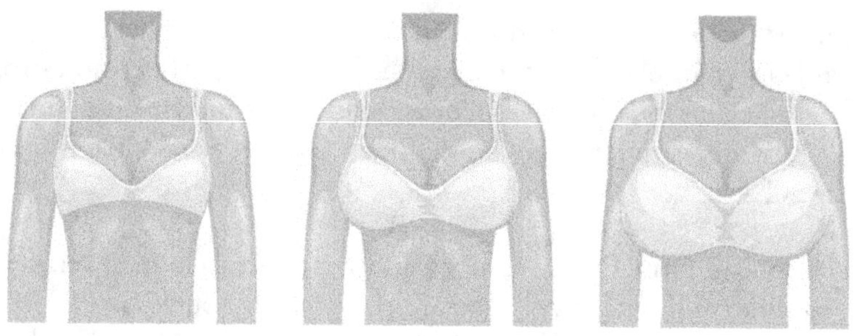

Figure 10- According to scientific studies, although breasts are among the most stared areas on the female body, their size does not play a significant role in women's attractiveness.

In fact, these two different preferences give us a significant clue as to how we should carefully evaluate scientific studies and their results. Because generalizations made in research sometimes lead us to different conclusions. Wonder how? Suppose the proportion of well-educated individuals in an average society is 20%. Suppose the percentage of those who are in good economic condition is also 20%. We can find the ratio of well-educated people with good financial status with a small calculation (20% x 20%) to be 4%. So, it is a pretty small minority. In scientific studies, since the majority that reflects the whole society is taken as average in the results, the rate of the preference of this 4% population influencing and changing the rest of the population's preference remains quite low.

In contrast, the proportion of low-educated population in societies is about 50-60%. Similarly, when we think the percentage of people with low economic potential is also around those numbers, this population makes up an average of 30-40% of the society. They can be almost 8-10 times more dominant than the other group, not only in terms of their power to influence the results of the experiment but also in terms of their voices and ideas to be heard in real life. According to a study by Farid Pazhoohi and his colleagues in Canada, men who think that big breasts increase the attractiveness of women are also revealed to have a sexist personality. Well, how accurate is it to hear the voice of this big breast-loving audience and shape your aesthetic preferences, or if your breasts are small, losing your self-confidence around their ideas? For example, are the males that women want to attract more by enlarging their breasts sexist men with low socioeconomic backgrounds? This is a big question mark! So, sometimes it is necessary to pay attention to such population differences and rates when interpreting the attraction criteria of the society.

According to scientific studies, although the small size of the breasts does not decrease the women's attractiveness, flat chests are an exception. There is an instinctive reason for this. When the subjects were asked to estimate the ages of women with this type of breasts when their faces were covered, scientists observed that people estimated the age of flat-chested women to be 12 years old on average. So, this type of breasts signals to the subconsciousness of men that the woman has not yet reached puberty and reproductive potential. When we consider the evolution of love, it is quite natural that such a feature is not found attractive by men.

Although breast size does not affect the attractiveness of women, we should not underestimate its effect on boosting their self-confidence due to the ongoing cultural beliefs. This rise in self-confidence can indirectly increase women's appeal.

Women with small breasts can wear push-up bras or silicone pads to make their breasts look larger than they are and can even permanently enlarge them with surgical interventions. In addition, a method used for a similar purpose is to make contour makeup on their cleavage. With this technique mainly applied by movie stars, it is possible to make small breasts appear a few sizes larger. Probably many of the women reading this book are aware of this trick. So, this information will be most useful for innocent male readers who cannot predict what makeup tricks can do.

Various parts of our body have different importance in the attractiveness of a person. So, which of these areas is more important? In an eye-tracking experiment, scientists revealed that men spend more time looking at the waist and breasts, but mostly on the breasts, than the genitals and the legs on the naked body of women. But is the more intensely looked breasts area more important than the waist-to-hip ratio, in terms of attractiveness?

Another study done in the previous years revealed that when male subjects evaluated photos of women with different breast sizes and waist-hip ratios, regardless of the breast size, they found mostly 0.7 WHR the most attractive. So briefly, men may look more at women's breasts, but WHR value is much more critical in terms of attractiveness.

SHOULDER-TO-HIP RATIO

The shoulder-to-hip ratio, as its very name signifies, is a feature that is calculated by dividing the shoulder circumference to the hip circumference. It significantly differs between genders.

Testosterone increases the shoulder-to-hip ratio in men by controlling the muscular structure, skeletal morphology, and fat storage areas. This gives men the typical "V" shape with wide shoulders and narrow hips.

Studies show that men with a high shoulder-to-hip ratio feel sexier and have higher self-esteem compared to their peers. Other men also think that those with high shoulder-to-hip ratio are more dominant and attractive. This view shows similarities in different cultures. That is why men all over the world want to have a more well-built and muscular body.

Women likewise find men with a high shoulder-to-hip ratio more attractive. This preference reflects positively on the sexual life of men with high shoulder-to-hip ratio. Studies found that men with high shoulder-to-hip ratio experience sexuality at an earlier age and have relationships with more partners compared to their fellows. However, research also revealed that women often prefer men with a high shoulder-to-hip ratio for short-term relationships.

The reason is high testosterone levels. While men with high testosterone levels show intense masculine characteristics, testosterone also reduces the effects of the bonding hormone called oxytocin. Thereby, women with the instincts of their primitive brain and experiences, may not prefer men that display high testosterone characteristics, for long-term relationships thinking, "Hmmm. This guy is very masculine, very attractive, but probably will cheat on me in the future." Instead, they are preferred in shorter relationships, which we can call playing around.

FEET

Feet are another element of charm on our body. Women generally prefer to have small feet. As a matter of fact, in Chinese culture, women's feet were bound and made smaller. The real reason for this practice, which started in the 10th century, is not known, but it is thought to be done for appeal. But these feet, which are bound from childhood, become seriously deformed since they developed abnormally. If you came across any photo of these women's feet, you have seen how deformed they are[2]. These deformed feet also make walking difficult for women. Thus, the most plausible theory of the reason for this practice is not because it increased feet' appeal with its distorted shape, but that it has emerged in China, where forced marriages were common, so women could not escape their husbands comfortably.

American scientists Jeremy Atkinson and Michelle Rowe have explored the effect of foot size on the attractiveness of women in an unusual way. They took facial photographs of women with small feet and big feet and morphed them into separate groups. So, there appeared two photographs. One was displaying the average facial features of the women with small feet and the other with the average of the facial features of the women with large feet. When the subjects were asked which photo was more attractive, 78% found the representational face photo of women with small feet more attractive. In comparison, only 22% thought that the representation face photo of women with big feet was more appealing.

Our sex hormones also affect our characteristic muscle, bone development, and fat distribution. Although a scientific study analyzing whether there is a relationship between estrogen/testosterone levels and foot length in women, has not been done to date, based on the findings of Jeremy Atkinson and Michelle Rowe, it is possible to think that there is a relationship between the foot size and the masculine and feminine characters on the face, probably due to this different level of sex hormones. Therefore, even though the feet are not an element of attraction except for fetish situations, it can be said that the faces of women with small feet carrying feminine lines are also more attractive for an important part of society.

BODY HAIR

It may be a shocking fact for some of you, but men and women have almost equal amounts of hair follicles. We have a total of 1 million 150 thousand hair follicles in both sexes, with an average of 10-20 thousand on our faces, 100-150 thousand on our heads, 425 thousand on our body, 220 thousand on our arms, and 370 thousand on our legs.

---

[2] I do not include a photo of the deformed feet of Chinese women in this book because it is a disturbing image. However, those who are curious about it can search for and easily find such photos on Google.

So, what is our difference? While most of the hair that develops from the hair follicles of women—especially those on the face—remains peach fuzz, those in men get a harder and thicker structure.

Women have been removing their body hair, especially in the last 30-40 years, in a way that makes this difference even more apparent. We can observe this trend most comfortably in Olympic athletes. Studies show that the hair removal rate of female athletes in the 1970s was quite low compared to the female athletes in 2012.

Hair removal in women has become a norm, especially in Western culture. Studies show that more than 90% of women remove most of their armpits, legs, and pubic hair. In other words, the probability of men meeting a woman who does not remove her hair is only around 10%.

Excessive hairiness is a factor that reduces the appeal not only in women but also in men. It would not be wrong to call pubic hair an exception to this dislike. In surveys, pubic hair appears to be acceptable and attractive in both genders.

TEARS

In the past, women accumulated their tears in small bottles, especially in the Far East. There are such bottles in Anatolia too. The tears shed after the dead were collected and placed in their graves since the Phrygians.

Tears also affect people's attractiveness. In a study published in Science by Noam Sobel and her team, a group of women were asked to watch a sad movie and collect their tears in a bottle. Later, when men were asked to smell these tears, it was revealed that this smell reduced their sexual appeal to women's pictures. Furthermore, after sniffing such tears, men's self-rated sexual arousal, physiological measures of arousal, and testosterone levels were also reduced. As for the control group where men smelled saltwater instead of tears, these reductions are not observed. In other words, women's tears can negatively affect male physiology.

In addition to the chemical effect of tears, crying has psychological effects on the opposite sex. Perhaps what strengthens the psychological effect of crying in men is that the tears make such negative physiological changes in them. The fact that the smell of tears reduces their sexual desires may awake anxiety or fear in their subconscious. This is probably why they mostly react to a crying woman negatively, such as anger!

Anger is an extension of fear and desperation. That is why some men do not know how to deal with this fear and distress they experience when their partners start crying; so, they start to scream and shout. On the other hand, other men try to stop the crying, thus the tears, by comforting the woman and saying soothing words. Whichever approach they adopt, these responses are probably men's efforts to get rid of tears, which have physiologically negative effects on them.

So, how do women react to tears? How do they feel when a man cries? Although there is no scientific study on the effect of tears on men's attractiveness, a crying man seems more humane to women. Perhaps one reason for this is that crying is mostly associated with women, and there is the existence of social conditionings like, "Men don't cry!" There is also an interesting study on this matter. Studies show that boys cry more than girls until the age of 7. But then, as a result of these social impositions, men level themselves about crying. Considering this situation, a woman may instinctively find a man who can cry occasionally more sincere, and therefore, more attractive.

VOICE

Our voice is another element of attractiveness. Studies reveal that people with beautiful voices seem more attractive than they are. The opposite is also true. We like the voices of attractive people more.

The music industry is also aware of this phenomenon. Thus, before putting the singers on the market, they make many touch-ups on their physical appeal. In fact, music groups consisting of handsome men or beautiful women with different attractiveness criteria are released to the market from time to time so that they can appeal to the most audience and make a profit. Almost everyone over the age of 30 will remember groups like *Backstreet Boys* and *Spice Girls* and their effects on people. Do you think it is just a coincidence that there were women in the *Spice Girls* group from brunette to blonde and ginger appealing to different tastes?

Considering the effect of the voice on our attractiveness, women find a low pitch, deep, and rich voice in men the most attractive. But again, studies show that women do not prefer men with such a voice for long-term relationships and stay a little distant.

Although we do not know the exact reason for this, perhaps it may be that men with such a voice have very high testosterone levels, and the negative effect of testosterone on fidelity activates an instinct in women that says, "This man is very attractive but will probably cheat on me in the future." Indeed, women's instinct on this issue is mostly right. In a 2020 study by Christoph Schild and colleagues on 816 subjects, both women and men with lower voice pitch reported having committed to infidelity more than their peers.

Another reason can be that women may think men with a deep voice are not attracted to them much because it contradicts the fight-or-flight response. As we will discuss in the next chapter, when we like someone, our body gives some physiological responses. One of them is the fight-or-flight response. One of our body's reactions in the fight-or-flight response is that our muscles contract slightly and experience tonus. Because of this contraction, we are ready to flee or fight. Since our vocal muscles that make up our vocal cords get this tonus as well, our voice becomes thinner when we talk to someone we like. From such hints, our subconscious perceives whether the person we are talking to is attracted to us. Since a low pitch voice will always be deeper than normal, the women's subconscious may mislead them to think that this person does not like them.

Unlike men, a high pitch and subtle voice makes a woman more attractive. Women with a masculine and deep voice seem more repulsive to the opposite sex. That is why some girls often instinctively thin their voices while flirting and imitate a child talking. Although studies show that slightly thinning the voice increases women's attractiveness, there is no scientific research that I know about whether thinning the voice with such an exaggeration by imitating a child is attractive to the opposite sex. However, according to my general observations, this kind of pretentious behavior harms attractiveness. Since I do not have clear scientific evidence, I cannot insist that you avoid doing it. So, the choice is up to you. But as a recommendation, I think it is useful to stay away from it. Besides, all men reading this book will now know that you do this instinctively because you are attracted to them.

Our body language is perhaps more effective than what we say in communicating with a person. Some studies claim that body language is 12.5 times more effective than our words, even though these results are still being debated. Although currently, we do not know the exact effects, it is a fact that body language has an essential part in communication. Naturally, in attractiveness too.

Especially in media such as Tinder and Instagram, where a person gets the first impression and judges us by our photos, our body language becomes even more critical. Although we will not be able to talk about every detail on body language because it is a book subject in itself, let us take a look at research done by scientists on how our body language in photos affects our attractiveness.

In their research in 2016, Dana Carney and her team from Stanford University took two pictures of the same individuals in certain places, both with an open and closed body language. They then created profiles on a platform like Tinder with these photos. If we analyze the details of the experiment, three women and three men were chosen and photographed in four different venues, one photo with a closed body language (for example, with their arms crossed), and one with an open body language (for example, arms open, palms facing forward). On a Tinder-like platform where liking was mostly by looking at photos, they created two different profiles for each individual: one with the photos showing open body language, and one with photos showing closed body language. So, in this experiment, the places are the same, the people are the same; the only difference is the body language of the same person in the photos. Then, they compared the number of likes each profile got.

According to the likings of approximately 3000 people, although the results support the open body language for both genders, the numbers are especially striking for men. While the rate of getting chosen for the profiles of men with open body language is almost 7 times higher than the profiles with closed body language, in women, profiles with open body language also brought 12% more likes.

We can see a similar effect in our daily lives. According to an observational study published by Lee Ann Renninger and her colleagues from the University of Vienna in 2004, men who received positive signals from women to talk to them in a bar environment showed some differences in their body language and behavior compared to those who failed. According to this study, these type of movements and behaviors were the keys to success: a dominant posture through which the space taken increases (the shoulders are upright, the hands take up more space, and the feet are slightly open); instead of scanning the entire room with the eyes frequently, a look towards the target, after the first catching each other's gaze, turning his eyes away but glance at her again in 5 seconds; avoiding movements that reduce the space taken (where the shoulders are low, the arms are crossed and the feet are close to each other); touching the other men in his group (throwing his hand on his shoulder, punching his friend in the shoulder, shaking hands, a high five, etc.) and not being stuck in the area, moving at least 1-1.5 meters. Scientists observed that when the men who did these dominant behaviors before approaching the women at the bar and then started to talk, they received a more positive attitude than those who did not.

IMMUNE SYSTEM

With the twentieth century, we met with an important privilege that our primitive ancestors did not have: vaccines. Vaccines have made us immune to diseases and have become the secret heroes that have saved millions of lives. Although our primitive ancestors did not have this privilege, the evolutionary process developed a system that would at least ease the lives of their children against diseases: falling in love with the right person.

The gene family called the human leukocyte antigen (HLA) is responsible for our immunity. The structure of these genes differs from person to person. This difference in HLA genes allows our body to recognize a wide variety of pathogenic organisms. If these genes did not differ and were the same in everybody, a virus or bacteria that would show up in the pre-vaccine time and the immune system would not recognize could easily wipe out the entire human race. However, the variance of these HLA genes among individuals significantly reduced this possibility; and diversifying it by falling in love with the right person also helped spread this situation.

Tissue typing is a term we are familiar with from organ transplants. If somebody is going to have an organ transplant, the tissues of the two individuals—more precisely, the HLA types—must match. So the recipient's immune system does not define this transplanted new organ as a foreign organism to the body and fights against it.

In compliance with the variety of HLA types, the probability of finding a matching tissue for a person is theoretically one in 600,000 individuals. As we are accustomed to the news of children with leukemia who are looking for bone marrow transplants, we often witness that matching tissues cannot be obtained from family members whose genetic structure should be the closest and can only be found with extensive research in registered donors worldwide. One reason children have many common features with their parents, from their physical appearance to their blood group, but their tissue types are often different from them is that during the evolutionary process, we have developed an adaptation of falling in love with the right person.

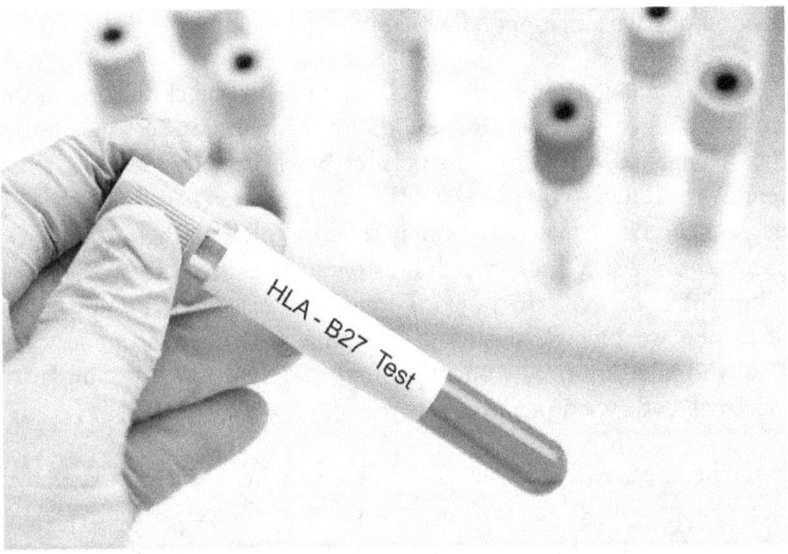

Figure 11-Human Leucocyte Antigen (HLA) enables our immune system to recognize foreign cells.

Scientific studies show that people prefer individuals whose HLA structures are different from theirs. Individuals instinctively increase the HLA diversity of their children by choosing partners with an HLA type that contrasts with theirs. In this way, different HLA genes from both mother and father strengthen the child's body defense against more kinds of diseases, thanks to the fact that we fall in love with the genetically correct person. Today, although this situation made it difficult to find a tissue-compatible individual in the organ transplant, it has provided us with an important benefit in the prevention of diseases in the past.

Some advantageous features are reflected in the person's physique and are decisive in our choice of partners. For example, fleshy lips are instinctively preferred because they indicate the high estrogen levels in women, and fats found in the hips are attractive because they help the baby's brain development during pregnancy. But as far as we know, HLA types are not reflected in our physical qualities. Besides, they are only found on the cell walls. Then, how can we detect the HLA type of our potential romantic partners?

Studies show that we perceive the differences of this protein by the smell of the person. We are not doing this consciously. Because as far as we know, HLA proteins do not have a distinct odor that we can smell.

When scientists made the subjects smell individually the clothes permeated by the natural smell of the opposite sex, the individuals whose smell was found attractive changed from person to person. Scientists later revealed that this preference was related to HLA-type differences between people. We can decide whether someone is attractive by simply smelling their clothes, even if we have never seen their faces. Those we find attractive are the people who have the most different HLA type than ours. Perhaps the reason we do not fall in love with everyone we like physically or feel an unidentified attraction towards someone who is not normally our type might be their HLA dissimilarity that only our smell and subconscious can perceive.

When scientists discovered that the differences in smell, and therefore the immune system, played a role in our partner choice, they made further interesting studies on this subject. For example, it was found that among the couples who had relationship problems and applied to the marriage counselor, the rate of saving the marriages of those who did not like the smell of each other was quite low compared to other couples. Another interesting finding of the scientific studies is that couples whose HLA types are close to each other, cheat on their partners more.

The fact that our body odor plays an important role in partner selection and relationships brings the question of the effects of the perfumes we use. Do the scents we use suppress our own smell? So, does it prevent us from accurately signaling our HLA type to the opposite sex?

Perfumes do not fit everyone in the same way. Although the content of a perfume in all bottles is the same, when different individuals wear it, the smell reflected around changes a little. We have experienced many times how we tried a perfume that our friend uses and then realized that we did not like it on us as much as we liked it on our friend. Thus, if we are a conscious consumer, although 300 new perfumes are launched on average every year, we get the smell that suits us best rather than fashionable perfumes. And we use the same or similar scents for years. The underlying reason for this choice is our HLA structure.

Research shows that when choosing a perfume to wear, our subconscious observes suitability to our immune system. If you buy a perfume not because it is fashionable but considering that it suits your skin, with this perfume, you both hold down unpleasant odors and make your potential partner smell your HLA type. For example, studies reveal that individuals with the HLA-A2 gene prefer perfumes with low rates of cedar, vetiver, and irises; and high rates of rose, cinnamon, and bergamot. Similarly, individuals with other HLA types prefer different odors. If we buy and use a perfume just because it is fashionable, this time because of their intense and possibly incompatible smell with our HLA type, we send the wrong HLA type signals to our potential romantic partners.

A few centuries ago, while the perfume industry was not so developed, personalized scents were made in perfume shops in Europe. Everyone had their personalized perfume, the formula of which was kept secret. After the link between our body odor, perfume, and partner selection was set forth scientifically, two companies have already obtained patents to produce scents matching people's HLA types. Perhaps soon, personally produced perfumes, whose content is hidden from everyone, will enter our lives intensely again.

When it comes to the effect of body odor on attractiveness, women have an advantage that men do not: the menstrual cycle.

Research reveals that when male subjects smelled the T-shirts that the same woman wore at different times of her menstrual cycle, they found the smell of the T-shirt worn during the ovulation most attractive. So, ladies, if you are going on a date with a guy you want to impress, timing it on your ovulation day will increase your attractiveness. Of course, this may not always be possible. But there is also a solution to this: the method that scientists use for storing clothes in their body odor experiments. If you wear the dress on your ovulation day and store it in the refrigerator in a closed glass container and wear it again on the date, it will retain its smell.

Besides the smell, the immune system has another effect on our attractiveness: symmetry. Our sex hormones, testosterone in men and estrogen in women, also have an immune-suppressing effect. With increasing levels of these hormones in adolescence, this suppression during development is felt more and causes slight deviations in the symmetrical structure of the person. Thus, when we examine the faces of people closely, we see that many do not have complete symmetry. If our immune system is strong enough, the negative suppression effect of these sex hormones is not reflected much, and our symmetry is mostly preserved. Consequently, if individuals with high sex hormone levels, hence, have a very prominent masculine or feminine look, and have also kept their facial symmetry during development, our subconscious appraises that their immune systems are strong. These individuals appeal to us more.

When it comes to the difference in symmetry, not only the front view of our face but also the side view can affect our appeal, more precisely from which side we are viewed. In the study of Zaidel and his colleagues, it was revealed that the paintings showing the right side of women's faces are seen as more attractive by men than the paintings showing their left sides. In the same study, there was no similar asymmetric difference in the attractiveness of men according to the face side. This remarkable finding of the study shows that this time our ancestors' instincts were wrong about attractiveness. Because in many medieval paintings, women are depicted with the left sides of their faces on the front.

PERSONALITY

We discussed the effects of our physical characteristics, such as our face and body, on our attractiveness. Well, what are the effects of non-physical factors such as personality, intelligence, and morality on our attractiveness? We will discuss them in this chapter.

DARK TRIAD

I want to begin this chapter with the most interesting and dangerous personality trait that affects a person's attractiveness: The Dark Triad. Narcissism, Machiavellianism, and Sociopathy (or Psychopathy) that make up the dark trio are defined as separate personality disorders, but they all have many common features. That is why they are called "the dark triad."

Narcissism, commonly known as egotism, is a disorder in which the person sees himself highly and superior to what he actually is. Interestingly, it is a hereditary feature in men. Research shows that the sons of narcissistic fathers are also narcissists. Actually, the expression "Like mother, like daughter" is true for women in terms of attractiveness and behavior, so for men, it is true to say "Like father, like son" for some bad characters.

Machiavellianism is the name of the personality disorder in individuals with the understanding "Every path to purpose is permissible." People with this type of personality disorder are the ones who accept and specialize in ignoring ethical, moral, and legal values, telling all sorts of lies, manipulating people to achieve their goals.

Sociopathy is a personality disorder that manifests itself especially in people with a lack of empathy and not feeling remorse for what they do. Since it is an important personality disorder, we will analyze its features in more detail on the following pages.

Women often describe men with these characteristics, called the dark triad in psychology, as the "bad boy" persona in their love life. The increased attraction of some women to men who have these personality disorders is actually a subject of scientific research.

In their studies, scientists have found various reasons for the causes of this attraction. The most important and interesting one is not so different from men preferring loose women for a short-term relationship. Studies revealed that women mostly prefer this kind of problematic men not for long-term relationships (e.g. marriage) but short-term relationships (e.g. one-night stands, playing around, etc.).

According to another study by Australian and British scientists, women who consider such individuals for long-term relationships show similar personality disorders. So, if a woman sees a man with a dark triad personality disorder as a potential husband candidate from the beginning, she similarly has a dark triad character. In a way, we can say that the birds of a feather flock together.

For short-term relationships, women mostly look for a man who will not be a burden afterward (they will not call, ask, overwhelm, find someone else, etc.). In fact, individuals with this dark triad personality may even be more attractive because of having both this indifference and self-confidence that comes with narcissism. Interestingly, women prefer men of this character more, especially when they are in the ovulation phase of their menstrual cycle. Probably the primitive instinct that says, "Let me find an (easy) partner when I'm already ovulating, and then we can mate and have a child" is effective. But women have very serious handicaps for this "getting attracted instinctively to a bad boy type for a short-term relationship." That is why such relationships often end with disappointment.

One of these handicaps is hormones. Women undergo some kind of perception shift for these type of men due to the effects of their hormones that change during the ovulation phase of their menstrual cycles. Normally women do not prefer these men for a long-term relationship because of the character flaws they have (e.g., lack of interest in his partner and future child, being selfish, the possibility of cheating, being indifferent, being a liar, etc.) However, with the perception shift caused by the hormones, women mistakenly believe that "Yes, he is that kind of person, but he will do it to others, never to me (and our child)!" In other words, scientific studies reveal that rather than the instinct to change the problematic man, women think this problematic man will not have the same attitude towards her (and his future children) because of the hormones in ovulation.

In fact, there is another factor for women that causes things to become complicated. That is sex, which is the natural result of a one-night stand. With orgasm, both sexes secrete a hormone called oxytocin, which enables us to bond with our partners. But the strength and effect of this hormone in attachment are slightly different in women and men. Testosterone in men is counter-effective with oxytocin in attachment. So, as long as the man's testosterone levels are high or remain high, oxytocin's bonding effect is not felt much. Although there is testosterone in women, its levels are quite low. Thus, oxytocin secreted after a one-night stand becomes much more effective. In other words, even if women do not plan it to be that way, they may get attached to the partner because of the oxytocin secreted after orgasm. Yet, this attachment is not observed in men. The only situation where the males' testosterone levels drop, so oxytocin's effects are felt stronger, is when they fall in love. Only then oxytocin secreted during orgasm has an impact on a man's attachment.

Therefore, the relationship with a man with a dark triad personality, even for a short-term or one-night stand, may lead to an unexpected point because the physiologies of both sexes are different: A manipulative, non-emphatic, problematic man and a woman who bonded with him unexpectedly.

Studies show that especially young women find men with this dark triad personality attractive. Perhaps women who face the destruction of this type by men caused in their younger years learn to stay away from such people in the future, albeit with some painful experience. I think in this situation, an example becomes better than precept. However, as we will study in detail in the breakup chapter, I am not sure if other physiological effects of this painful experience is really worth such a risk for the person.

Sociopathy, which is one of the basic elements of dark triad personality disorder, needs to be examined in more detail due to its importance. First of all, most sociopaths are smart and charming people. These qualities make them attractive. However, this attraction should not be perceived only physically. It is more accurate to talk about the appeal of these features blended with intelligence, self-confidence, and charisma, as they are manipulative and use words very well. So, in a way, they have the devil's own charm. Of course, in addition, some of those are physically attractive.

Another characteristic of sociopaths is that they are selfish. They only think of their own interests. In addition to their power to use words well, their charisma and charm also help them manipulate others. In cases where these are ineffective, the method they use is aggression!

Although they are generally sweet talkers, this feature is just an illusion. Because the main characteristic of all sociopathic individuals is that they lack empathy. This lack of empathy is too serious to be underestimated in sociopaths. With these characteristics, they do not hesitate to take advantage of you for their own interests, without worrying about how you will be on the hook or how much you suffer. Even if you are damaged by what they do to you, they do not regret it in any way.

To explain this with a different example; whether it is in business life or private life, there may be situations where almost everyone in their life has mistreated someone, lied to them, left them in a difficult situation, or hurt them knowingly or unknowingly. We, normal people, experience serious regret when we put our heads on the pillow at night if the other person is harmed or has the potential to be because of our actions. We feel guilty and regretful. Because we somehow empathize with the hard situation that the other person experiences. Sociopaths do not have such emotions.

Since they are completely selfish and do not empathize with others, even if somebody gets hurt by what they have done, they do not care in any way, do not feel regret or remorse, and continue their lives as if nothing has happened.

Sociopaths also tend to commit crimes if their charm and manipulation abilities do not help them get what they want. Depending on the situation, this tendency for crimes can range from fraud to document forgery, from bodily harm to murder. Even worse, the serious penalties for these crimes do not prevent sociopaths. If they think such crimes will somehow help them achieve their goal, they can easily commit these crimes without worrying about the possible punishment.

Since we know sociopaths with their extreme examples like Hannibal Lecter in The Silence of the Lambs, we are in an illusion to think that they are infrequent in society. However, sociopaths around us are actually much more than we think. Different studies found that their ratio in the society range between 1-5%, which I believe the 5% prediction on this scale is much more realistic. Because sociopathy is not a personality disorder in which a person sees a problem in themselves and goes to a psychologist or psychiatrist and to be treated. Therefore, it is not possible to determine and record the actual rate in the society.

Various characteristics of sociopaths, from their charisma to manipulation abilities, selfishness, and tendency to do things that are considered to be immoral or crime for others, help them to climb the ladders of success in business life quickly and comfortably. Thus, the rate of sociopathy among senior managers is higher than the general average in society. For example, studies show that 30% of companies' CEOs on the Fortune 500 list have sociopathic features. So, even if you do not encounter people with this disorder in your love life, your chances of facing them as a manager in your business life are high.

The annoying fact about sociopathy is that there is no cure for this disorder. Therefore, whether you have encountered a sociopath in your love affair or a business relationship, you cannot fix them. It is nothing more than a fantasy to believe that you can treat a partner with a disorder that medicine cannot treat, especially with your own efforts. Which is why, when you encounter such people, keep in mind to get away from them as quickly as possible instead of trying to fix them.

ALTRUISM

Let us now discuss the good characteristics that play a role in our attractiveness. The most important of these is altruism, namely selflessness. Altruism is the act of promoting someone else's welfare, even at a risk or cost to ourselves. Studies reveal that both sexes consider altruistic people as good characters, good partners, and good parents.

When we look at the studies on whether altruistic people are preferred for short-term and long-term relationships, we see that both genders prefer them, especially for long-term relationships.

In a 2016 study, Daniel Farrelly and his colleagues from the United Kingdom showed photographs of 12 physically attractive men and another group of 12 unattractive men to 202 women. Photos of men in these two groups were presented to women individually alongside rubrics of particular scenarios describing them high in altruism or low in altruism. According to these characteristics, the subjects were asked how attractive the person was for both short-term and long-term relationships.

They found that the rate of women choosing an ugly but altruistic man for a short-term relationship is almost the same as that of preferring an attractive but selfish man. Although it does not seem like there is a difference, this is an important detail that displays that the rates of approval of physically unattractive men, as long as they are altruistic, are equivalent to attractive but selfish men.

When women's preferences for long-term relationships were analyzed, this time, the results favored physically unattractive but altruistic men. The desirability rating of these men was about 30% higher than attractive but selfish men.

We can find the reason why altruism is important in attractiveness in the evolution of love. One of the essential features that women were looking for in the opposite sex was men to have sufficient resources. If a man is selfish, possessive, and stingy, that is, he uses his resources only for himself, or does not use them at all, this character will not be preferred naturally. Studies reveal that such features reduce the attractiveness of men. On the contrary, it is quite normal when we think about the evolution of love, as men who are altruistic and who use their resources for their entourage too are more attractive for women.

MORALITY

Another characteristic that affects our attractiveness is our morality. Morality refers to the principles concerning the distinction between right and wrong or good and bad behavior.

A joint study of Canadian and Chinese scientists in 2014 analyzing the brains of a group of 28 people comprising 14 women and 14 men revealed that some regions in our brains that were activated when we saw an attractive face were also activated when we see someone doing something morally right.

In addition, in the other part of the research, the photos of an attractive and ugly face were shown separately to the subjects, with a story of doing either a morally good thing or something normal, and they were asked to evaluate the physical appeal of the people in the photos.

While men thought good morals slightly increased the attractiveness of women, for women, good morality had a more positive effect on evaluating the physical characteristics of men. In other words, having good morals is a feature that positively contributes to our physical appeal and makes us look more attractive than we are. Although this effect is reflected in the attractiveness of both genders, it contributes more to men's.

INTELLIGENCE

Another factor that contributes to our attractiveness is our intelligence. Many people think that intelligence is an impressive feature and makes a person more attractive than they normally are. In line with our general observations in society, scientific studies also show that intelligence positively contributes to our attractiveness.

One of the fundamental features we get attracted to in a person was the positive contribution to future children's lives and healthy development. Intelligence is also critical in this respect.

Compared to people with limited intelligence, a smart person is a few steps ahead in finding and managing the right resources. Considering that the pen is mightier than the sword, intelligent people are also more likely to get rid of difficult situations or beat their opponents than those who use brute force. Besides, smart people are less likely to make mistakes that can cause problems for themselves or their children in the future. For reasons such as these and the like, intelligence is an evolutionary feature that makes a person more attractive.

Another factor that makes intelligence attractive is its connection to testosterone. High testosterone levels reduce the activation of logical thinking areas in our brains. So, in a way, we can say that intelligence and high testosterone are inversely proportional. As we mentioned earlier, high testosterone was also opposing to oxytocin, the loyalty and bonding hormone. Considering all of this together, it may be another evolutionary preference that more intelligent people will not have very high testosterone levels, and therefore, will be more faithful in a relationship than people with high testosterone levels. In support of this hypothesis, scientific studies reveal that intelligent people are indeed more loyal in their relationships than other people.

Interestingly, the halo effect also applies to intelligence. Not only are intelligent people perceived more attractive than they actually are, but we also perceive people with high physical attractiveness smarter than they are. Our brain thinks that good genes are always together and generalizes accordingly.

However, as our intelligence increases, our attractiveness does not increase in direct proportion. Studies reveal that there is a limit of intelligence level that has a positive effect on attractiveness. According to the research conducted by Karel Kleisner and his friends in Germany, in 2014, men with IQs higher than 140 were perceived as less intelligent than they were by their partners, and therefore their intelligence had less effect on their attractiveness.

Although the reason for the negative attraction to a very high IQ is not exactly known, it may still have an evolutionary basis. For example, recent research reveals that highly intelligent people are more susceptible to psychiatric diseases such as depression than normal people. In addition, highly intelligent individuals may find physically protecting and caring for their descendants and spouses a little more unnecessary than others. Looking at real-life examples, we also frequently observe that scientists generally marry later than their peers, have fewer children, and spend more time at work than at home. All these factors may cause very high intelligence to have a negative effect on attractiveness.

HUMOR

Humor, or simply funniness, is also one of our traits that affects our attractiveness. There is a question that has been discussed for years: Do women love funny men, or do they find men that they love funny? I think we will find the answer to this question when we evaluate the scientific studies on the effects of humor on a person's appeal. To find the right answer, it may be a wiser approach to focus more on neurological research in this section. Because self-reports of women in sociological surveys, which show that they prefer funny men, may not always be the case in real life.

First of all, a good joke on the spot is definitely an indicator of intelligence. So funny people have an extra appeal because of their intelligence. Moreover, brain scanning studies show that when we hear a good joke, the area of our brain called the ventromedial prefrontal cortex (vmPFC) is activated. The same area is one of the activated regions when we see an attractive person. In other words, a good joke affects our brains as if we saw a physically appealing face.

Interestingly, the effect of a good joke on vmPFC is slightly different in men and women. When men hear a joke, their vmPFC is more activated than women. In other words, being funny may increase women's attractiveness more than men's. In addition, studies reveal that women find smiling men less attractive. The exact opposite is true for women: Smiling women are found more attractive by men.

When we evaluate all these studies' results, we can say that being humorous and smiling increases the attractiveness of women more than that of men. Although humor also increases men's attractiveness because of the intelligence factor, it is most effective to settle for the clever jokes made in the right place at the right time without becoming a clown.

Therefore, if we come to the answer to our question in the beginning, whether women love funny men or find men they love funny, we can say that men who can be funny without turning into a clown are more attractive. However, when we consider the activation of vmPFC and the halo effect, it is also true that women find men they are attracted to funnier.

Another feature associated with humor is a smile. The smile of the person expresses their sincerity, accessibility, and positivity. Studies show that a smile is the most preferred characteristic in humans compared to other emotional states. Therefore, when we approach somebody that we do not know, their smile gives us a different strength and motivation. Although smiling is a preferred feature in both genders, over-smiling can have different effects on the attractiveness of the sexes. Studies show that men find smiling women more attractive, while women find smiling men less appealing. Perhaps, a constantly smiling man is not preferred by women, as it contrasts with the cultural and evolutionary seriousness imposed on the male gender.

The negative effect of the smile on men's attractiveness does not mean that men should wear a sullen and serious expression 24/7. It is only important to avoid grinning like a Cheshire cat constantly. In addition to this, although we will touch on this in the flirting chapter in more detail, a sincere smile brings extra credit to men, especially at the first meeting.

OTHER FACTORS

When deciding whether we like a person, we do not just evaluate their physical and personality traits. Other features also contribute to the attractiveness of the person. In fact, these can sometimes even move ahead of physical characteristics, depending on gender and expectation from the relationship. In this chapter, we will analyze these features that contribute to our overall attractiveness.

SOCIAL STATUS

Social status plays a significant role, especially in men's attractiveness. In most cases, it can surpass physical and personality traits for attractiveness because one of the most important criteria that women seek in the opposite sex is men to have sufficient resources for the health and future of children. They generally evaluate this with the social status of the person. Although what establishes social status in our early ages are criteria such as popularity in the classroom, in advancing ages, what determines the social status are the position and material resources that the person has and the accessories that point to these resources.

In 2012, Nicolas Gueguen and Lubomir Lamy from France conducted a study showing the effects of expensive cars, mostly a reflection of social status, on men's attractiveness. The results are impressive. In this experiment, they used three cars valued differently:

- A new Audi A5 Ambition Luxury (price EUR 58,000) for the high-value car

- A 1-year-old Renault Mégane (price EUR 24,000) for the middle-value car

- A 15-year-old Renault 5 Super Campus (price EUR 800) for the low-value car

Six attractive male confederates came out of three different types of cars at different times and approached the women walking nearby and asked for their phone numbers to have a date together.

With each car type, the confederates made this invitation to 180 women. So in total, they included the responses of 540 women in the experiment analysis. When the confederate asked for their numbers, 23% of the women complied with the request when he was with the high-value car. This ratio was 13% when he was with the middle-value car and 8% when he was next to the low-value car. The high-value car almost tripled the positive response rate from women.

However, we cannot necessarily associate these women's attraction to social status with gold-digging. Although there are also too many gold digger women, when we think about the criteria of evolutionary attraction, men with high economic and social status are one step ahead in having sufficient resources. Thus, high social status increases their natural appeal in the eyes of women.

The work of Michael Dunn and Robert Searle from Cardiff University in Ireland in 2010 is also one of the best scientific examples showing how social status increases men's natural attractiveness. It is actually my favorite study in this regard because this experiment is one of the few studies that examine the effect of social status on the attractiveness of both genders together.

In the study, both male and female models were photographed separately in two cars, one of which was cheap and the other one an expensive latest model. The opposite sex juries rated the attractiveness of the models out of 10. For the experiment to be objective, the juries that assessed male and female models in the cheap and expensive cars consisted of different people. In other words, four jury groups, two of which are composed of women and the other two of men, gave points to photos of the opposite sex model in different cars.

Two male juries that evaluated the female model's attractiveness in different cars both gave 7 points out of 10. The female jury that rated the male model's photo in the cheap car gave his attractiveness about 5.5 points out of 10. The other female jury assessing the same male model's attractiveness in the expensive car gave 7 points out of 10. So, the results revealed that the social status and economic power of women do not make a difference for men in evaluating their attractiveness, while the same criteria significantly increased men's attractiveness for women.

Although social status does not increase women's attractiveness, many women strive to have a higher status. We witness that they display their economic and social status with expensive cars, jewelry, and clothes. Even sometimes, they want to appear economically more powerful than they actually are with phones and other accessories they bought on loan. Why do women pay attention to these features that do not correspond to anything in terms of evolutionary and current attractiveness criteria?

Although this behavior also has different motives, such as the desire to make their peers envious, its advantage in terms of attractiveness is that it facilitates their access to men with higher social status. When women make themselves appear in a higher social status than they are and spend time in top-class locations, the probability of being noticed by potential partners with better resources increases. It also prevents men who do not have these qualities from approaching them: hitting two birds with one stone.

Research conducted by Devendra Singh of the University of Texas in the 90s studied the effects of men's income and their physical characteristics for their desirability, depending on the type of relationship sought by women.

In this study, scientists asked the female subjects to assess the desirability of men with different waist-to-hip ratios and income levels for a short-term or long-term relationship. When women evaluated men of different income groups and various WHRs for having coffee together, there was no significant difference in desirability.

But when it came to evaluating men's desirability for long-term relationships, the difference manifested itself clearly. Regardless of income, males with 0.7 WHR—which was, as we mentioned before, the most attractive for females but definitely not preferred for males—had the lowest value in attractiveness. The study also revealed that having a high income slightly increased the attractiveness of individuals with 0.7 WHR, but this effect was not significant. When it came to marriage, having low and middle income did not change the attractiveness of individuals with 0.9 and 1.0 WHR while having high income more than doubled their desirability in women's eyes.

If we evaluate the results of this research, we can say that for marriage, a high income does not alter the attractiveness and desirability of men who have physical qualities that diverge from masculine features, such as having 0.7 WHR. However, for men with masculine physical properties, receiving a high income increases their appeal for such relationships. For short-term and non-serious relationships such as drinking coffee or chatting, men's physical characteristics and income status do not affect their desirability.

The clothes we wear are another factor that affects our attractiveness. There is a lot of research done about how our clothes determine our perceived social status. However, in this chapter, I would like to tell an anecdote about something that I experienced, rather than studies on the importance of clothes.

When I first moved to Sweden as a new Ph.D. student, there was the intensity of learning a new subject and also the cost of establishing a new life with a research assistant salary in a new country where you only went with a suitcase. Thus, clothes were not, unfortunately, at the top of my list of priorities during the first months. One night, after finishing my experiments that lasted all day long, I was walking home tired and exhausted. I had comfortable clothes that I put on as they were the first things that caught my eye before leaving home without paying much attention to color harmony and fashion. I noticed an oncoming girl walking alone on the sidewalk. Of course, she also noticed me. Her first reaction as soon as she saw me at that time of night was to cross anxiously onto the pavement on the other side of the road. Since I knew who I was, it was an incredibly degrading moment for me, and I came to my senses.

After that incident, I realized that I should not put my clothes in such an insignificant position. I started putting dressing properly and personal care on top of my priority list. As a result, the behavior and approach of women have changed almost a hundred and eighty degrees.

You do not have to spend a lot of money to dress properly. You can wear affordable no-name clothes, and as long as they are clean, ironed, and match each other, you will be fine. Whether you are a woman or a man, when you dress well and properly, your attraction for the other person will increase positively.

Another element that affects our appeal is the color of the clothes we wear. Studies show that when evaluated by the opposite sex, red and black clothes make the person appear more attractive in both men and women compared to other colors. Interestingly, this effect is not observed if same-sex peers evaluate the attractiveness of the person. That is to say, opinions of our besties about picking a color may not be correct. Since for heterosexual individuals, the opinions of the opposite sex matter for attractiveness, it is beneficial to wear an outfit where red or black tones are predominant when going to any social environment.

In another leg of the research about the effect of clothing color on attractiveness, scientists photographed models in different colored clothes. Afterward, they showed these photographs to the subjects in a way that the color of the clothes would not be seen, that is, only the neck and face of the models were visible. Although the clothes' color did not appear in the photographs, the subjects interestingly found the model's photos taken while wearing red clothes the most attractive.

This effect may actually be similar to women's increased appeal due to the self-confidence that comes with applying makeup. By wearing red, people's mood may change. Thus, they may gain additional appeal because of their clothes' color. Some of us, especially males, may not like red, as it is a very garish and flamboyant color. This thought may even create a deep uneasiness in us while wearing red. When we consider the study's results, if we feel uncomfortable with wearing red, this may reflect on our self-confidence and facial expressions and decrease our attractiveness. In order not to encounter these negativities, it may be more appropriate to choose a black outfit. Of course, we can also combine this outfit with red accessories or details if we want.

Well then, what is the effect of other colors on our attractiveness? Research by Craig Roberts from the University of Liverpool in 2010 gives us the scientific answer to this question. In this study, photos of ten male and ten female models with various colored T-shirts were shown to 30 persons of each gender and were asked to evaluate them in terms of attractiveness. They revealed that the women found the same man as the least attractive in white clothes, while the male subjects found the women the least attractive in yellow and green clothes. When evaluating the results, we should keep in mind that this study is done in the UK, where most people have a lighter skin tone. Men with darker or tanned skin tones (e.g., the Mediterranean people) may look more appealing wearing white-colored clothes.

FLOWERS

Flowers evoke positive emotions in all humans, perhaps because they represent the spring, beautiful and sunny days. Various studies revealed that flowers have more positive effects not only in romantic settings but also in many different situations.

For example, a study showed that patients who had flowers in their rooms felt less pain after the operation compared to other patients, and their pulse and blood pressure values were closer to normal. Another result of the same study is that these positive effects were independent of the gender of the patients.

When we come to their effects on attractiveness, we see that not only the flowers themselves but also their use in accessories increases a person's appeal. For example, men approached women who wore a barrette with a flower more positively than women who wore no hair ornament. Not only barrettes, floral patterned dresses or accessories can also increase women's appeal. Of course, this does not mean to go out like a garland, but one should not ignore the positive effects of such wisely used details. For instance, especially on summer days, wearing a black or red dress with a floral pattern may be the right choice to increase their attractiveness.

Not only is the presence of flowers on us or giving them to a partner, but also their existence in our surroundings, can affect our subconscious about attractiveness. A study by Nicolas Gueguen from France clearly displays this effect of flowers.

In this study, a man from the research group approached 600 women in front of three different shops in a big mall: a patisserie, a women's shoe shop, and a flower shop. After introducing himself and telling them that he found them pretty, he asked their numbers to arrange a date later. The results are very interesting.

When this offer was made in front of the shoe store, 11.5% of women responded positively, 15.5% when made in front of the patisserie, and 24% when made in front of the flower store. In other words, even having flowers around has increased the positive response of women to the male confederate almost two times. Perhaps one should not underestimate this power of flowers, which is an indispensable part of the tables in romantic dinners.

TATTOOS

Tattoos, which are the permanent accessories we use on our body, also affect our attractiveness. However, their effect differs in men and women.

Studies show that both genders are negatively biased towards women with tattoos. Subjects of both sexes find the pictures of women with tattoos less attractive than those without tattoos. In addition, both men and women think that tattooed women are easier to get. The results of the research by Kaylee Skoda and her colleagues in Canada with 814 women, 391 of which are tattooed, strengthen the view that there is a grain of truth in these stereotypical prejudices.

According to the study results, women with tattoos are more open to casual sexual encounters than their peers without tattoos. They look more positively at sexuality experienced outside of a relationship or marriage (for example, one-night stands). In this study, scientists found that being more open-minded towards uncommitted sexuality has nothing to do with the number and size of tattoos the woman has. In other words, it does not mean that those who have more, or bigger tattoos are more open-minded about sexual issues. However, a remarkable finding in the study results was that the tattoo's location may affect their views on sexual openness. When women with tattoos are compared within themselves, scientists found that women whose tattoos are in a place that is normally not visible, such as the breasts, genitals, and lower back, are more sexually open than those whose tattoos are visible on places like the hands and face.

In men, the perception of tattoos is a little different. Prejudices against men with temperate tattoos are more positive, especially for short-term relationships. But too intense tattoos that cover most of the body also reduce men's attractiveness, as they reflect a negative image, such as gang membership or belonging to other marginal groups.

MENSTRUAL CYCLE

The menstrual cycle is a feature that men do not have but women have. Although women mostly dislike the fact that they have it, the menstrual cycle is another element affecting their attractiveness. Since women are the ones who suffer from the menstrual cycle, I think it is their right to enjoy its effect on attractiveness to the utmost.

In the previous sections, we mentioned that women's smell in their menstrual cycle's ovulation period is most attractive to men than the other days of the cycle. The effect of the menstrual cycle on women's attractiveness is not limited to smell.

Studies show that the photos taken during the ovulation period (that is, on the 13th-15th day after the start of menstruation if you have a regular and approximately 28-day period) appear more attractive to men than other days. Considering the results of this research, whether it is for getting likes on platforms such as Instagram, Facebook, Tinder, or for the CVs in job applications, using a photo taken on the day of ovulation compared to a photo taken on other days will bring women some more advantages because of the halo effect of attractiveness. There is a little more information I would like to add about the effect of the menstrual cycle on attractiveness. If you are interested in the neurobiology of love and do research on the internet outside of this book, you may find information relating to women liking different types of men in different periods of their menstrual cycles.

You will notice many articles stating that women like more feminine men when bleeding occurs, but they prefer more masculine men during the ovulation period. In studies with small experimental groups, such an effect was seen for many years. However, recent studies undertaken with larger groups of women reveal no such change in their preference. Therefore, the information you may find in the old sources can be misleading because it does not reflect the truth.

Although women's preference of men types does not change with the periods of their menstrual cycles, one factor affects this preference: the country's socioeconomic structure. A joint study conducted by an international group of scientists on 4483 subjects living in 34 different countries revealed that the country's socioeconomic structure affects women's preference for masculine men. According to this study published in early 2019, women in countries with high socioeconomic status prefer men of a more masculine type.

If we look at the evolutionary basis of this interesting finding, it should not surprise us. As we mentioned earlier, the most important features that women seek in their partners were whether they would take care of them and their children in the future, whether the potential partner had sufficient resources for this, and whether they would use these resources for them and their children. At the same time, we mentioned that the masculine characteristics of men are shaped by testosterone. Testosterone was also reducing the effect of oxytocin, which is the hormone for bonding. So, men with high testosterone levels probably would not be loyal. Consequently, despite instinctively choosing men with masculine characteristics for short-term relationships, women would usually stay away from them for long-term relationships.

However, in countries with a high socioeconomic level, women's income and labor force participation are high. Therefore, women living in such countries may not need a man's resources to care for themselves and their future child if they got cheated on and abandoned. With the self-confidence of standing comfortably on her feet and not endangering the future of her child, they can feel more attracted to masculine men, which they consider a riskier group. In countries whose socioeconomic levels are low, women prefer to avoid such risks. Thus, the personality traits of men become more prominent.

AGE

One of the features we look for and find attractive in the opposite sex is their age because it determines the reproductive potential the most. Since men can maintain their reproductive potential for very long years, this feature is more important in women whose reproductive years are more limited.

When we look biologically, the period when women have the highest reproductive potential is 20-22 years old. Even though girls' childbearing potential starts with their adolescence when they first menstruate, their bodies try to adapt to this metabolism change in the first few years. Women also have another problem in adolescent pregnancy. In our section on height, we mentioned that the female body has difficulty in allocating enough resources for both sexual maturation and growth during adolescence. It has to renounce one of them a little. With such limited resources, pregnancy becomes even a more immense burden for their body, and the healthy development of the fetus becomes almost impossible. Therefore, women have a high rate of miscarriage during this period when their bodies are not fully ready for pregnancy. In the advanced reproductive ages, the number of potential children they can have in total decreases each year, and the risk of having children with various chromosomal disorders increases.

For this reason, regardless of their own age, men find women in the early twenties the most attractive. In these ages, the number of women's suitors is the highest. Although this attraction is sufficient in terms of many types of relationships, in situations that require a much more serious decision such as marriage, most men also give importance to signs such as the personality of their partner and harmony in their relationships. As a result, we should not consider the extra appeal that women have in this age range as the criterion that every man cares the most about to marry.

As women get older, this appeal, and thus, the number of their suitors decreases. This is, unfortunately, an injustice of nature towards women. Because men's reproductive potential continues until much later ages, their ages are not as important as women's. On the contrary, social status and adequate resources, which are often a feature that women seek in the opposite sex, mostly increases as men get older. Thus, men can continue their appeal for longer periods and at a later age as long as they look after themselves. This appeal is also independent of women's ages. That is why even individuals like Johnny Depp, Brad Pitt, Keanu Reeves, George Clooney, etc., who live in the second half of their 50s, are still very attractive to most women in their twenties and embellish their dreams because of the social status and resources they have.

In our daily lives, people often restrict themselves because of the cultural norms. Some individuals even find it wrong to express their inclinations towards people that belong to such an age group, whereas they can comfortably do it towards individuals like movie stars, artists, etc., whom the society will overlook because of their social status. That is why people usually choose partners for their relationship in the age range that will not cause some raised eyebrows. When we examine married couples worldwide, we see that men are, on average, 3-5 years older than women. Most women prefer mature men, and psychological sciences associate this with prior problems with their father during childhood. However, explaining this preference with evolutionary attraction criteria is a better approach. For example, it is hard to say that the unemployed Uncle James, who sits in a coffee shop all day and eyes-up passers-by, is of the same age as Johnny Depp and has a similar appeal. If the reason for this attraction to mature men was not the social status but the age or only the problems with the father, as psychological sciences emphasized, Uncle James, who is probably a more fatherly figure compared to Johnny Depp, would have had a similar appeal.

The charm of the early twenties can sometimes cause a serious illusion for women. They can assume that the excess of their suitors at these ages will also continue in the later years. However, as women get older, especially by the late 20s, the number of suitors begins to decline rapidly. At the same time, many men get already married at those ages, so women's options will similarly be reduced. This includes the instinctive anxiety of the limited biological time left to have a healthy child and the social pressure in some cultures imposing them to marry soon. This anxiety can sometimes lead women to make wrong decisions: marrying—in a panic—a man who is not suitable for her. Most of the time, decisions made in this panic state underlie the making of incompatible couples or people that do not match each other.

Another option is to continue waiting for the ideal partner. This is mostly the situation that beautiful but confirmed bachelor women are placed in. Over the years, suitors and options decrease, but the ideal remains constant. In fact, this is a better behavior compared to panicked marriages. Because a relationship or marriage with the wrong person can cause significant harm to us. However, as time goes on, the possibility of experiencing love can be impossible. Therefore, it may be wiser to accept this injustice of nature and act accordingly. If you find the right person at an early age but think "I can find someone better in the future" or "I am still very young, I am not going to marry anyone until my 30s," you should not underestimate the possibility of being disappointed as you get older and regret the decision. Of course, things can go as you expected, or even better. But it is always worth keeping in mind that we are less likely to find the right person as we get older.

THE PHYSIOLOGY OF ATTRACTION

When we meet someone, we may get attracted to their personality, physical characteristics, or a harmonic combination of the two. At that moment, our brain and physiology undergo some changes. We will discuss these changes in this chapter.

Before we talk about the changes in our body and brain, it is useful to learn a little theoretical knowledge to understand the subject better.

Our sympathetic nervous system gets activated when we see danger and fear. If the threat is within our ability, we struggle with it. We fight. For example, when we see an insect, we often step on and kill it, since the perception of danger is not so great, as it cannot usually cause us instant damage. In this way, we eliminate potential future risks such as the harm it may cause by biting us while we sleep or carrying germs. However, if the danger is big and we think we cannot cope with it instantly, we escape from this danger. For example, when we see a big bear with her cubs while walking in the forest, if we do not have a weapon to protect us, we think we cannot cope with this danger. Thus, as soon as we see the bear, we run away as quickly as possible. This reaction, which we show in moments of danger or fear, is called "fight-or-flight response." Our sympathetic nervous system prepares us to escape or fight by making some changes in our body.

So, what are these changes or preparations in our body for fight-or-flight response?

First, our adrenaline level increases and our heart beats faster. This is an essential change for the fight-or-flight response. Because if we fight or run away, our muscles will need oxygen and energy. Our heart pumps blood faster to our body to better supply oxygen and energy.

Our pupils dilate. The enlargement of our pupils allows us to see further better if we are going to escape. It also helps us to see our environment better in dim light if we enter dark places while fleeing. Our sympathetic nervous system prepares our body for all these possibilities as soon as we give the fight-or-flight response.

Our muscles stretch slightly and get tonus. If they stretch a little more, we start shaking because of it. This is an important preparation. If we are going to flee or fight, it will be much easier and faster to start moving with slightly stretched muscles compared to a relaxed state.

When we are in danger, our sympathetic nervous system also causes our hands and feet to sweat. In fact, this is a very important preparation our bodies make before fleeing or fighting. We use muscle strength when running or fighting. Our muscles produce heat as they function. For the body temperature to be maintained at normal levels, this heat must be dissipated by sweating. This sweating is our body's early preparation against the heat that will be produced.

In addition to this, our mouth dries, again with the effect of our sympathetic nervous system. This is a change that our body makes to use the available resources effectively during the fight-or-flight response. Because when we sweat, our body loses water. We do not have a chance to take a break and drink water while fleeing or fighting. We usually do not have the possibility of drinking and storing water beforehand too. Therefore, our body pauses the unnecessary water use for our saliva to use it most effectively and efficiently so that there is enough water in our body to sweat.

Our sympathetic nervous system also makes some preparations in our internal organs. Although we will not address them individually in this book, it is sufficient to know that all these changes are also about preparing our bodies to fight or flee.

There is another situation where we give the fight-or-flight response: when we are attracted to someone. When the person we are attracted to is around us, our heart starts to pump faster, we become tense and tremble, our voice gets thinner with the tightening of our muscles, our palms sweat, and our mouth dries.

Fight-or-flight response

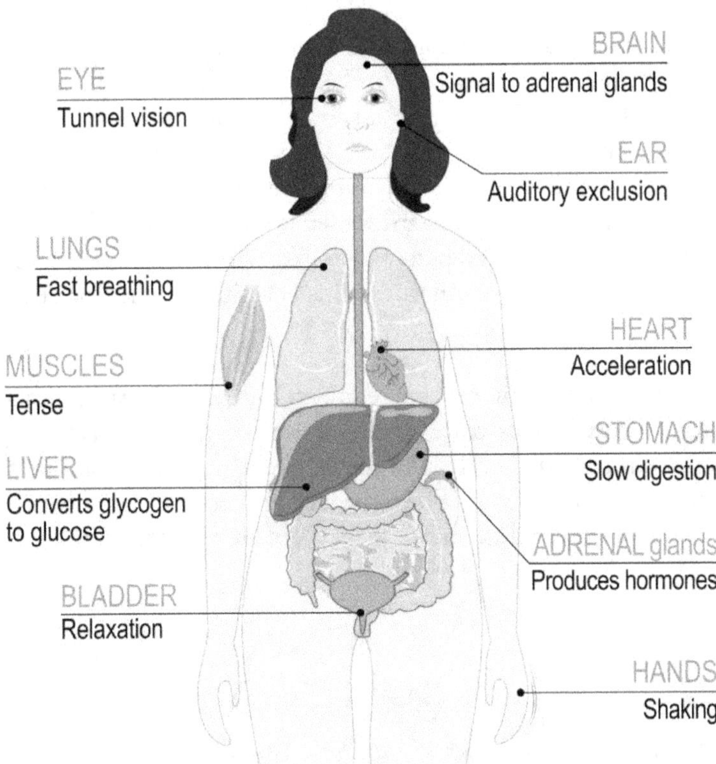

Figure 12- In the event of danger, our sympathetic nervous system gives "Fight-or-Flight Response" and causes some changes in our body.

Since our bodies show the fight-or-flight response when we are afraid in a moment of danger, why do we react when we are attracted to a person? Does our subconscious consider someone we like to be a danger to us? If we put aside individuals with a dark triad personality disorder, the people we like are mostly not dangerous. On the contrary, they often have features that make us dream beautifully. So why does our body react to them too?

The reason is fear. However, what we fear and see as dangerous is not our potential romantic partner! When we like someone, we are afraid of losing them, afraid of them not liking us, so we are afraid that our liking is one-sided! When we think generally, and somewhat metaphorically, the physical response we give is to fight or flee. When we like someone, we either talk to them and open up, so we face our fear and fight; or we bottle up our emotions and flee from our fear: fight or flight response!

When we are attracted to someone, we involuntarily dream about the future. These dreams vary, from how a beautiful couple we will be to how we will have pleasant times. If we are looking for a serious relationship, our dreams can be even about marriage and having children. We see the other person as the source of and the path to our happiness. The beautiful things we encounter in life or their possibilities are a kind of reward for us. It has a similar effect for our brain too. So, our brain sees the person we like as a reward. Therefore, the dopaminergic reward pathway in our brains is activated when we are attracted to someone.

The studies show that our ventral tegmental area, nucleus accumbens, and orbitofrontal cortex in this pathway are activated when we like a person. In addition, the ventromedial prefrontal cortex, the region in our brain responsible for encoding value, is activated. The more we like someone, the bigger and more valuable the reward is, and the more these areas are activated.

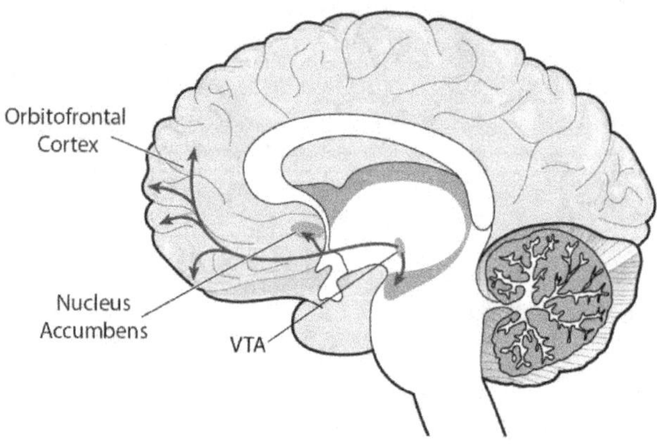

Figure 13-When we like someone, the reward system in our brain is activated.

FLIRTING

Every day, when walking on the road, sitting in a café, on TV, etc., we see maybe dozens of attractive people. But we do not fall in love with them because love is an emotion that usually passes through certain stages.

First, the person we are attracted to should be accessible to us. This means someone we can easily interact with. Because only when we communicate with a person, we get to know each other better and allow attraction to evolve towards love. We call this process flirting.

Flirting is the most misunderstood step and the step where most mistakes are made on the road to love. Because we can easily decide whether we like someone, but we are often unsure if that person is flirting with us, or if we are flirting, whether we are giving the right signals to them.

According to a research by scientists from the University of Kansas in 2014, only 28% of people can correctly understand whether someone is flirting with them. The remaining 72%, that is, almost three-quarters, do not know when someone is flirting with them, or they misinterpret it as flirting when someone is acting only sincerely.

The rate of understanding whether someone is flirting with them is lower in women than in men: around 18%. Men, on the other hand, can predict a flirting woman with a 36% accuracy. Still, almost two-thirds of men do not notice when a woman is flirting with them.

In the continuation of the same study, scientists asked a jury to watch the interaction between the two people and guess whether one flirted with the other. The results revealed that the probability of a third person's correct guess was even lower than the individuals themselves. So, when your friends say, "I think this boy/girl likes you." as an outsider looking in, their observations can even be more wrong than your instincts. That is why we must understand flirting well, especially for not missing opportunities due to misunderstandings.

In fact, although the way people flirt varies to a certain degree, it also has a lot in common, from America to Asia, from Africa to Europe.

In the 1960s, Austrian ethologist Irenäus Eibl-Eibesfeldt recorded the way women flirt around the world, using a hidden camera. When he examined the videos, he saw that all women have a common set of flirting behaviors. No matter where they are from and what their socioeconomic backgrounds are, women's flirting behaviors do not change from Amazonian rainforests to the salons of Paris.

Women first smile at their admirers and lift their eyebrows in a swift, jerky motion. They then open their eyes wide to gaze at him. This is followed by dropping their eyelids, tilting their heads down and to the side, and looking away. Frequently women also cover their faces with their hands, giggling nervously as they retreat behind their palms. The sequence of movements women perform when they are attracted to someone is so distinctive in almost every culture that Eibl-Eibesfeldt argues that this is an instinctive behavior of interest coded in women's genes, a universal flirting signal.

So, how do men flirt first when they like the opposite sex? They usually display a dominant and open body language. Bending forward while speaking, trying to stay closer than the normal communication distance, touching the opposite person, scanning often and for a long time with eyes, and smiling are the most common behaviors of men when they flirt.

FLIRTING MOTIVATIONS

One reason for the misunderstandings in flirting is that there are different flirting motivations according to the situation, time, and person. So, everyone does not flirt to have a relationship and to be lovers. In their research, scientists found six main flirting motivations. These are:

I.   Taking the relationship to the next level

II.   Sexual intent

III.   Exploring or curiosity

IV.   Having fun

V.   Raising the self-esteem

VI.   Material reasons

Let's discuss all these motivations one by one.

Flirting to take the relationship forward is the main subject of our book. The romantic flirting we do to get to know someone better and move on to the next step when we like them is the primary motivation in this type of flirting. We can flirt with someone not only to intensify our relationship but to fix the relationship if some things are not going well, and we are dissatisfied with it.

Another flirting motivation is flirting for sex. People with this motivation do not seek serious and romantic relationships. Their only goal is sexual satisfaction. We can list flirting for reasons such as one-night stands or finding a fuck buddy in this context. People can flirt with others to achieve these goals. As you can imagine, this flirting motivation is more common in men than in women.

Another flirting motivation is exploring or curiosity. Sometimes we receive various signals from others, but we may not fully understand what they mean. In such cases, people can flirt to encourage the other person and check what their true intentions are. In this way, they can understand people's motivations better and find answers to questions such as "Do they like me?" "To what extent are they interested in me?" "Is the reason behind their nice behavior toward me because they are sincere and want to be a good friend, or is there a romantic motivation behind it?" or "I wonder if they would like me; can I win them if I try a little?" Flirting in this context, which does not always have a romantic purpose, is called flirting for exploring.

Having fun is another flirting motivation. This is a more common type of flirting in women. Someone with this motivation often flirts with many people at the same time. However, what they are looking for is definitely not a romantic relationship. People prefer this type of flirtation to seek attention, establish a social environment, or strengthen ties with the person they are flirting with.

People may not prefer this type of flirtation for these purposes only. There may be other deep reasons behind it. For example, individuals who have been humiliated or bullied for various reasons in their social environment during adolescence or childhood may want to flirt with many people simultaneously to make up for their insecurity. Again, because of the same reason, they may distance themselves from all serious relationships because they fear that they will not be loved in return and will be disappointed if the relationship progresses. Similarly, they may have experienced severe traumas in their previous relationships and are afraid of being in love and getting hurt again.

Whatever the reason is, what we have to keep in mind is that the motivation of the people flirting for fun is not to have a romantic relationship. If we flirt with such a person for romantic purposes and eventually get disappointed, we should not blame ourselves.

Increasing self-esteem is another flirting motivation. People flirting with this motivation do not aim to have a romantic relationship. Ego satisfaction is one of its most important goals. Some people head for this type of flirting with certain expectations, such as, "Can I win over that boy or girl?" "How nice it would be if he were interested in me, flirting with me, and flattering my pride."

In addition, sometimes people can get out of a relationship, naturally depressed, in a mood where they feel bad. In such times, some people may prefer this kind of flirting motivation because they think someone else's temporary interest will make them feel better. Naturally, their purpose in flirting is not to have a long-term romantic relationship.

Let's come to our final flirting motivation, flirting to accomplish an instrumental goal. The material reasons that cause a person to flirt with others can be very diverse. For example, a free meal in a nice place or a free drink while at the bar are two of them. You can be a hardworking student and take good notes in the classroom. Your classmate of the opposite sex may flirt to get your lecture notes or make you study with them. Another frequent reason for this motivation is the money you have. If you are a well-off person, people can flirt with you to share your opportunities, and thanks to you, spend a higher level or more enjoyable time than they normally would.

If you play an active role in your institution, some people may flirt with you to get a title or promotion. Similarly, some students may flirt with their professors to get better grades. All these examples make up the primary motivations of people in flirting for material reasons. There are no romantic goals in this type of flirting.

The rate of encountering these six main flirting motivation types is also different. Although this rate varies from person to person and depends on the situation, studies reveal that 26% of flirting is done with the motivation of wanting a romantic relationship. In other words, only one of every four people who flirts with you in your life has the purpose of having a romantic relationship. This is followed by flirting for exploring and flirting for sex. The average rate of both is 23%. Afterward, there comes the flirting for fun. The rate of this type of flirting is 21%. While flirting to increase self-confidence covers 5%, material flirting is only 2%.

These rates, which reflect the average of society, can vary from person to person. For example, if you are a woman, the proportion of people flirting with you for sex will be over 23%. Similarly, if you are a well-off person, the rate of coming across a person flirting for material reasons would, unfortunately, be more than 2%.

When evaluating flirting motivations, we should not ignore the fact that people can have different dating motivations at the same time. While one person flirts with some people for fun, they can also simultaneously flirt with another person for material reasons. So, these flirting motivations are mostly situational rather than characteristics that persist throughout a person's life. Nonetheless, sometimes people can continue their single flirting motivation throughout their lives.

When we look at the figures, it appears how low the probability of having a romantic relationship is, even if there is an actual romantic flirting. On average, one out of every four people who flirt with us do it because they want a romantic relationship, and we can only accurately notice 28% of those who flirt. When we calculate, it is almost one in twelve. There are also additional factors that lower these rates. Do we like that person and want a romantic relationship? This is also important!

There are also some flirting that do not even start. You may think someone is interested in you, but you are not sure. That person may be shy and, therefore, may not step into a flirt: a flirting that cannot happen. In that case, if you are interested in them too, you should make them feel that they will not get a negative reaction from you. Everyone has a fear of rejection. As we mentioned in our preceding chapter, this fear activates our sympathetic nervous system. The person who is not afraid of being rejected does not really care about you after all.

Sometimes, your potential romantic partner may not trust you. This distrust may occasionally stem from your general behavior. For example, it is useful to check whether you are flirtatious with everyone with a motivation for having fun or whether there is such a perception about you in your circle. Because if people do not feel special in a relationship and think they will be cheated on and get hurt, they will hesitate to start a relationship.

The insecurity of the other person may not originate from your actions but may be more general. The problem may not be your behavior, but they may have a general distance to love and relationships, as they may have been hurt in their previous relationship. Those who have this kind of insecurity can actually be convinced. However, since they are persuaded but do not internalize trust, other problems may arise. This time, you will be the one who wears off more.

Sometimes, people may not be readily available to have a relationship with you. They may have a partner. They may be confused. In this case, forcing them to have a relationship may not be the right thing to do. Of course, being preferred in such situations makes us proud. However, according to studies, someone who has cheated on their partners in their previous relationships is three times more likely to cheat on their partners in their future relationships. So, someone who would leave their partner for you is very likely to leave you for someone else in the future.

We can increase the possibilities indefinitely. Therefore, I would only like to mention one of these without making this chapter any longer. If someone has flirted with you a little but has not gone further, this may be an exploration flirt. The person got the answer and is not interested in what comes next. We should not take this situation too personally. We need to continue our way, knowing that almost everybody experiences this on average in one of four flirting.

When we think of all these, finding love with the right person is not an easy task. But do not worry, this book is here to help you with that.

FLIRTING STYLES

Sometimes we do not understand whether somebody is flirting with us because the ways of flirting vary from person to person. In their studies, scientists identified five different flirting styles. These are:

I.   Traditional Flirting

II.   Playful Flirting

III.   Sincere Flirting

IV.   Physical Flirting

V.   Polite Flirting

Let us take a detailed look at these different flirting styles. People with traditional flirting style think that men should always take the first step. They say that the party that pursues the other in flirting should always be the man and think that the opposite is inappropriate. They are aware that the times have changed, and nowadays, women are also taking the first step and pursue men from time to time. But no matter what, they think it is wrong.

As you can imagine, it is women who mostly support this form of flirting. They probably demand this to avoid the fear of rejection so that life would be more comfortable for them. Interestingly, what women do does not exactly match what they want on this issue. Although they are the ones who defend this flirting style the most, this is not the style they use the most in real life.

Men with the traditional flirting style are interested in fewer people throughout their lives. To make this a little bit clearer, if a person is interested in a total of ten people in their lifetime, the men who prefer traditional flirting have a much lower number of women that they are attracted to than their peers.

Women who practice this flirting style complain that men do not notice their interest. In fact, this is something to be expected, in a sense. If you say that "I do not reveal anything until the man takes the first step, and it is always him who should be running after me in flirting," it is quite normal that your interest is not apparent to the other party.

Another type of flirting is playful flirting. People with this style think:

« Flirting is just for fun; people should not take it so seriously. »

« Flirting is a harmless form of entertainment. »

« I can also flirt with people I have no romantic interest. »

« The biggest reason I flirt is that it makes me feel good. »

Considering these, we can say that the motivations of those who prefer playful flirting style are generally for fun and increasing self-esteem.

Scientists have revealed that women do this type of flirting more than men. In other words, although women advocate mostly the traditional flirting style, they apply the playful style more.

Individuals with this flirting style are attracted to a greater number of people than average. So, if we open this up a bit again, if a person is interested in a total of ten people in their lifetime, people who adopt the playful flirting style are interested in much more than that.

People with this style of flirting do not have a problem expressing their interest to the other party. In the previous chapter, we have mentioned that people can understand if someone is flirting with them with only 28% accuracy. This correct prediction rate increases if the other person has the playful flirting style.

People who adopt this style find flirting flattering. So, they very much enjoy flirting and people flirting with them. Since men with this flirting style are likely to have a similar playful character in general, they complain that sometimes women misperceive them as flirting even they do not.

Our third style is physical flirting. People with this style use their body language well when flirting. They can easily express their sexual interest to others. If the other person has a sexual interest in these people, they can easily notice it.

Like those who adopt playful flirting, individuals with this physical style are also interested in more people than average. Similarly, they clearly show their flirt, and others easily notice them when they are flirting. They also find flirting flattering. They assume people are flirting with them wherever they go.

Sincere flirting, as the name suggests, is a style in which emotions are expressed a little more intimately than others. People who prefer this style think that there must be a mutual emotional connection to have a relationship with the person they are interested in. So, they do not flirt with others just for enjoyment or having fun. These individuals say that they find it exhilarating to notice a connection or common point with the other person while flirting.

In addition, these people take great pleasure in discovering whether the other person is interested in them. Of course, if this interest is mutual, the pleasure they get is probably greater. If they have a one-sided interest in the person, it should not be such an enjoyable situation. However, getting an answer should provide relief in any case.

People with the sincere flirting style only flirt with people they are interested in. Thus, they enjoy getting a good compliment from the opposite sex. In addition, if they are attracted to someone, they think it is best to show it to the other person and make it clearer. So, they do not pursue little plans or games like "Oh, I don't want to show that I like them; otherwise, they will fall out of love." "I shall reply to their messages late." etc.

Sincere flirting is the most honest form of flirting because it is practiced entirely with genuine feelings without any filters. This is not only the most honest but also the most effective way of flirting. Studies reveal that people who prefer sincere flirting have the highest positive response rate from the other person compared to other flirting styles.

The studies also show that people prefer the opposite side to adopt the sincere flirting style. So, the majority want other people to flirt with them in this style.

People who adopt this style find the flirt flattering. They do not complain about not being noticed. Whether a woman or a man, if the person is flirting sincerely, the other side can easily understand that the person is flirting with them.

Our last flirting style is polite flirting. People who embrace this style think, "In today's world, people should be careful when flirting." They advise it is best to think carefully and be sure about the other person's feelings before saying they like them. Probably, they do not want to get hurt after opening up to somebody and finding out that their attraction is one-sided.

People who adopt the polite flirting style believe that there are strict rules on how men and women should express their romantic interest. They are against going out of these rules. Moreover, they argue that people should always behave kindly and decorously on dates. If the other person unexpectedly acts physically more intimate while flirting, they immediately distance themselves from that person. When we consider all this, we can say that the people who adopt this flirting style are a little old-fashioned.

Compared to their peers, people who adopt the polite flirting style are interested in fewer people than the average. Considering their timid and self-controlling attitudes, this reduction in attraction should not be surprising. People who practice this flirting style also state that they have problems communicating their interest when they like someone.

People in this group do not find the flirt flattering. When someone they do not like flirts with them, they feel uncomfortable.

FLIRTING STAGES

No matter what flirting style we have, or what style the other person has adopted, it is necessary to go through specific and sequential stages on the way to a romantic relationship. Scientists observed the behavior of people during flirting and determined 12 common steps. The time spent in each of these stages is not constant. It can vary from person to person and from situation to situation. Sometimes all these steps are completed within hours (for example, in one-night stands), sometimes it can take weeks, months, or even years.

The first stage of flirting is that we eye someone's entire body from head to foot. In our chapter about attraction, we mentioned our eyes scan our potential partners in a few seconds. Our brains then decide whether we like them by doing various calculations about their character through their physical features, body language, and mimics. This is the step where this happens: The eye-to-body stage.

Table 1- Flirting is completed in twelve sequential steps.

FLIRTING STAGES	
1- Eye → Body	7- Mouth → Mouth
2- Eye → Eye	8- Hand → Head
3- Voice → Voice	9- Hand → Body
4- Hand → Hand	10- Mouth → Breasts
5- Arm → Shoulder	11- Hand → Genitals
6- Arm → Body (Waist, Legs)	12- Genitals → Genitals

If we feel attracted to someone, we try to make eye contact with them. By looking at their face and eyes more often, we try to make them notice our interest. If this interest or attraction is mutual, we exchange glances for a while, even if it is sometimes a furtive glance. This is the second stage of flirting, the eye-to-eye stage.

The next step after the eye-to-eye is the voice-to-voice stage. Talking is the first step in the communication of the two people who are interested in each other. This usually happens with the signals given by the woman in the previous stage. When looking at each other, women give cues such as having a positive body language and smiling to encourage the man to come and speak with her. Sometimes, she even creates the environment.

For example, if a girl is sitting in a café with her friends as a group and start to exchange glances with someone at another table, she can send her friends away for a while so that the man can come and talk more comfortably. If this is not possible, she can provide a more comfortable medium for the man to approach by being alone with excuses such as smoking outside or going to the toilet.

With the voice-to-voice stage, these two people talk and get to know each other. If the attraction continues, they move on to the next step: hand-to-hand. At first, the process starts slowly and evasively with the touch of the outer face of the hand and then continues with a romantic handhold.

The hand-to-hand stage is followed by the steps in which physical contact intensifies, with the arm being placed on the shoulder. After the shoulder, the arm comes into contact with other body parts, such as the waist, hips, and legs.

This sequence is not absolute, although all stages generally go by this order. Unless big jumps at the stages are taken, some steps can be skipped or switched. For example, after hand-holding, the arm can be put on the waist first and then on the shoulder.

However, when there are serious jumps during these stages, generally the other person negatively reacts. For example, if you put your hands on their hips immediately after the eye to eye step, you can expect being yelled at or even slapped, and the flirt ending at that moment.

These first six stages of flirting are entirely under the control of the woman. Girls give signals, provide an excuse or a medium for each step to happen. No matter what we call it, these are the processes that women initiate. If the man acts without receiving the signal or misinterprets it, he usually gets a negative reaction. This sometimes happens as scolding, but mostly the woman politely pulls herself away or withdraws. Usually, these messages are received by men, and no action is retaken without the right signal.

The next six stages are under the man's control with the woman's consent, rather than the control of the woman. Of these, only in the seventh step, the mouth-to-mouth stage, although control appears more in the man, the woman's control is almost equal to that of the man.

Twelve stages of flirting are completed with the hand going to the head after kissing, then descending from the breasts to other parts of the body, the mouth reaching the breasts, the hands reaching the genitals, and the genitals reaching each other in the last stage.

Scientists have interesting research that sheds light on who is in control at these stages. When they interviewed men and women from couples who have completed all of these flirting stages separately about how the events took place, scientists observed that women could tell about the first six stages with the finest details while having trouble remembering the details about the next stages. In contrast, men had difficulty remembering the details of the first six steps, while they were able to talk about the next steps in detail. So, depending on who was in control and whoever made plans to carry out a stage and move on to the next step, that is the one who remembers the details on that topic better.

For example, in a one-night stand, if the couple met in a bar, the woman can tell every detail regarding the first six stages, "This fool was eyeing me from a distance. I looked at him and thought he was okay. I smiled slightly and went to the bar. When he saw this, he came to me, and we started talking. Then, we went to the seats in the back and spoke. I slowly moved my hand closer and started touching his hand with the outside of my hand. He took courage and started holding my hand, etc." She cannot remember the details in the next stages clearly. The opposite is true for men. They cannot fully remember the details of the first six flirting stages, but they can talk about the following ones to the finest details.

Since we have learned all the details that make it difficult for us to understand the person's intent, from flirting motivations to their styles and stages, let's come to the most critical issue: flirting signals. How do we know if someone is flirting with us?

Although we had behaviors like pushing, pulling of the hair, throwing something at, or even hitting the person we like when we were a child, our way of flirting and signals improve and become less aggressive as we grow.

There are dozens of different flirting moves for each gender revealed in scientific studies (for example, there are at least 52 different flirting moves women do). It is impossible to address all individually. But let us take a look at the most important ones.

In our chapter on attraction, we learned that when somebody likes us, their pupils enlarge, their voice becomes thinner, and sometimes even tremble under the sympathetic nervous system's influence. But it may be a mistake to think of or search for these clues as the only indications of attraction.

Sometimes, people get nervous around us not only because they are attracted to us. There may be other reasons. Suppose we have a harsh temperament or are in a position to react negatively when they make a mistake or are just famous. In that case, they can get anxious talking to us. Therefore, it is quite wrong to take that anxiety as a sign of attraction alone. We should consider it with other signals.

Moreover, if someone likes us, do their pupils always have to dilate, their voice has to become thinner and tremble? The answer is no. Because, as we mentioned in the attraction chapter, these are the reactions under the influence of the sympathetic nervous system, and the real underlying cause is fear of dislike or loss.

When we think of it from this point of view, if the person is confident about themselves or sure about our feelings towards them, we may not see these reactions since there will be no reason for them to experience such fear and activate the sympathetic nervous system.

Another possibility is our closeness with that person. Love does not always develop between two people who have just met. Sometimes, friendships can turn into love. If you are familiar with that person, and they are comfortable around you, their sympathetic nervous system may not take action.

When people are with someone they like, they may tend to speak more and generally a little faster than usual, depending on their anxiety. Although this is an indication of interest, it does not contain certainty since it depends on the anxiety and the persons involved. For example, when some people are nervous, they can withdraw and talk less instead of talking more. Sometimes, even if they want to talk, they may be quieter than usual, thinking they have nothing interesting to talk about. However, studies show that people who are attracted to someone tend to talk more often and longer.

Exchanging glances and filtering with eyes is another sign of liking and flirting. However, studies show that short and quick gazes are not intended for flirting. If the other person likes us and wants to flirt with us, they gaze at us more and longer.

The intensity of the smile is another sign of flirting. If the other person smiles frequently, it is a good sign. Especially in women, a coy smile in which the person smiles as their eyes look at the floor is also a strong flirting indicator.

Like smiling, laughing loudly is also one of the signals of flirting. If someone bursts into laughter frequently, this may be a sign that they like us. At the same time, if men lean forward and get closer while laughing, their bodies are in a more open position and take up more space; this is one of the signs that the man is interested in you.

Women's slight tilting of the head to the sides during the conversation is another sign for flirting found by scientists. Men often think if a woman plays with her hair while talking, it is a sign of liking or flirting. However, studies show that this assumption is wrong. There is an exception to this situation. Studies have also found that women touch their own bodies more frequently while talking to the person they like. This includes the hair. Therefore, although it is not correct to say that a woman playing just with her hair is a sign that she is interested in the other party, we can say she is flirting if she also touches other parts of her body more often than usual while talking.

In the later stages of flirting, our movements change. We become physically closer. So, which of these are the most effective on the opposite sex?

According to a 2015 study by Joel Wade and Jennifer Stemp from Bucknell University in the U.S., men consider women kissing them on the cheek as the most effective flirting tactic. They say that they like the women rubbing against them, standing closer to them, and touching them in general as effective flirting methods that follow. In a word, from a very general point of view, the methods preferred by men and the most effective ones on them are mostly physical flirting behaviors.

So, which flirting behaviors do women find most effective and prefer the most? In the same study, scientists also investigated the answer to this question. They revealed that women prefer men to hold their hands the most. Women also reported men spending time with them, going out for dinner, kissing them, making them laugh, and taking care of them as other most preferred flirting methods.

That is to say, again from a very general point of view, the methods that women prefer and the most effective ones for men to steal women's hearts are some flirting behaviors that show interest in women or the ones in which the interest is made clear by the man.

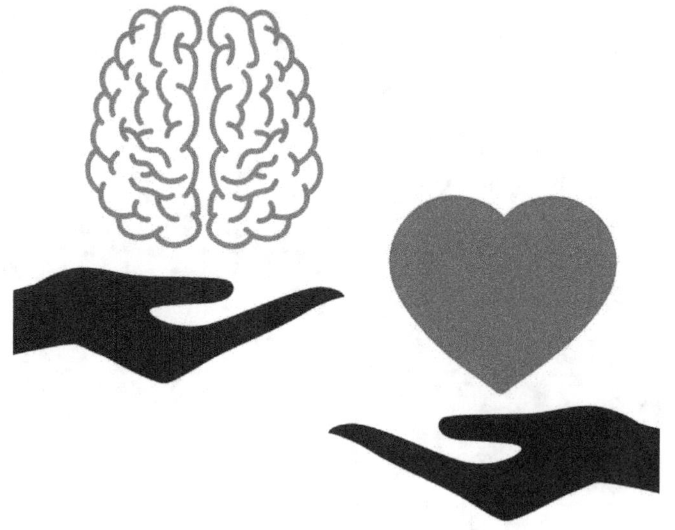

PHYSIOLOGICAL CHANGES WHEN WE ARE IN LOVE

At first, we get attracted to someone. By flirting, we get to know each other better, get closer, and strengthen this attraction. Now, we can say that the attraction is turning into love.

We talked about the activation in our brains that occurred when we were attracted to someone. Since love is a little more advanced and complicated than attraction, the changes in our brain and body increase.

Contrary to popular belief, these changes are common for everyone. Studies show that changes that happen when we are in love are the same for women and men, young people and the elderly, homosexuals and heterosexuals.

This probably happens to all of us; when we are attracted to or fall in love with someone, we do things rather ridiculous and unreasonable that we would not normally do. Maybe hours, days, weeks, or months later when it comes to our mind, we wonder, "Why did I do such a thing?" and get upset with ourselves.

Sometimes, in the later stages of the relationship, we blame our partners by saying, "You were not like this at the beginning of our relationship; you changed a lot!" Probably, we have also received similar complaints from our partners. We always have had that suspicion. We wonder if they have always been like this but pretended to be a nice person at first to steal our heart?

Do people really put on an act at first to steal someone's heart? Or do some of our actions and feelings have to do with the changes in our brains and hormones in the early days of the relationship? We will find the answers to all these questions in this chapter.

When we fall in love, testosterone is one of the first hormones that the amount changes in our body and thus affects our behavior. Although testosterone is known as a male hormone, it is produced in both sexes. It is more in males than in females. However, the effect of the same amount of testosterone on women is greater than its effect on men. We can analogize this hormone's impact on different genders to the effects of alcohol on different people. Some of us get drunk with five glasses of drink, while others can even get drunk with a single glass. The effect of the same amount of alcohol varies from person to person. The relative impact of testosterone on different genders is similar.

Testosterone increases the activity of the brain area called the amygdala. In addition to having many functions, the amygdala is especially the fear center in our brains. It is also responsible for aggressiveness. One reason that makes men more aggressive is that high testosterone levels in their bodies increase their amygdala activity.

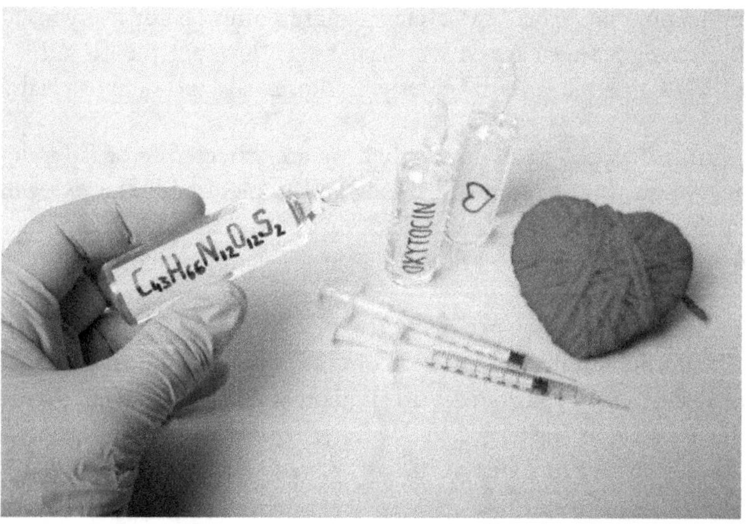

Figure 14-When we are in love, levels of various hormones in our body change.

When we come to love, testosterone levels change in different ways in both sexes. In the early stages of love, the amount of testosterone in men decreases, while its amount in women increases.

This decrease in testosterone reduces the amygdala activity; so, the man becomes calmer than before. This is the main reason why men are meek in the honeymoon period against the women they like. Later on, hormone levels are restored. Thus, men become a bit more aggressive when compared to the early stages of the relationship. So, women are, to a large extent, right when they say to their partners, "My love, you were not like this at first; you were more understanding and gentler." Of course, sometimes there will be men who pretend at the beginning. However, the main biological reason why most men are more malleable in the first months of the relationship is the drop in these testosterone levels.

This decrease in testosterone levels is actually an essential evolutionary adaptation for a relationship to flourish. Suppose the man is aggressive and unnecessary quarrels occur due to his high testosterone levels. In that case, the relationship may end even before it starts. However, being more understanding and docile with the falling testosterone levels appears to be a positive feature for the flourish of the relationship by increasing the couple's initial harmony.

Unlike men, women's testosterone levels increase when they fall in love. This increase raises their libidos. You may wonder why rising testosterone levels do not increase aggression in women but only affect their libido. This is because the oxytocin hormone levels that elevate when women fall in love reduce their amygdala activity and neutralize the effect of testosterone in this area. Therefore, the increase in testosterone levels in women shows its effect only as an increase in their libido. This change is also thought to have been developed as a result of an evolutionary adaptation in relationships. Previously, we discussed how love is a feeling based on a very advanced reproductive instinct. Here, this increase in testosterone levels in the early days of love is a stimulus for the woman to reproduce with the person she is attracted to. The body says, "Okay, you believe you found the right person, and that is why you fell in love. Then reproduce as soon as possible." Testosterone levels in women also return to their normal values after a while. With this change, the high libido of women begins to decrease as well. Thus, men do not see the same amount of sexual desire from their partners compared to the beginnings of their relationship. One of the biggest reasons for this is that the initially increased testosterone level in women decreases later in the relationship.

In our attraction chapter, we mentioned how our brain's dopamine reward system is activated when we like someone. When we fall in love, these areas activate even more. These increased levels of dopamine motivate us to pursue the person we are in love with. Dopamine secretion increases in our brain whenever we see them, hear them, or look at their pictures. This dopamine increase gives us pleasure. When these are absent, dopamine secretion stops. We begin to suffer deprivation. We cannot wait to see them and talk to them to increase the dopamine secretion in our brain again. Studies reveal that when we fall in love with someone, we sometimes think about that person in 85% of our day. The reason for this obsessive mood is the activation of our reward system. Dopamine not only motivates us to think of our partner but also makes us more energetic. In a sense, it also gives us the energy to chase the person we like.

Let us now come to probably the most special hormone for love: oxytocin. Although oxytocin's effect on love has begun to be understood in recent years, other functions of this hormone have been known for decades: it provides the uterine contractions at birth and triggers lactation.

That is why it gets its name from the Greek words Oxus = swift and tokos = childbirth. At delayed births, doctors give oxytocin to women to initiate uterine contractions. This hormone triggers not only birth contractions in the mother but also the onset of lactation.

Studies affirm that when we fall in love, the amount of oxytocin increases in both sexes, enabling us to connect with our partners. This increase is directly proportional to the love we have for our partners. Research by Israeli and American scientists in 2012 shows that the amount of oxytocin at the beginning of the relationship determines the relationship duration. So, if you ask your endocrinologist to look at oxytocin levels in your blood tests when you start a relationship, you and your partner will know in advance how long your relationship will last. Of course, it can be argued whether it is a good thing to know this in advance. Besides, based on the results of this research, we can say that if you concentrate on activities that will increase your oxytocin levels at the beginning of your relationship, your relationship may last longer.

The effect of oxytocin on bonding is not limited to romantic relationships. Oxytocin also allows mothers to connect with their children. This hormone is secreted in the father, too, with the birth of the baby. Thus, it is effective in connecting both parents to the child. When we think in terms of evolution, when parents are bonded with their children and take care of them, the child grows up safely. This effect of oxytocin probably has expanded in the evolutionary process in a way that would also allow couples to connect over time.

A surprising result found by scientists in their research is that the increase in oxytocin of newly in love couples is higher than the increase in oxytocin of new parents. So, if we are really in love, we get attached to our partner more than we are connected to our child.

Although oxytocin is a crucial hormone for bonding and plays a critical role in relationships, this hormone's increase can also bring some disadvantages.

Produced in the hypothalamus region of our brain and secreted from the pituitary gland, oxytocin has an opposite effect to testosterone. It reduces the activity of the amygdala, the fear center of our brain. This allows us to trust our partners more. Because of this trust and bonding to our partners, we sometimes do things that we normally would never do when we fall in love. Occasionally, we cannot understand our partner's true intentions, and sometimes we are cool with many things our partner does even if we are somebody who would not usually tolerate those kinds of things. It is the oxytocin increase in love, and accordingly reduction of our amygdala activity to our partner, that is responsible for almost all the negative things we do that could hurt us when we fall in love. So, oxytocin is the one to blame!

There is a saying that I like very much about love: "Love is giving someone the power to destroy you and trusting them not to." Love is undoubtedly such a feeling. Due to the increase in oxytocin, we unwittingly trust our partners more than we should. Therefore, sometimes we cannot see the parts of that person harming or could be harmful to us. If this person is the right one and the feelings are mutual, this trust is not a problem. Love is experienced with all its pleasure and pros. But otherwise, it can devastate us.

Certain actions cause the release of the oxytocin hormone that connects us to our partners. The most important of these is to touch. During the flirtation, the bodies of both sides release oxytocin every time we touch our partners intensely. For example, hand in hand walks and tight cuddles are such types of physical contact that make our brains secrete oxytocin.

In fact, oxytocin secretion by this physical contact affects all kinds of bonding. In addition to the bonds between lovers, those between parents and their children and between friends are also created by physical contact. Some of us even have pets. Those who have pets see them as part of the family, almost like their children. People are often incredibly attached to their animals. It is the secretion of oxytocin that creates this bond when we pet them.

Kissing also causes oxytocin release and allows us to connect a little bit more with our partners. It may be necessary to open a small parenthesis to the French kiss. Oxytocin is not only found in the blood. It also passes into saliva. Although there is no scientific study investigating this to date, the possibility of mutual exchange of oxytocin in the French kiss and thus the possibility of subconsciously detecting our partner's oxytocin levels might be making this kissing style more special for us.

In addition, other physical contacts such as massage and dancing also increase oxytocin levels in couples. Studies reveal that dancing increases our oxytocin levels by an average of 11%.

Sex is another activity that increases oxytocin levels in a person. My fellow men will hate me for saying this, but according to the studies, during an orgasm, the secretion of oxytocin in the body varies between genders. In 1987, Marie Carmichael and her colleagues from Stanford University revealed that the increase of oxytocin levels of men during orgasm was nearly 10%, while the increase in women was around 30%. Oxytocin levels are increased in direct proportion with the quality and severity of orgasms in women.

Over the years, the technology and research possibilities in science have developed. Thanks to these new developments, a brain scan study in 2013 at the Groningen University of the Netherlands confirmed the results of the biochemical studies showing that oxytocin levels in women and men increase in different amounts during sex. In their research, Hieu Huynh and his colleagues showed that during orgasm, the pituitary gland, which is responsible for the release of oxytocin in our brain, is not activated much in men but is markedly activated in women. Male sexual performance is also important in this way of activation in women. They did not observe any pituitary gland activity when women did not have orgasms or faked orgasms. Only real orgasms led to pituitary gland activation and oxytocin release in females.

Considering these and similar scientific studies, it seems like a great mistake that some women think that they can make men fall in love with them only with sexuality. In fact, when a woman is trying to make a man get attached to her by using sex, it is possible that the woman can be more romantically connected to that man who is not very interested in her. A good sexual life is, of course, an important building block of a healthy relationship. However, it is not very valid, at least according to the scientific data we have, to think of it as a way to romantically connect a man. Hence, there are many men who are connected to their partners without sexuality, and there are men that sexuality alone cannot attach them in any way.

Stimulation of the nipples also significantly increases the amount of oxytocin secreted. This stimulation and increase are not equal in both genders, and especially women are somewhat disadvantaged in this regard. In fact, there is a biological reason for this difference. We mentioned that oxytocin is responsible for the release of breast milk in women. When the baby is born, it instinctively sucks on its mother's breasts to feed, during which it stimulates her nipples. Nipples have a special type of nerves called mechanoreceptors. Those nerves reach the brain's hypothalamus region. When the nipples are stimulated during breastfeeding, those mechanoreceptors activate the magnocellular cells in the hypothalamus, causing them to secrete oxytocin. After this oxytocin increase, milk is secreted from the breasts. This is a body mechanism that is all about the care and nutrition of the child. But, at the same time, it enhances the mother's attachment to the baby because of the oxytocin's effect on bonding. Since the mechanoreceptors in the nipples and the magnocellular cells in the hypothalamus are present not only at the time of birth but constantly in the body, oxytocin secretion occurs whenever women receive stimulation from their nipples. If no milk has been formed in the breasts due to the lack of prolactin hormone, milk is not secreted. Still, this mechanism continues to work and shows its effect on bonding with their partners. In other words, women have a shortcut that causes them to release oxytocin in the relationship and enables them to connect more to their partners. This effect is not exclusive to women. Stimulation of the nipples in men, although not as strong as in women, also causes them to secrete some oxytocin and thereby attach to their partners.

MRI studies in recent years have revealed that the parts activated in our sensory cortex when the nipples are stimulated in both women and men overlap with those activated when our genitals are stimulated. Therefore, besides inducing oxytocin secretion, nipple stimulation in both genders also has an erogenous effect similar to genitalia stimulation.

There are currently 6495 mammalian species in the world. Interestingly, among mammalians, breasts are seen and used as a sexual commodity only in humans. Perhaps this is because our primitive ancestors had instinctively noticed the effects of these mechanisms, which are activated through the stimulation of the nipples, long before scientific research has revealed.

In our body, oxytocin is secreted not only by physical contact. Studies show that watching a tearjerker movie is the best oxytocin releaser. Researchers found that watching emotionally powerful movies increases our oxytocin levels by 47%. This increase is remarkable because studies show that normally a 10-20% oxytocin boost causes noticeable behavior changes. Almost four times the required oxytocin increase can be reached by watching such films. After a certain flirting period, if both parties want to take their relationship forward, then the type of movie couples will be watching together to speed things up seems certain.

In addition to all these, consuming certain foods may increase oxytocin production in our bodies. Although there is no clear scientific study on this subject, considering the synergistic production of oxytocin with hormones such as dopamine and estrogen, eating foods that boost those hormones may also increase our oxytocin levels. Dopamine boosting foods such as green tea, coffee, avocado, banana, chocolate, and animal products like cheese, etc., and phytoestrogen-rich foods such as peanuts, anise, thyme, parsley, and beer may be included in our diet in this regard.

There are also nasal sprays containing synthetic oxytocin. Its synthetic form has the same effects as natural oxytocin. Therefore, it is often used not only in clinics but also in many scientific studies on fidelity.

Nerve Growth Factor (NGF) is another hormone whose level changes in our brain when we fall in love.

Our NGF levels double in the first six months of the relationship and then return to normal values. The increase in NGF hormone levels varies proportionally to the intensity of love in persons. If someone is madly in love, their NGF amount will double. If they are not that much in love with their partners, the increase will be less. Because of this feature, one can determine whether someone is really in love and the degree of their love by measuring NGF hormone levels in the early stages of the relationship.

Italian scientist Rita Levi Montalci discovered Nerve Growth Factor in 1952. This discovery brought her the Nobel Prize in 1986. NGF, which is very important for our brain's functioning, plays a critical role in the formation, growth, and maintenance of new neurons. We will discuss in detail in the breakup chapter, but the increase of this hormone, which has a vital role in the healthy functioning of our brain, also has an impact that gives us a headache in a breakup.

In addition to its roles in the growth and protection of our nerve cells, scientists have also recently discovered that NGF reduces physical pain severity. So, if our partner faces a situation in which they suffer physical pain, being close to them will ease their pain.

Including the scientific papers, many sources mention that the serotonin hormone is involved in the feeling of love. Some state that when we fall in love, serotonin levels in our brain decrease similarly to patients with obsessive-compulsive disorder, and this change is the reason why we become obsessive about our partners when we are in love. Other sources claim that its amount increases when we fall in love, based on the myth that serotonin is a "happiness hormone." Unfortunately, both views are wrong! They do not have a proper scientific basis and are the result of incorrect interpretation of inadequate information.

First, let us look at the claims that suggest that the serotonin hormone levels in our brain decrease when we are in love. This opinion is the most common and is widely mentioned in scientific literature as well. This claim is based on a study by Marazziti and his friends in 1999. This is also the only experimental study to date that has examined the relationship between serotonin decline and obsession.

In this study, the researchers examined the serotonin transporter protein amounts in the blood of people in love and with obsessive-compulsive disorder. They found that serotonin transporter protein levels were lower in both groups than in normal people. They interpreted these results and concluded that our brain serotonin level decreases when we fall in love. And this interpretation has been expressed for years. Although this interpretation seems logical, it contains two serious scientific errors due to overlooking some critical facts.

The first problem in the study is that serotonin levels were not directly measured. The results were indirectly interpreted by measuring the amount of a transporter protein. When we look at the molecular mechanisms, the increase or decrease of a molecule and its transporter protein does not always change in direct proportion. So, even though such indirect measurements give us an idea, they are insufficient to speak precisely. But this is perhaps the smallest flaw of the claim. There is a much more critical problem in the study: the source of serotonin in our blood.

Even if we accept that the amount of serotonin in our blood increases and decreases in direct proportion to the transporter protein, as Marazziti and his colleagues assumed, the source of this serotonin is not our brain. Ninety percent of the serotonin in our body is produced in our intestines, 5% is produced in our platelets, and the remaining 5% is produced in our brain. Serotonin in our brains is mostly synthesized in a brainstem region called Raphe nuclei and the pineal gland.

There is a very special structure in our brains called the blood-brain barrier. This structure controls the entry and exit of materials into our brains. It only allows certain small molecules to pass. Serotonin is not a molecule that can cross this blood-brain barrier. Only serotonin produced in our pineal gland may theoretically mix into the blood since this gland is a special brain structure that is not isolated with blood-brain-barrier. However, the serotonin produced here is not related to love. It is synthesized as the precursor of the melatonin hormone. Then it is converted into the melatonin hormone, whose primary task is to regulate our sleep. Therefore, considering all these facts and molecular mechanisms, the decrease in our blood serotonin levels has no relation to the change in our brain when we fall in love.

Besides, in a study by Langeslag and colleagues from the Netherlands in 2012, it was observed that the serotonin levels in the blood vary in different directions in men and women who are in love. However, this study is also not very reliable since it was conducted on a small group of 20 people. Yet, they found that serotonin levels decreased in men, whereas it increased in women. Suppose the decrease in the serotonin hormone levels causes us to think more about our partners when we fall in love. In that case, its increase in women should make them not think of their loved ones as much as men. We all know that this is not true.

In addition to all these, although there is no method to measure the amount of serotonin in our brain with today's technology, the methods such as PET scan can look at the amount of serotonin transporter protein and serotonin receptors in the brain. Although the changes in love have not been studied, research on people with other addictions that resemble love, such as drinking, gambling, and drugs, did not find any difference in their serotonin transporter protein and serotonin receptors.

When we come to the view that suggests our serotonin levels increase when we fall in love, there is no single scientific study on this subject. In the 1980s, along with the marketing strategy of the drug Prozac, which is a selective serotonin reuptake inhibitor (SSRI) used to treat depression, serotonin was introduced as a "happiness hormone." It is marketed that the cause of depression in individuals is the decrease of this hormone, and if this decrease is prevented or reversed, the person will get out of depression and be happier. Thus, serotonin and happiness are coded almost synonymously in humans. Due to the successful effects of this marketing strategy, some sources claim that "When people fall in love, they become happy. If the happiness hormone is serotonin, then its amount should increase when we fall in love", even though there is no experimental data on this subject. On top of that, whether serotonin is a happiness hormone or not, therefore, SSRI use and its effects in treating depression is a hot topic that is being seriously debated in the scientific community recently. However, since it is out of our book's scope, we will not delve into this debate here.

The melatonin hormone can give clues about the reasons why we fall in love more in spring and summer. The amount of melatonin increases when the days become shorter and the daylight decreases in winter. This increase in melatonin hormone levels gives us general fatigue and sleepiness. It even affects about 20% of the population enough to get them depressed. This slowness, sleep state, and the limited use of our energy are all evolutionary adaptations to protect our body against the shortening of available food in winter. Some animals even hibernate as a more advanced response to this.

With spring, the days become longer, and the amount of sunlight we receive starts to increase. This increase in daylight leads to a decrease in our melatonin levels. Thus, we get rid of the tiredness of the winter months and become more energetic. In the meantime, flowers blooming in the spring, the arrival of the spring colors instead of the gray of winter, and the birds' singing make us release dopamine, putting us in a more pleasant mood. All these physiological changes make us fall in love more easily in spring and summer.

The amount of melatonin in our body does not just fluctuate seasonally. It also varies during the day. Its secretion starts to increase around 9 PM and reaches its maximum levels between 2-4 AM at midnight. After that, it shows a rapid decrease and is synthesized in minimum amounts in the morning hours. Although there is no scientific study on this subject, we may approximate the effect of melatonin's yearly cycle on being in love to its fluctuation during the day. Considering this cycle, perhaps the best activity for the first date may be a brunch in the morning hours when this hormone reaches its lowest levels during the day. Compared to dinner, brunch is both a more comfortable and acceptable date for the other party and also in the time frame when our melatonin levels are the lowest.

Cortisol is another hormone whose levels increase when we fall in love. Our cortisol levels also fluctuate during the day. Cortisol reaches its highest level in the blood 1.5-2 hours after we wake up, and then begins to decrease. Therefore, it usually reaches its highest level around 9-10 AM. This time interval is similar to the time frame in which melatonin hormone levels are optimal for love. This reinforces the accuracy of the decision of a late breakfast for the first date in terms of hormone levels.

Like serotonin, another frequently mentioned hormone whose levels change when we fall in love is phenylethylamine (PEA). Its structure is very similar to that of a drug, amphetamine, and has the same effects on the body. In his book "Chemistry of Love," published in 1984, psychiatrist Michael Liebowitz claimed that our PEA levels increase when we are in love, and this increase causes the drunkenness of love. Phenylethylamine triggers and regulates the dopamine and noradrenaline synthesis in our brain. Thus, we may assume that PEA levels also rise indirectly with the increase in these two hormones when we fall in love. However, to date, no serious scientific studies showed PEA increase in love and confirmed Liebowitz's claim.

Phenylethylamine is also found in chocolate. That is why many people assume that eating chocolate increases feelings similar to love. Perhaps this is why chocolate is an important element in Valentine's Day's gifts, along with flowers. However, the theory that these feelings will strengthen with the PEA in chocolate is incorrect because phenylethylamine in chocolate is quickly disintegrated in our digestive system. Therefore, the happiness of eating chocolate has nothing to do with PEA. Chocolate is a sugary food. Like all other sugary foods, it gives us delight by stimulating our brains' reward center by ensuring dopamine secretion.

Perhaps pheromones are among the molecules that are believed to have a remarkable effect on attraction. Pheromones are actually various chemical signals secreted by the body. Although generally found in insects, pheromones can be found in other species too.

A significant feature of pheromones is that they are species-specific. That is, a bee cannot detect the pheromone secreted by an ant. Similarly, a pheromone secreted by a bee is not felt by an ant or any other species. Each pheromone is only effective for its own species.

Studies reveal that animals perceive pheromones through a structure called the vomeronasal organ. In humans, the vomeronasal organ is inactivated with birth, even though it is there in the fetus period. Therefore, we adults do not have an organ that can perceive pheromones.

That is why, even though the effects of pheromones in humans are taken very seriously by the public, it is highly controversial in the scientific community. Some scientists think that even if pheromones exist, they will not be effective in humans since we do not have a vomeronasal organ. Other scientists believe that we can detect pheromones in another way than the vomeronasal organ.

Studies show that pheromones (or pheromone-like molecules) are found in our armpit sweat, urine, semen, vaginal fluid, and saliva. The most important pheromones found in humans are androstenone, androstadienone, androstenol, and estratetraenol. However, the effects of these molecules on us are not as significant as of those pheromones in animals and insects. For example, some pheromones, secreted by ants, signal the other ants in the colony where the food is. Some other mammalian pheromones signal when animals are ready to mate and create an aphrodisiac effect. No pheromone with such strong effects has been detected in humans so far.

For example, estratetraenol, which is secreted by women, is one of the strongest pheromones found in humans. However, its effect on men is quite limited. In a study, estratetraenol allowed male subjects to describe the movement of genderless graphics, which were similar to a stickman but consisting of only dots, as a female walk. This is so far the biggest impact of estratetraenol reflected in scientific research. However, hundreds of products that are claimed to contain pheromones and thus have an aphrodisiac effect are sold worldwide.

When we look at the contents of these products, all of which are manufactured under the counter, we cannot see in detail which molecules they use. If they use real human pheromones, scientific studies demonstrate that they do not have an aphrodisiac effect as claimed. If they isolate aphrodisiac pheromone of another species and use it in their content, considering that pheromones are species-specific signaling molecules, it is a fact that they will not work in humans.

Since we do not know their contents clearly, the possibility of containing an aphrodisiac pheromone of another species may also involve various dangers. Someone using such a product may send very different signals to these species, for example, when passing by a beehive or a pen. Therefore, in order not to endanger both your money and your health, it is beneficial not to be fooled by the marketing traps of such products and to stay away from them as much as possible.

BRAIN REGIONS

Like our hormones, some of our brain regions' activities also change when we fall in love. One of these regions is the ventral tegmental area (VTA).

The ventral tegmental area is located in the region of our primitive brain called the midbrain. It is a part of the reward system in our brains. Our reward system is activated when we are attracted to someone. It is activated even more intensely when we are in love.

Our nerve cells in VTA produce dopamine and connect with Nucleus accumbens, another part of our brain's reward system. This reward system's activation gives us a feeling of joy and happiness as we see the person we love. For this, we do not need to see the person in the flesh; even just looking at their photo is enough. Our reward system acts as if we saw them alive.

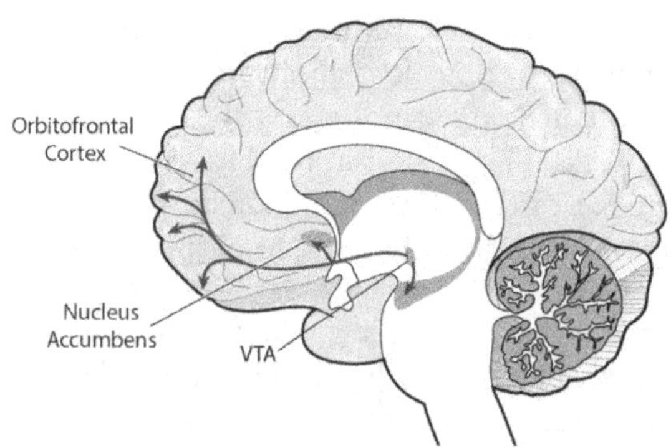

Figure 15-When we fall in love, there are changes in the activities of many regions in our brain, especially in the reward system.

When we fall in love, our Nucleus accumbens is also activated by signals rooting from our VTA. This region is responsible for not only the reward system but also our motivation and the sense of motherhood.

That is why when a woman sees a baby, her Nucleus accumbens gets activated, and it evokes motherliness. This brain region underlies women's more protective attitudes towards babies and children. As part of the reward system in our brains, neurons in the Nucleus accumbens also secrete dopamine. Therefore, we feel a sense of joy and happiness when this region is activated. This dopamine secretion is the reason for the positive mood changes, especially when women see babies. According to studies, photos of their own babies naturally activate women's Nucleus accumbens the most. The pictures of other babies also activate this region. Yet, this effect is not as strong as their own children's photos. The ugly babies of others are the unluckiest in this regard.

Addictive activities also strongly stimulate our Nucleus accumbens. We are delighted by actions such as taking drugs, gambling, and using social media that activate this reward center of our brain. For this pleasure state to continue, we feel the urge to do such activities frequently. Whether it is drugs, gambling, or social media use, the result is an addiction!

Variable-interval rewards activate our Nucleus accumbens the most. Thus, they cause the most severe addictions. This feature of our Nucleus accumbens sometimes gives us a headache when we are in love. However, with a few examples, let us first look at what this variable-interval reward is and how it seriously causes addiction.

People usually consume addictive substances like drugs, cigarettes, alcohol, etc., in definite amounts. These substances please us a certain amount when taken, but the pleasure we feel diminishes over time because of habituation. Since this pleasure decreases over time, people start to increase their dosage and use it a little more so that the joy continues. However, after a certain period, they give little pleasure as our bodies get almost insensitive. Yet, we have already become addicted. Even if we do not feel the pleasure much, we experience its deprivation. This time, we usually take them to avoid the unpleasant effects of deprivation.

In the variable-interval type, the reward and the pleasure received from this reward are variable. Sometimes you get the reward, and sometimes you do not. Good examples of such rewards are playing the lottery, sports betting, or gambling. Let us say you played sports betting. Sometimes your coupon stands a chance, and sometimes not. So, the reward is not always guaranteed. This creates the "interval reward" condition. When you are lucky, you sometimes earn small amounts, and sometimes much more. This is a good example of the reward being "variable." If the prize is so intermittent and varying, it causes a severe addiction in our brain. That is why those who play betting games are severely addicted. Such gambling is an important part of their lives. Sometimes they really want to quit, but often this is not possible.

Another current example of the variable-interval reward is social media. Whether we post something on Facebook or Twitter or share photos on Instagram, we get likes from our friends and followers in return. These likes are perceived as a reward in our brains and give us pleasure. However, the number of likes we receive on everything we share is not always the same. Sometimes our posts do not attract much attention, and sometimes they are quite popular. In other words, the reward is variable, and it is intermittent as the likes do not always come. That is why social media appears to be a severely addictive phenomenon these days. For this reason, most people spend most of their time on social media.

Let us come to love. The attention and love of the person we love is perceived as a reward by our brain and gives us pleasure. In a normal situation, this interest and love is mutual and more or less stable. We enjoy it a certain amount, just like when we smoke, but after a while, we get used to it. Although this interest and love gives us some joy, after some time, it does not give pleasure like it used to. In fact, if it is continuous and very intense for a long time, it may suffocate some of us, like eating an intense chocolate cake for every meal.

So, how would this love, the reward, be if it were intermittent and variable? Much more addictive, isn't it? Here, some people can exploit this mechanism consciously or only unconsciously because of their personality. Wonder how?

Let us say you are a woman and in a relationship with someone. And this person sometimes treats you very well, sometimes normally, and sometimes badly. So, the reward is variable and intermittent. Since you like him, when he treats you well, your reward system is activated, and you feel great. However, naturally, this pleasure does not occur when he treats you badly. Your brain is looking for that reward: him treating you well.

You find yourself thinking, "I wish he always treated me well. Why doesn't he always treat me well?" You ask yourself: "I wonder if I did something wrong? I wonder if I do not treat him well enough? Do I not show my love enough? Is that why he is like this? Would he treat me better if I treated him better?" You start doubting yourself and treating him better and sometimes depriving yourself. But he does not change. He sometimes treats you well and sometimes badly. This time you make more compromises by thinking, "I wonder why what I'm doing is still not enough?" However, the situation does not change again. Unfortunately, you are now an individual who is addicted to a variable-interval reward. And your relationship goes on like this until you realize that the problem is not you but him. Congratulations, you fell in love with either a manipulative or rather emotionally unstable person and became addicted.

Because of this addiction, it is hard to leave that person, even harder than letting go of drugs. You break up most of the time but make it up again. You are breaking up and making it up again, and this loop continues for a while. Until you finally realize that this relationship really harms you a lot. Only then can you completely finish things in your mind and get rid of your addiction to this manipulative or emotionally unstable person. Yet the break-up also devastates you for a while. Do not worry. You are not the only one experiencing this. In the previous chapter, we mentioned the dark triad personality. Such manipulative people often have this personality disorder, and their partners experience this vicious circle. Unfortunately, their numbers are quite high.

Let us come to another brain region whose activation changes when we fall in love: the amygdala.

Amygdala is an almond-shaped structure located in both hemispheres in the center of our brain. It is the brain region responsible for emotional learning and fear. It warns us about possible dangers and risks. However, when we fall in love, our amygdala does not do this task towards our partner.

This deactivation of our amygdala, mainly caused by oxytocin, prevents us from seeing the damage caused by our partner's behavior or the risks of potential harm that may be born out of some of our actions that we do by trusting them a lot. The misfunctioning of our amygdala towards our partner is the reason that makes love blind.

An interesting experiment U.S. scientists did in 2014 shows us how love blinds our eyes with this amygdala deactivation. In two different experiments by

Nathaniel Lambert and his colleagues, first 51 and then 43 different couples were taken into a room and asked to play a game. The experiment's game comprised one partner drawing a picture blindfolded and the other verbally helping on how to draw it. Before the couples were taken to the room for the experiment, they were also asked to answer a few secret questions. These questions included how much they loved their partners and whether they cheated on them.

In the second part of the experiments, these couples' blindfolded drawing games were recorded on video. Later, these three to five-minute video clips were shown to the jury of 6 people who had never known the couples before. According to the interaction they watched, the jury members were asked whether any of the couples were cheating on each other, and if they were cheating, which party they thought was the cheater. The results were unbelievable. The jury members were able to correctly guess in which couple there was cheating. They also correctly guessed who was the cheating partner, even by watching short video recordings of the interactions of people they had never known before.

It is astounding that even if those people were spending a considerable amount of time with their partners, they were not aware that they were being cheated on; however, complete strangers could guess correctly if there was cheating in a relationship and who was the cheating party by just watching their interaction videos for a few minutes. This experiment is a good example, showing how love is blind because of the 'amygdala deactivation' that happens when we fall in love. We rarely see the most harmful things our partner does, even if others can easily see it.

It may have happened to most of us; sometimes, our friends forewarn us against our partner on some issues. We usually reply, "No, dear, s/he wouldn't do such a thing." "You think wrong, s/he is not like that at all." However, after some time, we may have seen how right our friends were. The reason for their being right is that, as in the experiment by Nathaniel Lambert and his group, people in our environment whose amygdalas are working normally towards our partners notice some things easily about them that we cannot see because of our amygdala deactivation.

Therefore, it is often useful to listen to the warnings of the people around us. I specifically do not say "always" but rather prefer to say "often," because sometimes we do not choose our friends correctly either. Some may feel jealous of us and may want to sabotage our happiness. It is necessary to be wary of such possibilities. But if we choose our friends well, the right thing to do would be to pay attention to their advice.

When we fall in love, another important brain region whose activation changes is our orbitofrontal cortex. This part of our brain contains many features that make us human and separate us from animals. It is responsible for many things, from our logic to our attention, from memory to empathy, from our morals to comparing alternative scenarios.

When we fall in love, the activity of this region also decreases. Therefore, when it comes to issues related to our partner, we cannot think as logically as we normally would. Many of us have experienced this sometimes; while flirting and sometimes after a relationship ended, we realized how unreasonable some things we did were and regretted them. This is because the activity of our orbitofrontal cortex is reduced where our partner is concerned. Deactivation of both this region and our amygdala makes us much more naïve towards the person we love and their actions.

In fact, all these changes are crucial for us to experience love to the fullest and without thinking about unnecessary details. However, if we fall in love with the wrong person, this time, the same changes, unfortunately, allow our partner to abuse us easily.

HACKING THE BRAIN TO LOVE

Our brain is a fantastic organ. It is theoretically capable of processing 1 trillion operations per second and storing 100 terabytes of information. It is stronger and smarter than most of the latest phones and computers we have. However, it is also a stupid organ. It can be deceived very easily. Love is no exception to this. By tricking the brain, it is possible to make someone fall in love with us, or at least more quickly.

In 1974, U.S. scientists Donald Dutton and Arnold Aron conducted an interesting experiment on 85 males to show how the brain can be tricked about love.

In their work, some of the men passed through a 140-meter suspension bridge on a deep valley, while others similarly crossed a valley on a concrete bridge. As soon as the subjects crossed the bridge, the female assistant who was part of the experiment passed them a questionnaire and asked them to answer it. When the subjects were done filling out the questionnaire, she gave them her phone number so that they could call her anytime if they had any questions about the experiment. Although it may seem like a somewhat dull experiment so far, what happened afterward was quite interesting. Most of the men crossing the suspension bridge called the female assistant and wanted to have coffee. This behavior was not observed in male subjects who crossed the concrete bridge.

The only variable in this experiment by Aron and Dutton is the type of bridge: one is concrete, and the other is a suspension bridge. Concrete bridges are solid. If we do not have a massive fear of heights, we can easily walk on them. What about suspension bridges? They are bridges made of rope, swinging left and right, where it is difficult to balance. Crossing them makes most people anxious. Therefore, in this experiment, the adrenaline of the men crossing the suspension bridge increased, their hands were sweaty, their heartbeat accelerated, etc. That is to say, their sympathetic nervous systems were activated. This was not the case for those who used the concrete bridge.

Those who crossed the suspension bridge were still under the influence of this sympathetic nervous system activation when they came to the female assistant to answer a so-called questionnaire as part of the experiment. There is another condition in which our sympathetic nervous system is activated: when we are attracted to someone. When the subjects saw the female assistant as soon as they crossed the bridge, their brains confused the reason for this increase in anxiety and sympathetic nervous system activation. They thought, "When I saw this girl, my heart was beating faster, my palms were sweaty, and my adrenaline had increased. So, I should have been attracted to this woman." Therefore, those who passed the suspension bridge called the woman after the experiment and wanted to meet. Since the sympathetic nervous systems of men crossing the concrete bridge were not activated, there was no such confusion. Therefore, they did not call her to have a date after the experiment as much as the ones crossing the suspension bridge.

Although this experiment was conducted on male subjects, similar results in other studies show that this confusion effect is true for both sexes.

For example, in a study by Cindy Meston and Penny Frohlich from the University of Texas in 2003, the photograph of an average person was shown to people who were waiting in line at an amusement park to get on a roller coaster and those who got off the roller coaster, and they were asked to rate this person's attractiveness. Scientists observed that those who had just gotten off the roller coaster, so those whose sympathetic nervous systems were still active because of the excitement in that ride, gave higher scores for the attractiveness of the person shown in the photo than the other group who was waiting in line.

In other words, in order to trick their brain, it is not necessary to make someone perform dangerous actions such as passing the suspension bridge. Any situation or activity in which the person is anxious, and the sympathetic nervous system is activated may be sufficient.

For example, the sympathetic nervous system will be activated in a person who is concerned about their first day at work or school or someone who is nervously waiting in the corner at a party because they do not know anyone. When talking to these people as the opposite sex, similar effects and emotions may arise in them. But is it possible to achieve a similar effect in flirting that most of us encounter and which begins with a usual acquaintance? The answer is yes. Therefore, going to the amusement park or going to a thriller movie in the early stages of flirting may be the right choice because it will have similar effects by activating our date's sympathetic nervous system.

When we like someone, not only our sympathetic nervous system but also the reward system in our brain is activated. Our brains may also experience confusion in signals that activate our reward system, just as in signals that activate the sympathetic nervous system.

Everything that gives us joy and pleasure activates the reward system of our brain. More precisely, our brain's reward system has been activated with these inputs, and that is why we feel a sense of pleasure or joy. Music is one of these.

In the 2017 study of Manuela Marin and her colleagues from the University of Vienna, subjects were made to listen to different music types and asked to rate the attractiveness of people of the opposite sex from photographs. Scientists revealed that the women who listened to high-arousing music compared to those who did not listen to any music or those who listened to low-arousing music rated the attractiveness of the people in the photographs higher. Interestingly, researchers observed this effect only in female subjects in their study. Although music's positive power was also somewhat effective in male subjects, this effect was not as strong as in female subjects. We do not know why, but this difference may be because women generally enjoy listening to music a little more than men. Therefore, taking their partners to a nice concert in the early stages of dating or meeting someone at such a concert may increase men's chances a little more.

Figure 16- High-arousing music concerts especially cause women to rate the attractiveness of the people of opposite sex higher.

Although we have given the example of music, it is also possible to trick the brain's reward system with other activities. Exploring new places, engaging in fun activities, a good meal, even sweet words, sincere compliments, etc., activate our brain's reward system. We already do most of these often instinctively or culturally during the flirting phase.

So far, we have talked about tricking people's brains in attraction. Well, can we hack our potential romantic partner's brain so much that it will make them fall in love with us? Is there a shortcut for this?

According to the study by psychologist Arthur Aron in 1997, there is! In fact, with some subjects, in a way that ended in a marriage.

The method Arthur Aron found is not only very effective but also quite short. It takes only 49 minutes with this method for two complete strangers to fall in love with each other. The technique comprises 36 questions to be answered within 45 minutes and a four-minute eye contact afterward.

I will not write all the questions here; there is no need anyway. But let's look at some of them:

If you were to die this evening with no opportunity to communicate with anyone, what would you most regret not having told someone? Why haven't you told them yet?

If you could wake up tomorrow having gained one quality or ability, what would it be?

What is the greatest accomplishment of your life?

If you knew that you would die suddenly in one year, would you change anything about the way you are now living? Why?

How close are you to your family? What do they mean to you?

Of all the people in your family, whose death would you find most disturbing? Why?

What was your most embarrassing moment in life?

If you could change anything about the way you were raised, what would it be?

Have you noticed a common pattern in these questions?

Questions that go down deep in the person and ask them to talk about things they do not easily share with people. Isn't it? With these features, they are tricking the brain.

Normally we do not share deep subjects, secrets, and details about our life and past with someone we have just met or with our partners at the beginning of our relationship. For example, our thoughts about our family, regrets, and vulnerabilities, and so on often happen after the relationship has reached a certain point, after a certain intimacy and mutual trust have occurred.

When we analyze the questions in Arthur Aron's study, we see that these are usually about issues that would be talked about at much later stages of the relationship. This is the shortcut Arthur Aron has found. As someone answers these questions, their subconscious thinks, "If I am talking about the deepest subjects with them, I must have been really attracted to them and trust them well enough to talk about these things."

Participants in this study comfortably answered such questions to a person they have newly met because they knew that this was an experiment. But in our daily lives, if we ask such questions about their private life to someone we are attracted to but have just met or know little of, we will probably get a backlash. But if you do this gradually, you can speed up the intimacy process in your relationship, even if it is not in 49 minutes.

Not only the questions that enable them to open up about their private lives but also the last four minutes of eye contact is also essential for love to flourish. The 1989 study by U.S. scientist Joan Kellerman and her colleagues on 96 people shows that even just 2-minutes of exchanging glances allows us to like the other person more. But the most critical detail in their study results is that this glance to be mutual and deep. Conditions such as only one person gazing or looking to count the number of times the other person has blinked do not affect attraction levels.

The basis for exchanging glances to increase attraction is actually a phenomenon known since Darwin in the 1800s and has been the subject of numerous studies afterward: our actions shape our emotions. For example, if we were slouching and suddenly stand up straight, we feel more confident. If we put a smile on our face at any moment, we will feel more cheerful after a while. The fact that the mutual gaze increases our attraction does not differ from these other simple examples where our behavior and actions shape our emotions.

There is an important point to consider in hacking someone's brain to love. For such methods to work on people, they need to want to have a relationship or feel ready to have a relationship. As we mentioned at the beginning of our book, the willingness to have a relationship is the most crucial step leading to love. Because sometimes, we may not want a relationship in certain periods of our lives for various reasons. So, if you meet someone who feels this way, your efforts may not work out well.

RELATIONSHIPS

First, we get attracted to a person. Then, we get closer to them by flirting. Finally, we start having a relationship. In this chapter, you will find answers to questions such as how we can maintain a healthy relationship, what changes happen in our brain and body during a relationship, and how our personality affects relationships.

It is the dream of all of us; we want our relationship to last forever when we love somebody. Unfortunately, this does not happen often. After a certain period, arguments intensify, and the relationship becomes unbearable. Breakup and blocking on social media—as it is in fashion right now—take place. So why is that?

Usually, the problem is not you, but your hormones. When we first fall in love, we tend to see things through rose-colored glasses and perceive our partner as perfect with the influence of our changing hormones. This condition, called being drunk in love, starts to disappear when our hormones return to their normal values over time.

Many of our partner's negative features that we tolerate during this average 6-8-month honeymoon period start bothering us gradually when this period is over. For example, if our partner has been slurping their food, we find this cute at the beginning. But when our hormones return to normal levels and the head over heels period is over, such things become no longer cute for us or even annoy us.

However, we still secrete dopamine while we are with the person we love. Therefore, the feeling of happiness continues, albeit at a diminishing pace: about 12-18 months. At the end of this period, our brain is used to the continuous secretion of dopamine, and numbness develops, especially if the relationship is going monotonous, just like eating a chocolate cake all the time.

Although eating a chocolate cake gives us pleasure, we become numb if we eat it every day for every meal. We do not get the pleasure we got in the beginning.

Although the amount of oxytocin secreted in the first months of the relationship determines the relationship's duration, studies show that love lasts an average of four years. Therefore, when we look at the world, divorces in marriages and heated arguments in relationships are most common in the relationship's fourth year.

When we examine the primitive tribes that practice polygamy, we also see that this critical fourth year has an evolutionary basis. Scientists observed that couples who marry and have children in these polygamous primitive tribes repeat this process with another partner when the child is about three years old. Considering that love is a feeling based on children's care and reproduction, this behavior is actually not against this principle. Because a three-year-old child can walk, run, talk, and spend time on their own with other children in the tribe. So, it is no longer in need of parental care as much as before. That is why parents in primitive tribes also leave and find other partners at the end of these four years to diversify their gene pools.

Isn't it possible to have a long and happy relationship if love ends biologically after four years on average?

As Nazım Hikmet says in his poem "To a photograph":

"What matters is not to leave it to time,

It is not to leave it in time."

Is it possible not to leave our partner in time?

Yes, it is possible. In fact, if we do not make some mistakes during our flirting period and pay attention to certain points in our relationship, we can guarantee a happy relationship for at least four years.

In addition to all of this, the way to extend this is to accept that the feeling we call love scientifically has a certain length. We should not have unrealistic expectations for the future and think being drunk in love will last a lifetime, knowing that what we feel in the later stages of our relationship will not be the same as it was in the first place.

Bracing ourselves from the beginning and not having unnecessary disappointments is the key to having a long-term and enjoyable relationship for both parties. For such a long-term relationship, firstly choosing the right person is very important. Because of the changes in our body and brain in the first stages of love, our tolerance level towards this person will be at the highest level, no matter who we choose. In this period, we take an approach not to see the negative things that our partner does and forgive whatever happens.

However, most of the time, after the sixth month, our hormones that give the first drunk in love feeling begin to reach their normal values. Thus, our tolerance in those early times decreases. Arguments start to arise from incompatibilities. Thus, choosing a partner with whom we can maintain a compatible relationship is essential in having a good and long-term relationship.

Other foundations of happy relationships are, in fact, very interconnected: mutual love, respect, trust, understanding, and justice.

It is impossible to talk about trust, understanding, and justice where there is no mutual love and respect. In fact, this is somewhat similar to the chicken and egg paradox. Because the oxytocin hormone secreted when we fall in love not only allows us to connect to our partners but also reduces amygdala activity, causing us to have more trust in them. If we do not trust our partners, this may indicate a problem with our oxytocin level. Then we come across the dilemma of whether we are truly in love with our partner.

If someone is not masochistic or highly submissive, they want justice and equality in their relationships. Being the party that always makes an effort and tries hard for the well-being of the relationship forces the person's tolerance limits after a certain period. This condition reduces the quality and duration of the relationship.

Mutual understanding and empathy with our partners are indispensable for a good relationship. Of course, as free individuals, we do not have to change ourselves for our partners completely. However, this does not mean that we should definitely be uncompromising and inconsiderate in a relationship.

We all start our relationships by carrying some burdens of our pasts. Thus, some of us may be more sensitive to some issues than others because of the traumas we experienced in our previous relationships. Sometimes traumatic events in our family or our immediate environment also affect some of our behaviors in our relationships. Not only the traumas we experienced, but even our interactions with our parents in our childhood determine what kind of character we will assume in our relationships.

We all establish a bond with our parents in our childhood. With this bond, our parents are both our heroes who are with us in case of need for food and care, a safe haven that protects us from the dangers from the environment, and our guides that help us discover life. Their behavior in such situations forms the basis of the way we connect with other people.

If the behavior of our parents were consistent and reliable in our childhood, in our subconscious, we consider ourselves worthy of being loved. This makes it easier for us to connect with our partners. For example, if our parents gave us milk and food when we were hungry and calmly comforted us when we were worried and afraid, we place reliance on them and other people with whom we are connected later in life. On the contrary, if our parents did not treat us adequately in such situations, we encounter problems in trusting our partners.

In fact, the reason for this trust issue may be the growth of our amygdala due to neglect and lack of love experienced in early childhood. Our amygdala is the area of our brain responsible for fear and anxiety. Individuals with larger and active amygdalas show more fear, anxiety, and aggression. Its size also varies between genders. One of the reasons for aggression in men is that their amygdalas are bigger than women's.

In a 2010 study, Nim Tottenham and her colleagues from Cornell University discovered that neglect and lack of love in childhood increased the size of the amygdala in children. To show this effect, Dr. Tottenham and her team compared the amygdala size of children growing up in an orphanage and children growing up with families. Comparing MRI scan images, they revealed that the amygdalas of the children who stayed in the orphanage for more than 15 months were larger than their peers. Interestingly, when the children stayed in an orphanage for less than 15 months and were adopted afterward, their amygdala size did not differ from those of other children who grew up in family environments. This study is an excellent example of how a lack of early parental care and love can shape our brain structures and affect our behavior.

Moreover, a 2020 study led by Baylor University revealed that people who were children when their parents were divorced showed substantially lower oxytocin levels in their adulthood than those whose parents remained married. Decreased oxytocin levels may play a role in having trouble forming attachments. Indeed, the study results also showed that lower oxytocin levels correlated with responses on several measures of attachment in those individuals. Those who experienced parental divorce during childhood were less confident and less secure in relationships.

In 1991, based on children's attachment styles, Kim Bartholomew and Leonard Horowitz identified four different attachment styles for adults: Secure, preoccupied, dismissing, and fearful.

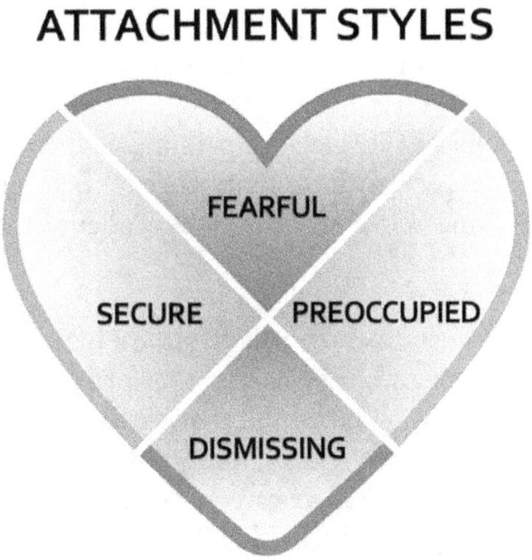

ATTACHMENT STYLES

Figure 17- There are four different attachment styles that determine our attitude towards our partner in a relationship.

People whose parents were always with them and cared for them during their childhood have the secure attachment style. Feeling that their parents love them and fulfill their emotional needs leads these people to express themselves and their feelings more comfortably throughout their lives. People with this attachment style trust and value both themselves and others. Their approach to mutual relations and relationships is positive. They have less avoidance and separation anxiety in relationships. When their relationship ends, they will be sad but will respond with understanding and maturity to those who leave.

People whose parents were emotionally present with them as a child most of the time but who did not or could not do this continuously for various reasons, and people who could not find their parents by their side whenever they needed them often have the preoccupied attachment style. For the person, this situation creates an anxious attachment characteristic in their relationships. Therefore, individuals with a preoccupied attachment style have little self-worth and trust. In contrast, the value they give to others is high. They are afraid of being abandoned and left alone. They are obsessively attached to their partners. While this obsession causes them to want to be closer to their partners and spend more time with them than usual, it also causes them to complain about their partners not being close enough and not being interested in them. Therefore, they experience a relationship that is somewhat overwhelming, controlling, and one with jealousy attacks.

The dismissing attachment style usually involves individuals who were emotionally neglected by their parents during childhood and whose parents were cold and unresponsive. This lack of parental care causes them to become self-sufficient. These people only have confidence in themselves, even as a child. As a result, they become self-confident, independent, and unwilling to get attached to people.

Individuals with dismissing attachment style place a higher value on themselves than usual. On the other hand, they deem other people worthless. They have an increased fear of rejection. They think that getting rejected will lower their self-worth. So, mostly they may even choose not to have a relationship with various excuses like focusing on their career, not trusting people, etc. In their relationships, they avoid attaching to their partners due to their mistrust in others and remain distant. This lack of bonding prevents them and their partners from having a happy relationship.

Individuals with fearful attachment style are those who were physically, emotionally, or sexually abused by one of their parents in their childhood. Their other parent is often emotionally present, but this does not prevent them from having trust issues in the future. Therefore, individuals with fearful attachment style, like those of dismissing attachment type, escape from relationships. Unlike them, however, this escape is not only because they do not value others, but also because they deem themselves unworthy of being loved. Due to traumatic interactions with parents experienced as a child, they wish their partners to meet their emotional needs in their relationships. Still, on the other hand, they experience serious concerns with trusting in and connecting to their partners.

The proportion of people with these four attachment styles in different societies also varies. Many groups did numerous studies showing this variance in attachment styles among cultures. For example, according to the study of Sumer and Gungor in 1999, these rates among U.S. students are 45% for secure attachment, 10% for fearful attachment, 20% for preoccupied attachment, and 24% for dismissing attachment, whereas, among Turkish students, the rates are 43% for secure attachment, 9% for fearful attachment, 28% for preoccupied attachment, and 19% for dismissing attachment.

So, does our attachment style affect the features we are looking for in our partner to have a happier relationship?

There are three different hypotheses about people's attachment styles and the features they are looking for in a partner. One of them is the similarity hypothesis. It states that people prefer partners who have a similar attachment style to theirs. Another theory, the complementarity hypothesis, suggests that the individuals prefer partners who do not have the characteristics that they have and have the opposite attachment style. The last one is the safe harbor hypothesis. This hypothesis suggests that people prefer someone with a secure attachment style to establish a strong bond in their relationships regardless of one's own attachment style.

A 2009 study by Bkarn Holmes and Kimberly Johnson from the U.K. revealed that although people say they prefer individuals with the secure attachment style or a similar attachment style to themselves in hypothetical situations, their actual preferences in real life differ. So, when people said, "I want to have a relationship with a person having this attachment style" in surveys, scientists observed that this hypothetical preference did not occur when their real partners' attachment styles were examined. In short, what people say and what they do regarding attachment style preference in their partners mostly differs.

In this study, Holmes and his colleagues revealed that regardless of their attachment style, in real life, most people have relationships with individuals who have the opposite attachment style, which is in a way complementary to their own. Perhaps, as our ancestors say, opposites really attract each other more when it comes to attachment styles.

However, researchers did not survey the happiness levels of these couples in their relationships. Hence, we cannot conclude from this research that although opposite attachment styles attract each other, such couples always have a very harmonious and happy relationship. Because most of the time, individuals who know what they want and only have a relationship with a partner that meets these features can find happiness more easily.

Although our attachment style is determined by the relationship with our parents in childhood, research shows that these types may not remain constant throughout one's life. What we experience in our relationships can also change our attachment style later. For example, if an individual with the secure attachment type is cheated continuously in their relationships or has experienced other serious traumas, their attachment style may change in their subsequent relationships.

This is because what we experience in our relationships can change our amygdala size, therefore our behaviors. This change is similar to the change in children's amygdala size related to their parental love and care conditions. Although there is no direct research on how love and breakups affect the size of our amygdala, there is a remarkable study about how stress levels change this region's size in adults.

A 2010 study by Britta Hölzel and her colleagues from the U.S. revealed that when people with high-stress levels were treated, and their stress levels were reduced, their amygdala size decreased in parallel with these low-stress levels. Thus, since a good relationship with the right person will dispel our various anxieties, it would reduce our amygdala's size with a similar effect and make us look at life more positively. In contrast, stressful relationships with the wrong people would increase our amygdala size and lead us to look at life and relationships more negatively in the future.

Therefore, it is essential in a relationship to be aware of the issues that our partner may be sensitive to due to various old traumas, even if they are not caused by us. In order to get rid of these effects, and thus, to increase the duration and quality of our relationship in the long term, we should be as encouraging and reassuring as possible against our partner's sensitive issues.

There is another element for having good long-term relationships that seems to contradict others: arguing! To be honest, I have not come across any scientific study on this subject. It may have escaped my notice. However, based on my experience, I can say that small arguments from time to time are actually beneficial for relationships. I even experienced this situation myself. I was definitely against arguments in the past, whether I was right or wrong. I always made compromises and refrained from arguing so that there would not be any discomfort. One day after an argument in which I kept it down again, my girlfriend furiously said, "Oktar, I hate you! We can't have an argument with you in any way, but I want to fight sometimes!" I felt the need to question my attitude when I saw those sparks of "not being able to fight" in my girlfriend's eyes.

Mutual understanding is crucial in relationships. Yet, it also made sense that unburdening our hearts from time to time with mild arguments to prevent things from piling up in our partners or in us would throw negative electricity away. After all, none of us are perfect. Of course, we sometimes do things that annoy our partners. This does not mean we should continuously be fighting like cats and dogs. If you are already in such a relationship, it is better to reconsider your love and relationship. However, I think occasional mild arguments that do not hurt our partners may strengthen the relationships.

Mutual love, respect, trust, understanding, and justice are not only the basis of a healthy romantic relationship but also of a good friendship. This friendship and connection generally form the core of maintaining our relationship for many years, even when our hormones return to normal levels.

Figure 18– Sometimes the activation of a special region in our brain ensures two people to stay deeply in love with each other for decades.

Although long-term relationships are based upon friendship and companionship that continue after love ends, in some cases, the activity of a particular region of our brain, Periaqueductal gray (PAG), may be the secret of everlasting love.

In 2012, Bianca Acevedo and her colleagues from the U.S. did a brain scan study on 17 people who had over 20 years of happy relationships and said they were still deeply in love with their partners. Researchers revealed that, besides the brain areas that are typically activated when we are in love, those peoples' Periaqueductal grays were also highly activated. The amount of activation in this area was also related to the length of their relationship to date. Although the researchers presented this finding only as an observation and did not discuss its cause, we can interpret its reasons by considering some features of Periaqueductal gray.

PAG is the pain center in our brain. If we mention it without the detailed mechanism, when we encounter a painful situation, this region decreases the pain we feel by secreting molecules called endorphins, which have a similar effect to morphine. Moreover, PAG's nerve connections with the brain's reward center also ensure dopamine secretion in our brain. That is to say; our brain has developed a defense mechanism that both reduces pain and makes us feel a little better when we face pain. Periaqueductal gray is one of the key areas of this mechanism.

Because of this defense system, marathon runners get into a pleasure state called "runner's high" with the effect of endorphins and dopamine, which they secrete with the pain they experience toward the end of the run. This feeling often causes addiction to those people. The same is true for those who train for long hours in the gym. The examples can be multiplied. The common point of all is that they always want more because of the addiction created by the pleasure developed against this pain.

Although our brain is a highly developed organ, we said it was deceivable enough to mix things up. The Periaqueductal gray region is no exception. PAG responds not only to physical pain but also to emotional pain. Disappointments, heartbreaks, betrayals, sadness, or other emotional distresses that we experience also activate this brain region to protect us from such feelings' bitterness.

This mechanism against pain affects even the kinds of music we listen to. Most of the time, we enjoy the effects of the secreted dopamine when we listen to upbeat and cheerful music. Some people, on the contrary, often enjoy listening to painful and sad songs. Endorphin and dopamine secretion while listening to the emotional pain in these songs give us pleasure and cause addiction, just like upbeat songs do. In fact, people who intensely listen to this kind of music sometimes do not settle for the emotional pain to activate this system. From time to time, they increase this effect they experience with the physical pain they add by cutting themselves with a razor.

Regarding the effect of the Periaqueductal gray in long-term relationships, we probably will not be able to know for many years the exact reason why this area is activated more in people who have such a relationship. However, when we think that everyone's brain activity is different, perhaps this significant activation of PAGs may be an innate feature of those who have a happy long-term relationship. This innate activation may lead them to be more tolerant to pain, especially emotional pain. Thus, they might be tolerating the problems they experience in their relationships much more. Considering the role of PAG in dopamine secretion as well, we can also think that they can maintain their romantic love longer. Since we do not know the exact reason for the activation of the Periaqueductal gray in long-term relationships, this is only an interpretation. Yet, this is not an analysis that contradicts the current scientific data we have.

We can benefit from our brains' weaknesses not only in the stage of attraction and flirting but also for a more peaceful and long-term relationship. One of the biggest problems in relationships is not to trust our partners. The basis for this is our partner's potential to cheat on us, or briefly, our risk of being cheated. Suspicions of infidelity are generally pointed toward men. So, is there a way to make men more loyal in relationships?

In 2012, an interesting study was carried out at Bonn University in Germany, showing oxytocin's effect on men's fidelity. In this study on 86 men, Dirk Scheele and his colleagues experimented on single men and men in a relationship as two separate groups. While randomly, some men in these two groups were given oxytocin in the form of nasal spray, the others were similarly given saline solution as a placebo. Later, men in both groups were taken into a room to interact with an attractive woman. In the group of men who had a relationship, scientists observed that those given the placebo approached the woman as closely as possible. In contrast, those who received oxytocin remained more distant from this attractive woman and maintained their social distance.

In single men, both those given the placebo and the group given oxytocin stayed as intimate as possible to the woman.

The results of this experiment show us that if a man's oxytocin levels in the relationship have not risen enough, he is more likely to cheat. But if a man in the relationship has high oxytocin levels, even made higher just before a circumstance that involves the potential to cheat, this time, he retains loyalty. I think this study contains an essential tip for women who have suspicion or fear of being cheated. What do you say?

We do not see the effect of oxytocin only in fidelity. According to another study by the same group of researchers in 2013, oxytocin also causes men to see their partners more attractive. Another result of the same research is that this effect of oxytocin in men occurs only toward women with whom they have a romantic relationship. No such effect was observed with other women.

There is a famous Arabian Nights tale that most know: Layla and Majnun. When Majnun's great love for Layla becomes notorious in the country, one day, the sultan calls Mecnun to his side. He is curious about Layla's beauty. "Majnun, I want to see Layla for whom you have fallen into the deserts," he says. The news is released, and Layla is summoned to the palace. When Layla enters, the disappointed sultan leans over to Majnun and says, "Is this the Layla you are madly in love with? Where is her beauty?" Majnun sighs deeply and says, "Oh sultan, I wish you could see her the way I see." This is precisely the effect of oxytocin in men who have a relationship.

The fact that oxytocin increases fidelity in men brings to mind whether it has the same effect on women. Compared to men, it is not easy to find the answer to this question in women because oxytocin levels in females vary during their menstrual cycles. Therefore, it is not possible to conduct a controlled experiment in them as much as in men. The exception is those who use birth control pills. The amount of oxytocin in these women does not differ significantly during their menstrual cycles. However, using contraceptives can also have some other side effects because it interferes with their hormonal cycle. Therefore, precise results may not be obtained in such studies.

The same group at the University of Bonn that did the oxytocin and fidelity research on men conducted a similar experiment on women in 2014. But interestingly, this time, unlike their work on men, they did not separate female subjects into two groups as "singles" and "in a relationship." We clearly do not know why they preferred to do so. Maybe in the first place, they may have performed the experiments in two separate groups, but when they did not get the results they expected (in which birth control pills may have an impact), they may have chosen to combine the groups to re-analyze the data and preferred to publish them like that. Unfortunately, this is sometimes done in scientific studies. Therefore, it is necessary to be a little careful and questioning when examining such studies.

As for the study results, scientists observed that women who received oxytocin preferred to stay closer to the man in the experiment than women who received the placebo. Since the women in the experiment are not grouped as "in a relationship" and "single," these results should not be considered as an inclination toward unfaithfulness. The most accurate interpretation may be that "the oxytocin increase in women who use contraceptive pills, reduces their social anxiety against males." If you are a woman using a birth control pill and have social anxiety, increasing your oxytocin levels may help you solve this problem.

In order to have a long healthy relationship, oxytocin has effects beyond fidelity. A 2009 study done by Swiss scientists revealed that giving oxytocin to couples before their arguments reduces people's negative attitudes during an argument and makes them more constructive. Given that violent and disruptive fights damage relationships, oxytocin's softening effect on this issue seems crucial for healthy and long relationships.

I will not repeat it here since I have already mentioned the activities that increase our oxytocin levels. If we care to carry out these activities intensively during our relationships, we will be taking important steps on the path to living a healthy and long relationship.

LONG-DISTANCE RELATIONSHIPS

Sometimes as an extension of the digital age we live in and sometimes out of necessity, we often encounter long-distance relationships. Thus, we need to discuss long-distance relationships in two separate groups.

First, there are couples who have to go to different cities, even countries, and live physically apart for reasons such as career or school change for a certain period during their relationships. The other one is the couples who establish their relationships through channels like social media first, without physically getting close to each other because other socialization possibilities around them are limited for various reasons.

Let us first discuss the relationships that start on social media because social media is now a fact of our time. Indeed, it is now the starting point of most of the flirtations. Can those social media flirtations turn into true love?

Social media has many limitations compared to face-to-face meeting and dating. However, these limitations can sometimes turn into serious advantages for people. For example, when we first meet someone only on social media, we mostly see them with photos taken from the most beautiful angles and flaws hidden with various filters. Thus, most of the time, we are physically attracted to that person more than we normally would be in real life.

What a physically appealing person says seems more credible, honest, and sincere to us because of the halo effect. The only exception to this is when people's body language does not match what they say. Therefore, what is said in social media flirtation can be more convincing because of the increased credibility of the person we are highly attracted to and because we cannot read the inconsistencies in their body language at that moment.

In addition, in the previous chapters, we mentioned that our brains complete the unknown features of the person we like positively. What we know about someone that we only communicate with on social media is limited to what they show to us. If we like someone physically, our brains positively complete the rest. There are even some extreme examples where people can introduce themselves in different genders with fake photos on social media and easily gain others' trust. In short, attraction, which is the first step of love in long-distance relationships on social media, can occur easily, even at a higher level than it would normally be in real life.

Figure 19- Social media is a channel in which most long-distance relationships are built up today.

Things that are often ordinary in a physical relationship are seen as a privilege and achievement in social media relationships, further stimulating our brain's reward center. For example, it is quite common in a normal relationship to see our partners' faces, touch, and smell them. However, with a social media flirt, let alone doing these regularly, sometimes even getting an instant photo of them can be a difficult wish. Therefore, the extra effort we put into just getting such ordinary things makes our online partners even more valuable in our brains.

Let's come to the other important step of love: bonding. As we have mentioned in many examples before, the oxytocin hormone, which is necessary for our attachment to our partners, is mostly secreted by physical contact. However, its levels can also increase a little in long-distance relationships because our brain often cannot clearly distinguish between imagination and reality and gives similar responses. Thus, oxytocin is also secreted whenever we imagine spending time that includes physical contact with our social media flirts. Maybe it is not secreted as strongly as usual, but some oxytocin is secreted. As these thoughts continue and diversify, its secretion gradually increases.

Moreover, oxytocin is also a hormone linked to the dopamine system in our brains. When our dopamine system is activated, oxytocin is also released. That is why whenever we see a beautiful photo of our social media flirt and whenever we have a pleasant conversation with them, we secrete some oxytocin along with dopamine. This oxytocin secretion enables us to connect with them. Due to the lack of physical contact, maybe this bonding develops slightly slower than normal but eventually happens.

When we consider all this, it is possible to get attracted to our flirts on social media, even if we never really see them, and then get attached to them and fall in love. Perhaps in most circumstances, this love will grow a little later than usual. Still, we may even love our social media flirt more strongly in some cases than we would normally love.

In social media relationships, we encounter two problems when we fall in love. One of them is the effort. As we mentioned above, in social media relationships, we strive to achieve some things that are ordinary in a normal relationship. Our brains see them as rewards and achievements. Although these rewards impact positively at first by causing dopamine secretion, if we are the ones who demand these mostly, this thought can settle in our subconscious, "I worked hard in this relationship. It was always me who tried hard." This feeling of injustice can sometimes drag us into unnecessary touchiness and lead us to argue and leave our partners for insignificant reasons. There is also the opposite possibility. Sometimes, despite needing to leave that relationship because things are not going well anymore, we postpone breakups so that all those efforts we made are not wasted.

Another problem is that if we do not meet with our social media flirt at the right time and turn it into a physical flirt, we are starting a risky relationship. Suppose we meet without knowing the other person enough. In that case, the probability of encountering someone with the potential to harm us physically may be higher than in other conditions. Therefore, first dates following social media flirtation should generally be in daytime and crowded environments. If possible, we should meet after searching about and verifying the information about them in various ways. We should find out more information than they tell us on social media.

On the other hand, if we delay the physical meeting time for various reasons and start dating after we fall in love with our social media flirt, this time, our amygdala and orbitofrontal cortex activities would be decreased for that person. We will lose our chance to evaluate them objectively. This means if that person is not the right one, we will start a relationship in which we risk suffering physical and emotional harm. When we think of all this, social media is a channel that increases our chances of finding a potential partner and offers us great opportunities in this regard. Flirtations that begin here can turn into beautiful relationships and passionate love. However, we can enjoy these benefits of social media only when we approach it consciously without ignoring its negative aspects. Otherwise, it has much greater risks than a relationship we would have in our everyday life.

Another type of long-distance relationship is the couples who have to separate their distance in a certain period of their relationship. Although this situation has various disadvantages for relationships, it also has its advantages.

Let us talk about its advantages first. When we move to a digital relationship for a certain period while in a physical relationship, just like in social media relationships, what we normally experience, such as holding hands and walking hand in hand, becomes a reward for us and is much more valuable. This increases the value of our partners in our brains.

It can be better understood if we explain our reward system's similar reaction to some other examples in daily life. Smoking, if you are a tobacco addict, or eating chocolate cake if you are not, can be good examples. Smoking is an action that activates our reward system and therefore gives us pleasure. However, we do not feel much pleasure when we smoke every day because we get used to it. Smoking becomes ordinary for us. When we quit smoking and do not smoke for a while, we feel an uncontrollable desire to smoke again. The very first cigarette that we light when we succumb to our desires and give up our determination gives a lot of pleasure to us.

Similarly, since chocolate cake is a sugary food, it gives us pleasure while eating because it activates our reward system. However, when we eat chocolate cake every day, it becomes ordinary for us, and we do not feel the pleasure we used to get. If we take a break from eating chocolate cake for a while, its value for us increases again, and we enjoy it when we eat it. In fact, this is what we experience with distances in a relationship. Even holding hands, which is normally very casual, gives us great pleasure when we meet weeks or months after separation.

The long-distance relationship also has some drawbacks. Let us say the relationships resemble a brick wall and assume that three bricks disappear from this wall every time we fight. Usually, in our normal relationships, we release oxytocin with physical contact. Thanks to this hormone, those three bricks that fall out of the wall after a fight are glued back into their place. Since there is no physical contact in long-distance relationships, the amount of oxytocin that we secrete by imagination is limited. Thus, only one of those three bricks that disappears from the wall after the fight can stick back; two bricks are missing. If we are away from each other for a long time and we fight frequently, these bricks decrease by two, causing the wall to collapse faster than usual. The way to prevent this in long-distance relationships is to meet physically often and attach the missing bricks on that wall back with the oxytocin we secrete at those times.

When we consider all these, long distances can even bring benefits to the relationship rather than harm if managed wisely. It can extend the duration and quality of the relationship. Even in normal relationships, instead of living in each other's pocket every day, meeting at certain intervals, such as every few days, positively affects the relationship. Of course, in cases where this is not possible, such as marriages, going on vacations separately, or if this is not possible for some reason like having children, socializing at least a few days a week separately has a significant benefit for the quality and duration of the relationship.

In the case of the opposite, when partners live together, disagreements and intolerance may increase, especially if you do not have a relationship with the right person. The most recent example of this situation is the lockdown announced in China because of the COVID-19 outbreak and its effect on relationships. The strictly enforced lockdown caused couples to share the same environment for a long time. When the lockdown was over, the number of divorce lawsuits reached record levels. Since there is no detailed research on the reasons for this increase while this book is being published, we cannot draw a definite inference. We can say that some of these are cases that were already planned but postponed due to the lockdown. However, probably a significant part is because the couples who were forced to live together in a closed environment for weeks had lost all their tolerance for each other.

BREAKUPS

$\mathbf{M}$ost of the time, not everything goes the way we want in relationships. Sometimes breakups are inevitable. Studies show that 85% of people experience a breakup in at least one of their relationships, while 95% are rejected at least once by the person they have fallen in love with or reject someone who has fallen in love with them. So, if you are not in that lucky group of that remaining 5%, you will find a lot about yourself on the following pages.

In this chapter, we will talk about the general reasons for breakups and how we can prevent them. We will also discuss some other important matters like the changes in our body and brain when a relationship is over and how we can overcome breakup pain more easily by understanding these changes and forget about our ex-partners more quickly.

Sometimes our mistakes or lack of certain things in our relationships cause breakups. Sometimes, even if we do everything right in a relationship, our partner's character leads to separations.

Although infidelity seems to be the primary reason for most breakups, other relationship problems usually lie behind it. However, sometimes, even if everything is perfect, the difference in our partner's brain structure can also lead to unfaithfulness. A 2014 study on 7400 twins in Finland found that 62% of men and 40% of women who cheated on their partners had a genetic tendency to do that. Of course, this is not an exact reason or excuse for cheating because cheating on a partner is a choice. But our genes and genetic differences that affect our brain's functioning sometimes have a hand in our tendency to cheat.

With this Finnish study in mind, let us look at a 2017 study by Kayla Knopp from the University of Denver in the U.S. In this study, which was conducted by following hundreds of people's relationships for five years, scientists found that people who cheated on their partners in their previous relationships were three times more likely to cheat in their later relationships than those who had never cheated on their partners. Scientists also noted that this increased probability is independent of the relationship type.

Thus, assumptions like "Their previous relationships were not serious, but we will get married. When we get married, they will not cheat" do not have much validity. This is true for both sexes. Whether men or women, someone who cheated on their partners before is very likely to cheat on their lovers in their subsequent relationships. That is to say, the importance of choosing the right person, which is one of the key elements that ensure a happy and long relationship, also appears here. When it comes to these types of people, our self-confidence in not being cheated needs to be controlled. Because every infidelity can bring us serious traumas that we will carry into our future relationships. While there are seven billion people in this world, it is not logical to choose a person who can hurt us and be like turkeys voting for an early Christmas.

People sometimes cheat on their partners due to various problems in their relationships. However, if we consider the results of the study in Finland, regardless of who their partner is, sometimes some people can easily cheat because they do not feel the attachment we have for our partner since their brain functions differ from ours. Therefore, we need to consider this possibility from time to time not to be upset by blaming ourselves.

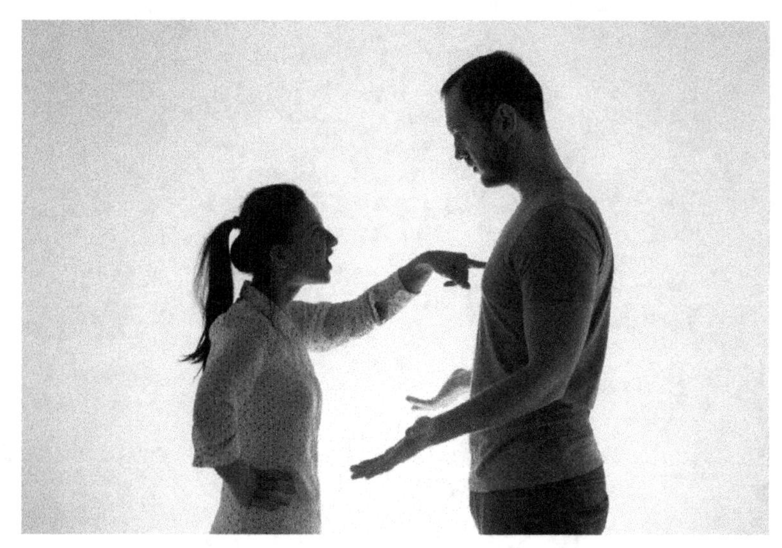

REASONS FOR BREAKUP

Violent arguments are at the top of the reasons for breakups. Sometimes jealousy and sometimes lack of harmony in couples lead to constant and violent arguments in relationships.

Especially these days, social media use is among the major factors that trigger arguments and breakups in relationships. Since Facebook was the first social network established and used extensively for a long time, most scientific research is on the effects of this medium on relationship health. Many studies show that intensive use of Facebook decreases the relationship's quality, leading to jealousy-based arguments, breakups, and divorces.

There are also studies showing similar results with those who use Twitter intensively. Compared to Facebook and Twitter, there is not much scientific study about the effect of Instagram on relationships since it is a social network that has been used more frequently only recently. However, a limited number of studies reveal similar results in using Instagram. For example, according to research by Jessica Ridgway and Russell Clayton from Florida State University, those who post more selfies on Instagram experience more intense arguments and breakups in their relationships.

So, why is that?

Tens of thousands of years ago, humankind lived in small tribes of 80-100 people. Our ancestors lived in villages of more or less this size hundreds of years ago. Nowadays, although we sometimes live in cities with a population of millions, our social circle is mostly limited to 80-100 acquaintances from our school, neighborhood, and work. So, for thousands of years, we often choose our close friends and partners from this limited social circle.

Since human beings have always lived in such a limited social environment from the earliest periods until recent times, our brain has been shaped to handle only this much social input comfortably. With the recent growth of social media, we can now reach almost anyone we want, regardless of their location. Similarly, people from all over the world can easily reach us.

Since physical distances are now removed, and people can easily be reached, we naturally become interested in more people. While in the past, we only found our partners from a limited environment such as work, school, neighborhood, we can now flirt with anyone from anywhere in the world via the internet. Although this seems like a fantastic opportunity, it can often move people away from true love.

First, let us talk about its damages to those who are not in a relationship and seek love.

The likes we receive on our social media posts activate the reward system in our brains. Thus, they are addictive, just like gambling or drugs. On top of this addiction, our reward system is activated more with the interest, compliment, and flirtation we get from our followers. This is the biggest reason why we enjoy the attention, especially from people we like or respect. However, as in all other addictions, once we get used to the attention we receive on social media, we always seek it and spend more time and energy to get it.

However, in a relationship, it is necessary to concentrate and spend effort for love to develop and sprout on both sides. Both parties should feel special.

So, how possible is it to concentrate on one person while texting and flirting with many people at the same time on social media just to make ourselves feel better or to increase our options? Not really! Apart from social media, we see similar examples when we look around in our daily lives. Probably everyone has a very familiar acquaintance whom you always find attractive, who always has suitors, but is a confirmed bachelor. The fact that many suitors are constantly interested in them is a trap that many attractive confirmed bachelors fall in. When we have so many options, we get confused and cannot fully concentrate on any of them. Since we cannot show enough interest, these suitors fall out of love with us, and then we often become alone for this reason.

We can compare this situation to the all-inclusive, open buffet meals of five-star hotels. The options are so many that we often cannot decide. We fill our plates little by little from almost all dishes. Perhaps we will be full again at the end, but since we are getting small amounts from all those nice dishes, we cannot fully enjoy any of them. Sometimes we even mix the food so much that we become so full, and we experience severe stomachache and indigestion afterward. Most of the time, we cannot even eat some of the food we put on our plates. Just like the effort spent on some flirting, they go to the trash. On the other hand, we still fancy the dishes we could not taste because there was no place on our plate. However, when our options are more limited, we know what we want to eat and fully enjoy that dish.

The negative impact of social media may not only be due to the relative abundance of options. A study by a group of scientists in the U.S. on daily life interactions can give us some clues about the other effects of social media. In the first stage of their study, the researchers placed an ad in a newspaper to recruit subjects. They announced that they needed young and single women for their research and that the experiment consisted only of a personality test. What volunteer subjects did not know was that this study had nothing to do with a personality test.

The selected female subjects were taken to a waiting room by themselves before the personality test. Meanwhile, a handsome young man from the researchers' team entered the room, introduced himself as a subject to take another test, and started chatting with the women. The researchers who watched the entire interaction with a hidden camera entered the room after the conversation intensified and took the female subject to another room for the personality test. They applied this procedure separately for all female subjects.

The personality test for these women in the other room was not a real one. When the so-called personality test was finished, the researchers gave fake results to the female subjects. They randomly said, "Your personality test turned out very well" or "Your personality test turned out to be pretty bad." Later on, these female subjects were directed back to the exit through the waiting room with the collaborating handsome man. Meanwhile, the handsome collaborator approached these women, who were single according to the selection criteria of the experiment and asked them out on a date with kind words like, "It was a very pleasant conversation, but it was left half-finished. I would like to get to know you more. What if we have a coffee or something later?"

Regardless of their beauty, the women, who received fake positive results in the personality test, rejected this offer with the thought and self-confidence that they deserve better than this handsome man. However, the women, who received fake negative results in the personality test, again, regardless of their beauty, accepted this handsome man's offer. Perhaps a similar situation is the reason why some women of average appeal, who are overwhelmed by the interest and compliments of tens of men on social media every day, miss the right opportunities because of this inflated self-confidence; who knows?

One of the essential elements of any relationship is trust. When our partner feels that our concentration and attention are not on them because of our excessive social media use, they begin to question our love towards them. They create millions of scenarios in their head. One of these scenarios—and the most predominant one because it awakens the most potent negative emotion—is the doubt over being cheated. Because social media is a medium that facilitates cheating. We are all well aware of this. This doubt leads to the loss of their trust in us, hence undermining our relationship's health.

Cheating that occurs in our social environment shaped around acquaintances of 80-100 people from work, home, and school is usually noticed and quickly heard about. As a natural consequence of this, our relationship ends. This risk of being caught causes people to restrain themselves, even if they desire to cheat. Studies show that the most critical factor that stops individuals who want to cheat their partners is the risk of getting caught and the fear of the consequences arising from being caught.

However, when social media is concerned, the risk of getting caught is much less. With a second e-mail address to be opened in a few minutes and the fake profiles created accordingly, people can easily flirt with anyone through these profiles with the phone in hand, even when their partner is in the same room. Therefore, the more intensely someone uses social media, the more suspicious their partners become about these possibilities.

Of course, we can use social media. However, this use should not be excessive. It should not cause us to neglect our partners. It should not make them feel insecure. According to the studies, social media use in the right amount does not cause problems in relationships.

While some arguments and disagreements in the relationships are because our tolerance for our partners decreases with the end of the honeymoon period, some may occur as a natural result of some of our behaviors at the beginning of the relationship or even during the flirting phase. What we do, do not do, and do wrong during the flirting period may influence the health of our relationship in the future. What are these behaviors? Let us take a look at a few.

There is a complaint that many people have expressed during the relationship or flirting period: "He was running after me all the time, but when I showed him that I liked him, he fell out of love with me." The vast majority of us have heard many similar anecdotes from friends or social media. If we are in the flirting phase, we usually take advice from our friends, such as, "Do not show that you like them. Take it slow, or they will lose interest" as a tactic to prevent this.

In fact, making someone run after you, playing hard to get, is an effective tactic in the short term. After all, as our ancestors say, "We pursue that which retreats from us." However, its later effects may actually be the opposite of what we desire. It may be the major reason why our partner loses their interest in us just when we express our love. Wonder how?

The flirting period is a process where people get to know each other better and get closer to each other. If one party applies a tactic such as taking it easy during this period, it becomes arduous for the other person to get to know them. In this case, our brain fills the gaps itself.

So, when we like someone physically, our brain accepts their other characteristics as positive. It creates an imaginary hero, an imaginary love, of which it fills the spaces itself. A playwright, Civan Canova, actually realized this when he said," We place our dream soul in a body we fancy and call this nonsense love." Since these imaginary qualities, which are created and idealized by our brains, mismatch with our partner's characteristics, we fall out of love and break up as soon as we realize what is idealized and what is actually there do not agree with each other. Therefore, if both parties behave openly in a way that allows their partners to get to know them adequately and ensure that they are bonded during the flirting period, a long-term relationship with strong foundations can be established. Hence, premature separations can be prevented.

In the previous chapters, we mentioned that our brain's reward system is activated when we like someone. In a way, our brain sees our possible romantic partners entirely as a reward. Therefore, as we get to know them, discover their new and beautiful features, and spend time with them, our brain's reward system takes action and releases dopamine. This dopamine release gives us pleasure. The same is true for them.

If not calibrated properly, some tactics we use during the flirting period may sometimes mislead the reward perception in our partner's brain. When we play hard to get for a long time or do not show that we are attracted to them, the reward perception in their brain can be reduced to the actualization of only these things, instead of us as a whole. When we say that we love them, this one-time reward is received, and the game is over. They no longer care about us like before.

It is also crucial for the hormonal synchronization in the relationship that the two parties are gradually bonded by getting to know each other. In our previous chapter, we mentioned that there would be some changes in our brain and hormones when we fall in love with our partners. These make us experience the change we call the honeymoon stage. However, the honeymoon stage fades away, with our hormones returning to their normal values within 6-8 months. If one side pulls back during the flirting period, the other party idealizes them because of this withdrawal and falls in love more quickly than they should be. So, in a relationship, it is sometimes possible to talk about a partner who fell in love months ago and the other party falling in love months later. Thus, there may be a few months-long synchronization problem between partners' honeymoon stages.

Considering that this period is usually a six-month course, the synchronization problem continues not only in the honeymoon stage but also thereafter. In other words, while the party pulling themselves back is just starting to experience the honeymoon stage, this period may even be over in their partner. Therefore, since the initial state of that person with head over heels feeling does not continue, their attitudes may also change, and this situation may bring along arguments. A breakup can be more challenging and traumatic for the person who begins to experience it than the one whose honeymoon stage is over. Because the person who is head over heels in love at the moment of the breakup is physiologically more in love with and more attached to their partner. The party who loves more also gets more heartbroken in separations.

Women are slightly more disadvantaged than men in this regard because the characteristics that both genders value in the opposite sex for long-term relationships are different. Men value physical qualities more since they are indicators of reproductive potential and health. On the other hand, women look for indicators such as whether the man will provide her and their children with adequate resources and whether he can help her during childcare. These features can mostly be understood with the man's personality traits.

While we can see the physical characteristics of a person in two shakes, it takes us longer to understand their personality. Thus, women instinctively act a little slower to get to know the man's personality before they fall in love. They try to figure out the man's real purpose, tolerance for difficult situations, character, and possible future paternal characteristics. They instinctively look for answers to questions like, "Is this man sincere?" "Does he have the potential to cheat on me and leave me?" "He seems to have the resources, but is he parsimonious?" Therefore, women generally do not enter into a long-term serious relationship until they are sure of all this. While this criterion difference between genders makes men fall in love much more quickly, it takes some more time for women.

This difference not only brings women a disadvantage for hormonal synchronization during love but also creates hesitation in relying on their possible romantic partners. As women do not fall in love at similar speeds because of the difference in attraction criteria between the sexes, they sometimes cannot make sense of the man's love, which usually happens faster. As a result, they may experience hesitations in trusting the sincerity of their partners' feelings. This leads to spending more time and not starting the relationship until they get to know their partners well and build trust. However, we should also keep in mind that some men whose flirting motivations are not romantic can lie about their feelings and motivation. In fact, in some cultures, the number of men who use the promise of marriage as a tactic to win women should not be underestimated. Therefore, women should question the sincerity of their partners by using other clues in our book. However, while doing this, women must keep in mind that men also fall in love more quickly.

Sometimes, making someone run after you for a long time can also be used to test whether that person is really interested in you. Actually, this is a logical approach. If someone is genuinely interested in you, they will not give up quickly and fight for it. However, an improperly calibrated and prolonged chasing time involves two major risks. First, the person can get tired of running after you and move away from you, which is quite normal.

The other risk is much more problematic. The person may not get tired of chasing you for a long time, but this constant and prolonged chase may not indicate the greatness of their love, as it is thought to be. They may be obsessed with you. Considering that the percent of people with obsessive love disorder (OCD) in society is almost as high as other personality disorders, this possibility should not be ignored. After so much chasing, you can be convinced that this person really loves you and start a relationship. After a while, you may want to end your relationship for various reasons.

Well, the biggest risks and troubles can begin after that. Compared to other candidates, this person who has been chasing you for a very long time, not because he loves you the most, but because he is obsessed with you, will not leave you alone after the relationship ends. Harassment and discomfort will continue for a long time after the relationship. Some people also view being left as a threat to their egos. They can add verbal and physical violence to their abuse and persistence when they fall into despair to regain you after the relationship. Current or former romantic partners commit nearly half of the femicides around the world. Moreover, according to the National Coalition Against Domestic Violence (NCADV) data, 1 in 7 women have been stalked by an intimate partner during their lifetime to the point in which they felt very fearful or believed that they or someone close to them would be harmed or killed. For this reason, if a man continues his physical and verbal harassment after rejection, which is beyond trying his luck again, you should be cautious about it. Especially when it comes to people with ego problems, this kind of behavior may not be a sign of the greatness of their love or masculinity, but a strong indication of possible physical violence you may experience in the future!

Another tactic we apply during the flirting period to speed things up or bond our partner to ourselves is to make them jealous. However, if this tactic, which can be effective during the flirting period, is not calibrated correctly, it may return to us with negative consequences later in our relationships. Suppose we flirt with others to make our partner jealous or look like we are flirting. In that case, it is likely that they will unconsciously consider us as "someone who flirts with others while also being into me." This, in turn, can trigger arguments in and out of season on the theme of distrust and jealousy in our relationships. These fights both disturb the relationship's peace and become unbearable after a while and accelerate the breakup. However, when we do not seek for little games from the beginning and place such an image in our partner's subconscious, we are more likely to experience a happier and long-term relationship, where the problem of trust is much less.

In fact, such games and tactics are extremely effective when they are correctly calibrated. Of course, there should be some coyness and jealousy during flirting. However, we behave far from keeping such tactics at the right level most of the time. This miscalibration prevents us from having a relationship of quality in the future. So, before we blame our partners, it is always good to know our faults first. At least not to make similar mistakes in the future so that we can have better relationships.

Arguments are among the most important reasons that bring breakups in relationships and divorces in marriages. Disagreement, dispute, and conflict of the couples are the reasons for almost half of the divorces in the world.

There may be various reasons for such conflicts in marriages. Although we do not know the exact ratio of the causes of those conflicts, some statistics can provide us with valuable data on a very intriguing subject: Is the age difference between spouses an underlying factor in conflicts?

In marriages, the woman can be younger or older than or at the same age as the man. The woman being older than the man or the man being more than a few years older than the woman carries with it concerns that the couples will not get on with each other. If we examine the marriage and divorce data, we can understand whether these concerns are a reality reflected in the divorce rates or just a superstition. When we analyze the ratio distribution of millions of marriages and divorces according to the age difference between partners, we see that both scatter similarly (Fig. 20). There is no value difference to be taken into account except for small changes of one or two points[3]. Thus, contrary to prejudices, the age difference between spouses does not appear to be an important factor in divorce and its causes, regardless of its direction and gravity. People's personalities, the way they look at the relationship and their partners, make up the biggest cause of the problems in conflict.

Along with the arguments, infidelity is another important reason that ends relationships. In fact, getting cheated on is often more traumatic than the arguments for the person.

So, why do people cheat on their partners in a relationship?

Studies reveal different cheating motivations for both sexes. Therefore, it is useful to analyze them separately.

---

[3] Although the statistical analysis of this large data using the ANOVA method shows a difference in some groups because it includes millions of marriages and divorces, it is still not correct to say that such small percentage differences have a meaningful equivalent in real life.

The causes of infidelity do not contain gender differences only. Reasons for cheating and their orders also vary in different cultures.

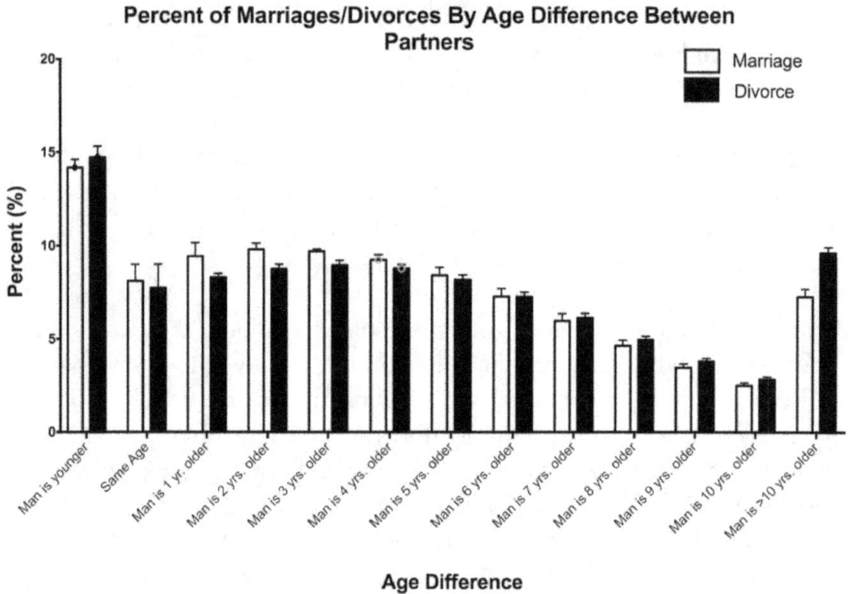

Figure 20- When the last 19 years marriage and divorce statistics are analyzed, the age difference between spouses is not involved as a remarkable factor in divorce and its reasons.

European women cheat the most when their partners stop being interested in them. For American women, their partners' loss of interest is also the number one reason for cheating.

The second leading cause of infidelity among European women is "the third person being very handsome." This reason is ranked fourth for American women.

"Having doubts about the relationship" ranks third among the reasons to cheat for both European and American women.

"The third person was with me when I needed someone" ranks fourth among the reasons European women cheat. This reason is in the second place for American women.

While the fifth reason for cheating among European women was "I needed to feel sexy," boredom is placed fifth among the most common causes of cheating for American women.

Although the most common reasons for cheating of women differ from each other when looked at one by one, if we write them side by side and analyze the whole picture, they have one thing in common: not getting attention from their partners in the relationship, or rather not getting attention as before. When we even think of the excuse about the third person being very handsome, an underlying reason for this might be restoring the self-confidence shaken by their partners' indifference and feeling special again by being with someone appealing.

When we come to the reasons for the cheating of men, both Europeans and Americans report "the third party being very attractive" as the most common reason for cheating.

While European men placed "the third party being with them when they needed someone" second among the reasons for cheating, American men placed "the third person being interested in them romantically" in this rank.

European men rank "the sexual life between partners being over" third among the most common reasons for cheating, and this reason appears as the fourth among American men. American men rank having doubts about their relationship in the third place.

The fourth most common cause of infidelity among European men is boredom.

"Their partners have stopped giving attention to them" is the fifth most common cause of infidelity in both European and American men.

When the most common causes of cheating among men are examined one by one, there seem to be some differences between them. However, the big picture again points out relationship problems and their partners not being interested in them as before, just like women.

Of course, there are sometimes other reasons people cheat on their partners. However, when we look at the overall picture, what lies behind women and men cheating on their partners is related mostly to the relationship's quality.

An interesting risk on cheating reflected in research is one's own attractiveness. Although being attractive often increases the chance of finding our dream partner, various studies show that good looks have a negative effect on relationships. Interestingly, the studies show that men with more symmetrical faces, hence more attractive, cheat on their partners more. This cheating is also irrespective of the type of relationship they are experiencing. Similarly, more handsome men are found to have shorter marriages than their unattractive fellows. This negative effect of attractiveness on relationship length is not only for men. In the same study, scientists also examined the relationships of celebrities and found that the marriages of attractive celebrities last shorter than those of other celebrities.

If we are attractive, our suitors often do not hesitate to try their luck even if we are in a relationship. In such cases, our attitude toward these third parties determines our relationship's health and future. According to the studies, in cases where such third parties threaten the relationship, peoples' tendency to perceive their partners more attractive and derogate the third party's attractiveness protects relationships.

A 2017 study by Christine Ma-Kellams and her colleagues from Harvard University revealed that attractive individuals in a relationship do not derogate attractive suitors who try their luck and threaten the relationship, but rather see them as more attractive than they actually are. Interestingly, this effect was not seen when attractive individuals were single.

Similarly, a recent study reveals an interesting finding about women's beauty and the health of relationships. According to the research results, if women deem themselves more attractive than their partners, then the relationship is on the rocks. In other words, if a woman thinks she is more attractive than her partner, she questions their relationship more. The results of the study affirm that women who think like this do not fully commit to the relationship, cheat on their partners more often. Even if the relationship is not very problematic, they want to leave their partners when they find someone more attractive, that is, someone they think they deserve. Perhaps the most important emphasis in this study is not whether the women being researched are actually beautiful or not. Those women think, are made to believe, or feel that way.

Although these studies have focused on sexual infidelities, we do not have to cheat on our partners only sexually in relationships. Sometimes we can be unfaithful emotionally too. While in a relationship, we can even like and flirt with a third person without having sex. The reactions of both genders to these two types of cheating can be different.

According to research, heterosexual men find their partner's sexual infidelity much more unforgivable than their emotional infidelity. For heterosexual women, the opposite is the case. Women react much more seriously to their partners' emotional infidelity than their sexual infidelity.

According to the study by American scientists David A. Frederick and Melissa R. Fales, 35% of women are upset more with their partner's sexual infidelity, while this rate is 54% for men. When it comes to emotional infidelity, the rate of being upset is 46% for men and 65% for women. In other words, while men can forgive their partners' emotional infidelity more than women do, women can forgive their partners' sexual infidelity almost twice as much as men.

As we mentioned in our first chapter, these results are not surprising when we think of the different needs of the sexes as the feeling of love has evolved. Women instinctively prefer men who have sufficient resources to care for them and their children. From this point of view, a man only sexually cheating on a woman is not as negative as him falling in love with another woman and directing all his resources to her. On the other hand, men instinctively want to use their resources for their own children's care and healthy growth. Therefore, compared to the risk of caring for someone else's child that would be born as a result of women's sexual infidelity, pure emotional infidelity, which does not have such a possibility, can be tolerated more by men.

PHYSIOLOGICAL CHANGES AFTER A BREAKUP

Often our relationships end in a breakup, whether because of arguments, cheating, or other reasons. So, what changes happen in our brain and physiology when we break up? In this chapter, we will discuss how we can ease our separation pain by understanding these changes, forget our ex-partners more quickly, and prevent the mistakes we make after a breakup.

Breakups create similar negative physiological and psychological reactions both when we are rejected by someone we like and when our partners leave us. However, their severity is not equivalent to each other.

In fact, not only those who are left or rejected (rejectees) but also those who reject and leave (rejectors) experience negative emotions. Their social circles can see rejectors as ruthless, heartless, and non-empathetic. Such thoughts negatively affect the rejectors' values in their peers and their probability of finding a partner in that social circle in the future. Thus, to avoid these negative repercussions of rejecting or leaving, people often choose to reject or leave without hurting the other party and act as if they empathize. In addition to these, if there are certain mutual communions, not only the rejectee but also the rejector often get in a depressed mood after the breakup.

Nevertheless, those who are left feel the separation pain more than the ones who leave. Being left lowers their self-esteem. They become more depressed. However, this depression and agony also help them make more explicit assessments of themselves and others meanwhile.

According to the research results, after the breakup, rejectees cry and plead more than the rejectors and try harder to persuade them to get back together and get a second chance. In their efforts to retain their ex-partners after a breakup, men resort to physical abuse, such as using force and going to women's locations. In contrast, women use more remote harassment methods such as texting and online stalking.

Not only the methods but also the results of persuasion efforts are different for both genders. Research shows that if men put more effort into their relationships and increase their commitment, they recover the relationship more often than women in similar situations do.

Especially when severe problems arise in marriages, and there is a rapid acceleration towards separation, persuasion efforts are not the only method tried to save the relationship. People often think that having children will get their marriage back on track. Although research has shown that childless couples have shorter marriages than couples with children and divorces decrease in proportion to the number of children couples have, most of the time, having children does not turn a problematic marriage into a happy relationship. Divorce is usually delayed only until the child is older. Sometimes divorce is renounced just because of the child. Hence, a couple who cannot tolerate each other has to live together throughout their lives. Children may even bring additional arguments and quarrels to this already incompatible couple about the distribution of duties between the parents regarding the children's care. That is why an unhappy marriage can even turn into torment for the parties when a child is made.

A child made with the idea of saving a troubled marriage brings disadvantages to women beyond these problems. One of these is the advancing age of the woman due to the postponement of the divorce. As we mentioned before, young age is an important factor for women's potential to find a partner. A divorce postponed because of a child born in an unhappy relationship decreases women's chances of finding a new potential partner with the passing years. In addition, the custody of children is usually given to mothers after divorces. This is another factor that decreases women's potential to find a new partner after the divorce. Because not only humans but also the males of other species in nature do not instinctively want to look after someone else's offspring. Thus, women with children are less preferred. So, women should think through all these possibilities before trying to have a child to save an unhappy marriage.

Sometimes, no matter what we do, relationships cannot be saved, and separations occur. Studies show that, following a breakup, the rejectees mostly try to make their ex-partners jealous. Rejectors, on the other hand, avoid their ex-partners more. Research also reveals that the rejectors start a new relationship more quickly than the rejectees. Perhaps breakups in a problematic relationship are accelerated by rejectors finding alternative partners before ending the relationship.

Although men and women mostly experience similar feelings after breakups, sometimes they differ. While men who leave their partners report being happier and more indifferent than women, women who leave report feeling jealous more often. When we evaluate this emotional difference together with the research results showing that rejector men cheat on their partners before breakups more than rejector women, we can conclude that finding an alternative partner before deciding to leave is a more frequent factor in rejector men than rejector women.

When we look at the reactions given after the breakup, we see that women and men display similar behaviors. Both parties can show behaviors ranging from discussing troublesome points in the relationship to physical harm. From crying to pleading, even the threat of suicide, various behaviors to dissuade the other from their opinions are observed more intensely in the rejectees.

When these reactions do not work, and the relationship ends, the most significant behavioral difference between sexes, whether they are rejectors or the rejectees, is shopping. After ending a relationship, women buy clothes, shoes, jewelry, makeup, etc. Thus, they increase their attractiveness and restore their self-esteem. Although it is not mentioned in research results, going to the hairdresser, whether it is to change the hairstyle or color or to have a nice blow-dry, is an activity that women similarly do after a breakup. In men, generosity and spending more money are observed after a separation.

All these behavioral patterns actually have a connection with the difference in evolutionary attraction criteria between sexes. Since physical attractiveness is more important in women, they display behavior patterns that increase these characteristics after separation. On the other hand, social status and having resources are more important criteria in male attractiveness, so men's behavioral patterns that give signals to their environment that they have these qualities increase after the breakup.

When it comes to the changes in our body during a breakup, we can examine them in two phases. The first phase of the breakup is called protest or denial. At this stage, we do not accept getting left or the breakup because of the changes in our brain and physiology. We do our best to win back our partners and relationship.

In fact, our behavior at this phase also has an evolutionary basis. If we are not someone who is quick to fall in love, being attracted to someone new, going through a flirting phase with them, discovering that they are suitable for us, and then starting a relationship takes months or even years. However, human life is limited. When we consider that love is a feeling associated with the reproductive instinct, our age range in which we have reproductive potential is even more limited. Especially in our ancestors, who matured late due to malnutrition but died mostly in their 30s because of wars, wild animal attacks, epidemics, and various other diseases, this reproductive age range was even more limited. So, the time spent in each failed relationship is a waste of our precious but limited reproductive years. In fact, this situation is so ingrained in our subconscious that perhaps this is why one of the most heard sentences in breakup arguments is "I gave you my youth!"

One basis of our behaviors in the protest phase is that our brains compel us to struggle for our old relationship to save from this process, instead of risking the similar months and years that will pass in a new relationship after the breakup. Besides, our brain always tends to go the way it knows, rather than trying new things. Relationships are no exception to this tendency. A relationship to try with someone new after a breakup is darkness for us. Thus, it is outside of our comfort zone. However, even if we do not get along, we know the behaviors of someone we have been with for a long time. Our brain prefers what it is familiar with, even if it does harm to it, instead of embarking on a new adventure since it is afraid of going outside its comfort zone.

The evolutionary basis of the denial or protest phase is not limited to this. Our primitive ancestors lived in small tribes or groups. Hence, their options for finding a mate were limited. Losing their partners often meant not finding a new mate and losing their reproductive chances. This is why the adaptation to struggle to save, rather than immediately accept, broken relationships also enabled our primitive ancestors to continue their reproductive possibilities.

Today, we also have arguments many times in our relationships and experience breakups. Although sometimes we intend to break up completely in the heat of the moment, most of the time, we implement this decision for just a few days or at most weeks. After that, we make it up, and the relationship continues. If our adaptation to save the broken relationships had not developed in the evolutionary process, we would have been leaving many relationships that ended for trivial reasons. Thus, we would have run out of our potential partner candidates over time and mostly live alone.

In the denial phase, we excessively release dopamine and noradrenaline for our ex-partners. The increase in these hormones is more significant than when we first fell in love with them. Thus, our ex-partners' value increases, especially after that initial anger and rage pass. It drives us to love them more than we normally do.

In fact, in this respect, breaking up creates reactions similar to the feeling of deprivation in letting go of an addiction. For example, if you are a smoker, you will not feel that much pleasure while smoking. Most of the time, you want to quit smoking because of the financial damage and health problems. However, especially in the first weeks of quitting, you constantly crave a cigarette. You always think of how pleasant it was to smoke. Since withdrawal symptoms after breaking up create the same reactions in our brain, they cause similar effects and illusions.

The only thing that hurts us in a breakup is not just the excessive increase of dopamine and noradrenaline. The effects of the Nerve Growth Factor (NGF) hormone often push us to make the wrong decisions when we break up. Wonder how?

As we mentioned in the previous chapters, our NGF hormone levels are increased in the first six months of love. In general, NGF has an impact that makes the nerves stronger, healthier, and more enduring. Our nerves and synapses with which we keep our memories are not exempted from this effect.

The first six months of love is the honeymoon period. These are the times that people generally enjoy their partners and the relationship most. Therefore, our memories of our partners and the relationship during this period are mostly positive. With the effect of increased NGF, our memories of those times are encoded in our brains stronger than others. Therefore, although there are events that lead us to a breakup in the following months, they are often not remembered as strongly in the post-breakup period. Instead, our positive memories, which are more strongly coded with the NGF effect, are remembered more.

That is why even if we break up after serious arguments, heartbreak, and even being cheated, we mostly recall the positive memories after our first anger passes. Hence, we think, "Actually, they were not a bad person at all. We were having such good times and fun" and tend to forgive our ex-partners.

Studies show that regardless of the duration of the relationship, people tend to reunite most in the first six months after breaking up. About one-third of couples who break up make up again within the first nine months. Considering the couples that reunite in the later periods, the rate of those who try again goes up to 65%. However, about half of those who try to re-engage with their ex-partners are unable to maintain their relationship as expected and break up again. Interestingly, a third of those who try a second relationship with the same partner and break up again want to have a relationship with that person again. So, most of us do not come to our senses because of the influence of these hormones! We hope that toxic people and relationships will always get better the next time.

So, how can we fight this illusion? How can we prevent someone who has harmed or could hurt us from becoming more valuable than they are because of some changes in our brain and possibly making the mistake of returning to them, which will end negatively again?

First, we need to target our dopamine system. When we break up, our ex-partner seems to us more attractive and better than they are because of the extreme increase in our dopamine levels. To prevent this illusion, we need to do things to neutralize this boosted dopamine's effect.

For this, it may be useful to write a list of our ex-partner's features that we dislike, cannot tolerate, and wear us out. Thus, we can look at this list and see a more objective picture of our ex-partner when their good sides predominate and start to mislead us because of extremely increased dopamine. Additionally, everyone has a poor photo of themselves. After the breakup, we should delete all their photos but keep a picture of our ex-partner in which they look bad. When they come to our mind, we can look at this unattractive photo and neutralize their increased appeal because of the elevated dopamine levels when we broke up.

Another way we can forget our ex-partner a little more easily during post-breakup is to stay away from the activities we did together. For example, if we were going to a certain café or restaurant and spending time there together during the relationship, even if we only pass by that place after the breakup, those strongly engraved old and pleasant memories will always swim before our eyes, and our forgetting process will lengthen out. Avoiding a song that we loved to listen to together, turning to another activity instead of an activity we enjoyed together, and avoiding the places where we can run into our ex-partner—including not only physical environments but also blocking them on social media—will help us in this process.

If we have decided to break up with our partners, there is usually a good reason for that. Sometimes being cheated on and sometimes arguments becoming intolerable are the primary reasons for a breakup. However, while the negativities we experience during our relationship do not come to our mind much after a breakup, positive memories that are strongly encoded in our brains with NGF's effect are remembered almost constantly. This situation may mislead us in our decisions, and we can go back to a problematic ex-partner. One other way to deal with this is to write down negative memories in a notebook, such as whenever our ex-partner offended us, verbally or physically abused us, and made us feel bad. When we are inclined to think of only pleasant memories due to the NGF effect, going through these notes and remembering the reality will help us forget them.

Deleting WhatsApp correspondence is also important to forget our ex-partners. However, before deleting our entire conversation history, taking screenshots of our arguments and keeping them can again be useful to remind us what they can make us feel if we go back to this person. In short, developing tactics against the effects of the NGF hormone on breakups will protect us from making the same mistake again.

The second phase of a breakup is resignation. At this phase, we are completely convinced that the other person will no longer return to us or that we will not return to them. When we accept the breakup, various changes occur in our brain. This time, our dopamine drops significantly to clinical depression levels.

In fact, this post-breakup period also has an evolutionary basis. In a breakup, we often end a relationship that lasts for months or even years. In other words, as I mentioned before, we waste the months or years of our limited reproductive period for someone, all for nothing. This means serious disappointment for our subconscious. Moreover, the uncertainty of finding someone new, and if found, the risk of similar things happening, brings us anxiety and depression.

Studies show that the stress and anxiety we experience in a breakup get an average of 36.06 points according to the "Impact of Event Scale (IES-R)" test used in measuring the amount of traumatic stress. This score is the same as people's stress and anxiety levels after a severe earthquake, heart surgery, or a major traffic accident. Depending on the magnitude of the love and, therefore, disappointment they experience, this score may be slightly lower in some people and higher in others. Scientific studies show that people who suffer from traumas with an IES-R score above 40 do not have their immune systems functioning properly, and this problem continues for years.

With the depression experienced after the breakup, we are actually sending the signal, "Help me heal all these wounds!" to our social circle. Therefore, our friends and family are extremely important for us to overcome this period easily. Because a person with depression normally does not want to do anything, even if they do, they cannot find that energy in themselves.

Therefore, the support of our environment and our friends, their calming suggestions, and fun activities that will put back our falling dopamine play a crucial role in getting through this period without any problems. Our decreased dopamine during this depressive period should be increased with activities such as going to a concert, an amusement park, a fun movie, or a vacation with our friends or family. Otherwise, we may turn to harmful activities such as alcohol, gambling, drugs, or smoking to restore our dopamine.

Some of us can also devote ourselves to eating as a dopamine-releasing activity. Yet, this is mostly directed at unhealthy foods like junk food. Therefore, it is harmful to our overall health.

Studies show that religion and worship also stimulate dopamine secretion in our brain. In fact, studies reveal that the relapse rate decreases among people who turn to religion after quitting drugs. In other words, worship replaces the dopamine secreted in drug intake, which is another addiction like love. Thus, some people instinctively devote themselves to religion after traumatic breakups. Religion and worship usually are not harmful to a person. However, people who are feeling depressed and empty after a breakup may suddenly find themselves in the traps of various marginal sects and congregations.

There are also various easy and effective activities where we can increase our dopamine levels on our own during this resignation stage. One of them is to look at cute baby photos. These photos activate our Nucleus accumbens, causing our brains to secrete dopamine. We do not have to be depressed to do this. Whenever we are bored and joyless, we can surf the internet for some cute baby photos. A smile will spread on our faces, and our mood will be lifted. Although not as effective as cute baby photos, videos of funny animals, like cats, also have similar effects.

This depression experienced in the resignation phase of the breakup also has positive contributions to us. When depressed, we go through a more grounded thinking process. We review our mistakes and make better decisions regarding our future relationships. In fact, when we look at it from this perspective, breakup pain that is not very traumatic appears as a fruitful experience for our self-development.

Sometimes, after a breakup, one of the things we do to forget our ex-partners is to find someone else immediately. If this person is someone we like and we are having a pleasant time, it will also be useful in overcoming depression as it will activate our dopamine system. However, before we do that, I think there is a question that everyone should sincerely ask themselves and answer with the same sincerity: If my ex-lover wants to reunite, would I quit this relationship and go back to them?

If you intend to return to your ex-partner and use this relationship only to get over the breakup pain or to make your ex-partner jealous, I think you are doing a great wrong to that person. They may have started or already fallen in love with you. It does not seem like the right approach to me to make that person experience the breakup pain at an unexpected moment for a reason that has nothing to do with them or the relationship.

Reminding ourselves that most people are selfish and live their lives free of ethical concerns can also prevent our hearts from being broken. Hence, it is necessary to be a little cautious before starting a relationship with someone who has just ended their relationship, considering the reuniting rate is up to 65%. Waiting for them to overcome their breakup pain will reduce the likelihood of that person returning to their former partner while having a relationship with us. This will, to a large extent, prevent us from experiencing a breakup at an unexpected moment.

The last phase of the breakup is returning to normal. At this stage, we forget our ex-partner and overcome depression. Our dopamine levels return to their typical values again. We are now ready to set sail for new loves!

So how long do these breakup phases last in total? Many criteria, such as the relationship's length, the person's character, and the degree of love, can affect this period. Therefore, we cannot pronounce a universal time. Even the age of the person can affect the duration of this forgetting phase. According to research, overcoming our partners usually lasts more than one year for those over 50. In contrast, it lasts 3-6 months between the ages of 18-24.

From the evolutionary perspective, it is quite normal that the periods of forgetting our ex-partners vary in different age groups. In our subconscious, we perceive breakups as a waste of valuable time in our reproductive potential. Since the reproductive potential of people between the ages of 18-24 will continue for a more extended period, they are less affected by breakups and can overcome them more quickly. However, as it is too late for many things at much later ages, it often takes longer for older people to overcome the trauma of a breakup pain and forget their ex-partners.

One situation that also prolongs forgetting our ex-partners is emptiness. Not having started another relationship after a breakup and loneliness can lead us to think about our ex-partner longer and more intensely than usual. When we are single, we may be unable to get them out of our minds. Especially if our ex-partner has also not started a new relationship, this process may take longer because we will preserve our possibility of reunification in our subconscious. Therefore, starting a new relationship after overcoming the breakup pain will make it easier for us to forget our former partner.

AFTERWORD

Love change us more than we think. Every person we take into our lives and every love we experience leaves traces on us. While these traces are positive in relationships with the right people, toxic relationships can be destructive enough to affect us for a long time. What we go through changes not only our psychology but also our physiology. That is why a healthy relationship with the right person is crucial for our well-being.

A happy, stress-free relationship with the right person reduces the size of our amygdala, the part of our brain responsible for fear and anxiety. This change turns us into less anxious and calmer people. Strong relationships also positively affect our hippocampus, the part of our brain responsible for memory, and the neural stem cells in the hippocampus. This enables us to become more comfortable and more successful individuals. Research found that a happy relationship is even effective in protecting us from various diseases. Besides its positive physiological effects, all of which cannot be listed here, a happy and trusting relationship also alters our childhood attachment style. If we have a fear or anxiety-based attachment style, a strong relationship will help to transform it into a trust-based style, which will have a constructive effect on our future romantic relationships and daily social interactions.

On the contrary, toxic relationships filled with anxiety and stress have the opposite effects. Our amygdala grows and becomes more active. We become more aggressive and anxious. The stress we experience also reduces the size of our hippocampus, causing memory and learning difficulties. A lack of concentration and energy brought on by depression even affects our success at work or school. Its negative effects on our immune system, which sometimes last for years, can make us more susceptible to infections and some chronic diseases. Considering the negative effects of the traumas experienced in such relationships and breakups on our attachment style, we may experience difficulties in our social and romantic relationships in the future.

We completely decide who to take and why we take someone into our lives. Sometimes we get attracted to a person's mere physical appearance or popularity. Sometimes it is just the thought, "Everyone around me has a lover; I should have one too." By thinking this, we may have a relationship with the first person we come across. Sometimes we can start a relationship with someone for the sake of winning a competition with a fellow. The aftermath of such behaviors, which we can do to gain experience or self-confidence, or just to get flattered with a little attention and feel good, can be detrimental if we are not with the right person. On the contrary, a pleasant relationship with the right person can add enormous benefits to our lives.

Love is a big and important part of our lives. This book was written to tell you about all aspects of love and help you make informed decisions. It aimed to present scientific studies, which were only accessible to a limited number of scientists until today, in the most understandable way to a broad audience. Of course, it is impossible to mention all the tens of thousands of studies on attraction, flirting, relationships, and breakup in one book. Therefore, although I included topics and studies that concern the majority as much as possible, the information everyone needs is different. These small details I excluded, since they do not concern the majority, would cause some crucial information in the book to be lost and overlooked. They would also result in this book being an arduous work for you to read and comprehend. However, unfortunately, sometimes, the devil is in the details. Thus, on some issues that you cannot find answers to in this book, it is better to stay away from people like self-proclaimed relationship coaches and some nonscientific information on the internet. Instead, please consult real professionals or do your own scientific literature research.

Thank you so much for reading *The Science of Love and Attraction*. I hope you enjoyed reading the book as much as I enjoyed researching and writing it. If you enjoyed this book (or even if you didn't) please visit the site where you purchased it and write a brief review. Your feedback is important to me and will help other readers decide whether to read the book too.

Wishing that you to experience love as much as possible, with the right people.

M. Oktar Guloglu, Ph.D.

December 2020

BIBLIOGRAPHY

Aharon, I., Aharon, I., Etcoff, N., Etcoff, N., Ariely, D., Ariely, D., et al. (2001). Beautiful faces have variable reward value: fMRI and behavioral evidence. *Neuron*, *32*(3), 537–551.

Allen, C., Havlicek, J., & Roberts, S. C. (2015). Effect of fragrance use on discrimination of individual body odor. *Frontiers in Psychology*, *6*, 1115. http://doi.org/10.3389/fpsyg.2015.01115

Aron, A., Melinat, E., Aron, E. N., Vallone, R. D., & Bator, R. J. (1997). The Experimental Generation of Interpersonal Closeness: A Procedure and Some Preliminary Findings. *Personality and Social Psychology Bulletin*, *23*(4), 363–377. http://doi.org/10.1177/0146167297234003

Bakmazian, A. (2014). The Man Behind the Beard: Perception of Men's Trustworthiness as a Function of Facial Hair. *Psychology*, *2014*(03), 185–191. http://doi.org/10.4236/psych.2014.53029

Banca, P., Morris, L. S., Mitchell, S., Harrison, N. A., Potenza, M. N., & Voon, V. (2016). Novelty, conditioning and attentional bias to sexual rewards. *Journal of Psychiatric Research*, *72*, 91–101. http://doi.org/10.1016/j.jpsychires.2015.10.017

Bartels, A., & Zeki, S. (2000). The neural basis of romantic love. *Neuroreport*, *11*(17), 3829–3834.

Bartels, A., & Zeki, S. (2004). The neural correlates of maternal and romantic love. *NeuroImage*, *21*(3), 1155–1166. http://doi.org/10.1016/j.neuroimage.2003.11.003

Bartholomew, K., & Horowitz, L. M. (1991). Attachment styles among young adults: a test of a four-category model. *Journal of Personality and Social Psychology*, *61*(2), 226–244. http://doi.org/10.1037//0022-3514.61.2.226

Bereczkei, T., & Mesko, N. (2007). Hair length, facial attractiveness, personality attribution: A multiple fitness model of hairdressing. *Review of Psychology*, *13*(1), 35–42.

Berridge, K. C., & Kringelbach, M. L. (2015). Pleasure systems in the brain. *Neuron*, *86*(3), 646–664. http://doi.org/10.1016/j.neuron.2015.02.018

Bickart, K. C., Wright, C. I., Dautoff, R. J., Dickerson, B. C., & Barrett, L. F. (2011). Amygdala volume and social network size in humans. *Nature Neuroscience*, *14*(2), 163–164. http://doi.org/10.1038/nn.2724

Bielfeldt, S., Henss, R., Koop, U., Degwert, J., Heinrich, U., Jassoy, C., et al. (2013). Internet-based lay person rating of facial photographs to assess effects of a cleansing product and a decent cosmetic foundation on the attractiveness of female faces. *International Journal of Cosmetic Science*, *35*(1), 94–98. http://doi.org/10.1111/ics.12010

Bleske-Rechek, A., Kolb, C. M., Stern, A. S., Quigley, K., & Nelson, L. A. (2014). Face and body: independent predictors of women's attractiveness. *Archives of Sexual Behavior, 43*(7), 1355–1365. http://doi.org/10.1007/s10508-014-0304-4

Boccia, M. L., Cook, C., Marson, L., & Pedersen, C. (2020). Parental divorce in childhood is related to lower urinary oxytocin concentrations in adulthood. *Journal of Comparative Psychology (Washington, D.C. : 1983)*. http://doi.org/10.1037/com0000248

Bovet, J., & Raymond, M. (2015). Preferred Women's Waist-to-Hip Ratio Variation over the Last 2,500 Years. *PloS One, 10*(4), e0123284. http://doi.org/10.1371/journal.pone.0123284

Bovet, J., Lao, J., Bartholomée, O., Caldara, R., & Raymond, M. (2016). Mapping female bodily features of attractiveness. *Scientific Reports, 6,* 18551. http://doi.org/10.1038/srep18551

Brak-Lamy, G. (2015). Heterosexual Seduction in the Urban Night Context: Behaviors and Meanings. *Journal of Sex Research, 52*(6), 690–699. http://doi.org/10.1080/00224499.2013.856835

Braun, M. F., & Bryan, A. (2016). Female waist-to-hip and male waist-to-shoulder ratios as determinants of romantic partner desirability. *Journal of Social and Personal Relationships, 23*(5), 805–819. http://doi.org/10.1177/0265407506068264

Bruckert, L., Liénard, J.-S., Lacroix, A., Kreutzer, M., & Leboucher, G. (2006). Women use voice parameters to assess men's characteristics. *Proceedings of the Royal Society of London B: Biological Sciences, 273*(1582), 83–89. http://doi.org/10.1098/rspb.2005.3265

Bui, K. K., Rinchuse, D. J., Zullo, T. G., & Cozzani, M. (2015). Perception of facial attractiveness following modification of the nose and teeth. *International Orthodontics, 13*(2), 195–209. http://doi.org/10.1016/j.ortho.2015.03.001

Burton, A. C., Nakamura, K., & Roesch, M. R. (2015). From ventral-medial to dorsal-lateral striatum: neural correlates of reward-guided decision-making. *Neurobiology of Learning and Memory, 117,* 51–59. http://doi.org/10.1016/j.nlm.2014.05.003

Busetta, G., & Fiorillo, F. (2013). Will Ugly Betty Ever Find a Job in Italy? *SSRN Electronic Journal.* http://doi.org/10.2139/ssrn.2336608

Bzdok, D., Langner, R., Caspers, S., Kurth, F., Habel, U., Zilles, K., et al. (2011). ALE meta-analysis on facial judgments of trustworthiness and attractiveness. *Brain Structure & Function, 215*(3-4), 209–223. http://doi.org/10.1007/s00429-010-0287-4

Chaix, R., Cao, C., & Donnelly, P. (n.d.). PLOS Genetics: Is Mate Choice in Humans MHC-Dependent? *Journals.Plos.org, 4*(9), e1000184. http://doi.org/10.1371/journal.pgen.1000184

Chauhan, N., Warner, J. P., & Adamson, P. A. (2012). Perceived Age Change After Aesthetic Facial Surgical Procedures. *Archives of Facial Plastic Surgery, 14*(4). http://doi.org/10.1001/archfacial.2011.1561

Cheng, Y., Chen, C., Lin, C.-P., Chou, K.-H., & Decety, J. (2010). Love hurts: an fMRI study. *NeuroImage, 51*(2), 923–929. http://doi.org/10.1016/j.neuroimage.2010.02.047

Clayton, R. B. (2014). The third wheel: the impact of Twitter use on relationship infidelity and divorce. *Cyberpsychology, Behavior and Social Networking, 17*(7), 425–430. http://doi.org/10.1089/cyber.2013.0570

Clayton, R. B., Nagurney, A., & Smith, J. R. (2013). Cheating, breakup, and divorce: is Facebook use to blame? *Cyberpsychology, Behavior and Social Networking, 16*(10), 717–720. http://doi.org/10.1089/cyber.2012.0424

Cloud, J. M., & Perilloux, C. (2014). Bodily Attractiveness as a Window to Women's Fertility and Reproductive Value. In *Evolutionary Perspectives on Human Sexual Psychology and Behavior* (pp. 135–152). New York, NY: Springer New York. http://doi.org/10.1007/978-1-4939-0314-6_7

Collins, S. (2000). Men"s voices and women"s choices. *Animal Behaviour, 60*(6), 773–780. http://doi.org/10.1006/anbe.2000.1523

Confer, J. C., Perilloux, C., & Buss, D. M. (2010). More than just a pretty face: men's priority shifts toward bodily attractiveness in short-term versus long-term mating contexts. *Evolution and Human Behavior, 31*(5), 348–353.

Coricelli, G., Coricelli, G., Nagel, R., & Nagel, R. (2009). Neural correlates of depth of strategic reasoning in medial prefrontal cortex. *Proceedings of the National Academy of Sciences of the United States of America, 106*(23), 9163–9168. http://doi.org/10.1073/pnas.0807721106

D, M. M. M. P. (2010). Courtship signaling and adolescents: "Girls just wanna have fun?" *Journal of Sex Research, 32*(4), 319–328. http://doi.org/10.1080/00224499509551805

DAILEY, R. M., PFIESTER, A., JIN, B., BECK, G., & CLARK, G. (2009). On-again/off-again dating relationships: How are they different from other dating relationships? *Personal Relationships, 16*(1), 23–47. http://doi.org/10.1111/j.1475-6811.2009.01208.x

Davey, C. G., Allen, N. B., Harrison, B. J., Dwyer, D. B., & Yücel, M. (2010). Being liked activates primary reward and midline self-related brain regions. *Human Brain Mapping, 31*(4), 660–668. http://doi.org/10.1002/hbm.20895

DeLecce, T., & Weisfeld, G. (2015). An Evolutionary Explanation for Sex Differences in Nonmarital Breakup Experiences. *Adaptive Human Behavior and Physiology, 2*(3), 234–251. http://doi.org/10.1007/s40750-015-0039-z

DiDonato, T. E., & Jakubiak, B. K. (2016). Strategically Funny: Romantic Motives Affect Humor Style in Relationship Initiation. *Europe's Journal of Psychology, 12*(3), 390–405. http://doi.org/10.5964/ejop.v12i3.1105

Dixson, B. J. W., & Lee, A. J. (2020). Cross-Cultural Variation in Men's Beardedness. *Adaptive Human Behavior and Physiology, 6*(4), 490–500. http://doi.org/10.1007/s40750-020-00150-4

Dixson, B. J. W., & Rantala, M. J. (2016). The Role of Facial and Body Hair Distribution in Women"s Judgments of Men"s Sexual Attractiveness. *Archives of Sexual Behavior, 45*(4), 877–889. http://doi.org/10.1007/s10508-015-0588-z

Dixson, B. J. W., Lee, A. J., Blake, K. R., Jasienska, G., & Marcinkowska, U. M. (2018). Women"s preferences for men"s beards show no relation to their ovarian cycle phase and sex hormone levels. *Hormones and Behavior, 97*, 137–144. http://doi.org/10.1016/j.yhbeh.2017.11.006

Dixson, B. J., & Brooks, R. C. (2013). The role of facial hair in women"s perceptions of men"s attractiveness, health, masculinity and parenting abilities. *Evolution and Human Behavior, 34*(3), 236–241. http://doi.org/10.1016/j.evolhumbehav.2013.02.003

Dixson, B. J., Dixson, B. J., Duncan, M., Duncan, M., & Dixson, A. F. (2015). The Role of Breast Size and Areolar Pigmentation in Perceptions of Women's Sexual Attractiveness, Reproductive Health, Sexual Maturity, Maternal Nurturing Abilities, and Age. *Archives of Sexual Behavior.* http://doi.org/10.1007/s10508-015-0516-2

Dixson, B. J., Grimshaw, G. M., Linklater, W. L., & Dixson, A. F. (2011). Eye-tracking of men's preferences for waist-to-hip ratio and breast size of women. *Archives of Sexual Behavior, 40*(1), 43–50. http://doi.org/10.1007/s10508-009-9523-5

Dixson, B. J., Grimshaw, G. M., Ormsby, D. K., & Dixson, A. F. (2014). Eye-tracking women's preferences for men's somatotypes. *Evolution and Human Behavior, 35*(2), 73–79. http://doi.org/10.1016/j.evolhumbehav.2013.10.003

Drury. (2010). Immunity and mate choice: a new outlook. *Animal Behaviour, 79*(3), 7–7. http://doi.org/10.1016/j.anbehav.2009.12.023

Dunn, M. J., & Searle, R. (2010). Effect of manipulated prestige-car ownership on both sex attractiveness ratings. *British Journal of Psychology (London, England : 1953), 101*(Pt 1), 69–80. http://doi.org/10.1348/000712609X417319

Dunne, S., & O'Doherty, J. P. (2012). Choosing for me or choosing for you: value in medial prefrontal cortex. *Neuron, 75*(6), 942–944. http://doi.org/10.1016/j.neuron.2012.09.005

Dutton, D. G., & Aron, A. P. (1974). Some evidence for heightened sexual attraction under conditions of high anxiety. *Journal of Personality and Social Psychology*, *30*(4), 510–517. http://doi.org/10.1037/h0037031

E, A., A, F., N, G., M, S., & FT, B.-P. (2015). Early Social Environment Affects the Endogenous Oxytocin System: A Review and Future Directions. *Frontiers in Endocrinology*, *6*(4), 32–32. http://doi.org/10.3389/fendo.2015.00032

Eibl-Eibesfeldt, I. (1971). Love and Hate, translated by G. Strachan.

Eisenbruch, A. B., Simmons, Z. L., & Roney, J. R. (2015). Lady in Red: Hormonal Predictors of Women's Clothing Choices. *Psychological Science*, *26*(8), 1332–1338. http://doi.org/10.1177/0956797615586403

Emanuele, E. (2011). NGF and romantic love. *Archives Italiennes De Biologie*, *149*(2), 265–268. http://doi.org/10.4449/aib.v149i2.1367

Esch, T., & Stefano, G. B. (2011). The neurobiological link between compassion and love. *Medical Science Monitor : International Medical Journal of Experimental and Clinical Research*, *17*(3), RA65–75. http://doi.org/10.12659/msm.881441

Etcoff, N. L., Stock, S., Haley, L. E., Vickery, S. A., & House, D. M. (2011). Cosmetics as a Feature of the Extended Human Phenotype: Modulation of the Perception of Biologically Important Facial Signals. *PloS One*, *6*(10), e25656. http://doi.org/10.1371/journal.pone.0025656

Fagherazzi, G., Fagherazzi, G., Vilier, A., Vilier, A., Boutron-Ruault, M. C., Boutron-Ruault, M. C., et al. (2012). Height, Sitting Height, and Leg Length in Relation with Breast Cancer Risk in the E3N Cohort. *Cancer Epidemiology Biomarkers & Prevention*, *21*(7), 1171–1175. http://doi.org/10.1158/1055-9965.EPI-12-0130

Fales, M. R., Frederick, D. A., Garcia, J. R., Gildersleeve, K. A., Haselton, M. G., & Fisher, H. E. (2016). Mating markets and bargaining hands: Mate preferences for attractiveness and resources in two national U.S. studies. *Personality and Individual Differences*, *88*, 78–87. http://doi.org/10.1016/j.paid.2015.08.041

Farrelly, D. (2013). Altruism as an Indicator of Good Parenting Quality in Long-Term Relationships: Further Investigations Using the Mate Preferences Towards Altruistic Traits Scale. *The Journal of Social Psychology*, *153*(4), 395–398. http://doi.org/10.1080/00224545.2013.768595

Farrelly, D., Clemson, P., & Guthrie, M. (2016). Are Women's Mate Preferences for Altruism Also Influenced by Physical Attractiveness? *Evolutionary Psychology*, *14*(1), 1474704915623698. http://doi.org/10.1177/1474704915623698

Fink, B., Neave, N., Manning, J. T., & Grammer, K. (2005). Facial symmetry and the "big-five" personality factors. *Personality and Individual Differences*, *39*(3), 523–529. http://doi.org/10.1016/j.paid.2005.02.002

Fisher, H. (2005). Why We Love. Henry Holt and Company.

Fisher, H. (2009). Why Him? Why Her? Henry Holt and Company.

Fisher, H. (2016). Anatomy of Love: A Natural History of Mating, Marriage, and Why We Stray (Completely Revised and Updated with a New Introduction). W. W. Norton & Company.

Fisher, H. E., Brown, L. L., Aron, A., Strong, G., Strong, G., Mashek, D., & Mashek, D. (2010). Reward, Addiction, and Emotion Regulation Systems Associated With Rejection in Love. *Journal of Neurophysiology*, *104*(1), 51–60. http://doi.org/10.1152/jn.00784.2009

Fisher, H., Aron, A., & Brown, L. L. (2005). Romantic love: An fMRI study of a neural mechanism for mate choice. *J Comp Neurol*, *493*(1), 58–62. http://doi.org/10.1002/cne.20772

Foo, Y. Z., Simmons, L. W., Perrett, D. I., Holt, P. G., Eastwood, P. R., & Rhodes, G. (2020). Immune function during early adolescence positively predicts adult facial sexual dimorphism in both men and women. *Evolution and Human Behavior*. http://doi.org/10.1016/j.evolhumbehav.2020.02.002

Fraccaro, P. J., O'Connor, J. J. M., Re, D. E., Jones, B. C., DeBruine, L. M., & Feinberg, D. R. (2013). Faking it: deliberately altered voice pitch and vocal attractiveness. *Animal Behaviour*, *85*(1), 127–136. http://doi.org/10.1016/j.anbehav.2012.10.016

Frederick, D. A., & Fales, M. R. (2016). Upset Over Sexual versus Emotional Infidelity Among Gay, Lesbian, Bisexual, and Heterosexual Adults. *Archives of Sexual Behavior*, *45*(1), 175–191. http://doi.org/10.1007/s10508-014-0409-9

Frederick, D. A., Frederick, D. A., Hadji-Michael, M., Hadji-Michael, M., Furnham, A., & Swami, V. (2010). The influence of leg-to-body ratio (LBR) on judgments of female physical attractiveness: Assessments of computer-generated images varying in LBR. *Body Image*, *7*(1), 51–55. http://doi.org/10.1016/j.bodyim.2009.09.001

French, M. T., Popovici, I., Robins, P. K., & Homer, J. F. (2014). Personal traits, cohabitation, and marriage. *Social Science Research*, *45*, 184–199. http://doi.org/10.1016/j.ssresearch.2014.01.002

Garver-Apgar, C. E., Gangestad, S. W., Thornhill, R., Miller, R. D., & Olp, J. J. (2006). Major Histocompatibility Complex Alleles, Sexual Responsivity, and Unfaithfulness in Romantic Couples. *Psychological Science*, *17*(10), 830–835. http://doi.org/10.1111/j.1467-9280.2006.01789.x

Gelstein, S., Yeshurun, Y., Rozenkrantz, L., Shushan, S., Frumin, I., Roth, Y., & Sobel, N. (2011). Human tears contain a chemosignal. *Science*, *331*(6014), 226–230. http://doi.org/10.1126/science.1198331

Gibson, L. S. (2015). The Science of Romantic Love: Distinct Evolutionary, Neural, and Hormonal Characteristics. *International Journal of Undergraduate Research and Creative Activities*, *7*(1), 1036. http://doi.org/10.7710/2168-0620.1036

Gleeson, G., & Fitzgerald, A. (2014). Exploring the Association between Adult Attachment Styles in Romantic Relationships, Perceptions of Parents from Childhood and Relationship Satisfaction. *Health*, *2014*(13), 1643–1661. http://doi.org/10.4236/health.2014.613196

González Álvarez, J. (2015). Men dissociate sexual attraction from moral judgement more than women. *International Journal of Psychology*, n/a–n/a. http://doi.org/10.1002/ijop.12228

Greengross, G., & Miller, G. (2011). Humor ability reveals intelligence, predicts mating success, and is higher in males. *Intelligence*, *39*(4), 188–192. http://doi.org/10.1016/j.intell.2011.03.006

Griffey, J. A. F., & Little, A. C. (2014). Infant's visual preferences for facial traits associated with adult attractiveness judgements: Data from eye-tracking. *Infant Behavior & Development*, *37*(3), 268–275. http://doi.org/10.1016/j.infbeh.2014.03.001

Gueguen, N. (2012). "Say it...near the flower shop": further evidence of the effect of flowers on mating. *The Journal of Social Psychology*, *152*(5), 529–532. http://doi.org/10.1080/00224545.2012.683463

Gueguen, N. (2013). Effects of a tattoo on men's behavior and attitudes towards women: An experimental field study. *Archives of Sexual Behavior*, *42*(8), 1517–1524. http://doi.org/10.1007/s10508-013-0104-2

Gueguen, N. (2015). Women"s hairstyle and men"s behavior: A field experiment. *Scandinavian Journal of Psychology*, *56*(6), 637–640. http://doi.org/10.1111/sjop.12253

Güroğlu, B., Haselager, G. J. T., van Lieshout, C. F. M., Takashima, A., Rijpkema, M., & Fernández, G. (2008). Why are friends special? Implementing a social interaction simulation task to probe the neural correlates of friendship. *NeuroImage*, *39*(2), 903–910. http://doi.org/10.1016/j.neuroimage.2007.09.007

Guéguen, D. N. (2011). "Say it with flowers": The effect of flowers on mating attractiveness and behavior. *Social Influence*, *6*(2), 105–112. http://doi.org/10.1080/15534510.2011.561556

Ha, T., Ha, T., Overbeek, G., Overbeek, G., Engels, R. C. M. E., & Engels, R. C. M. E. (2010). Effects of attractiveness and social status on dating desire in heterosexual adolescents: an experimental study. *Archives of Sexual Behavior*, *39*(5), 1063–1071. http://doi.org/10.1007/s10508-009-9561-z

Hall, J. A., & Xing, C. (2014). The Verbal and Nonverbal Correlates of the Five Flirting Styles. *Journal of Nonverbal Behavior, 39*(1), 41–68. http://doi.org/10.1007/s10919-014-0199-8

Hall, J. A., Carter, S., Cody, M. J., & Albright, J. M. (2010). Individual Differences in the Communication of Romantic Interest: Development of the Flirting Styles Inventory. *Communication Quarterly, 58*(4), 365–393. http://doi.org/10.1080/01463373.2010.524874

Hall, J. A., Cody, M. J., Jackson, G., & Flesh, J. O. (2008). Beauty and the Flirt: Male Physical Attractiveness and Approaches to Relationship Initiation.

Hall, J. A., Xing, C., & Brooks, S. (2013). Accurately Detecting Flirting. *Communication Research, 42*(7), 939–958. http://doi.org/10.1177/0093650214534972

Harris, S., Kaplan, J. T., Curiel, A., Bookheimer, S. Y., Iacoboni, M., & Cohen, M. S. (2009). PLOS ONE: The Neural Correlates of Religious and Nonreligious Belief. *Journals.Plos.org, 4*(10), e7272. http://doi.org/10.1371/journal.pone.0007272

Haviland-Jones, J., Rosario, H. H., Wilson, P., & McGuire, T. R. (2005). An Environmental Approach to Positive Emotion: Flowers. *Evolutionary Psychology, 3*(1), 147470490500300. http://doi.org/10.1177/147470490500300109

Havlicek, J., & Roberts, S. C. (2009). MHC-correlated mate choice in humans: A review. *Psychoneuroendocrinology, 34*(4), 497–512. http://doi.org/10.1016/j.psyneuen.2008.10.007

Hämmerli, A., Schweisgut, C., & Kaegi, M. (2012). Population genetic segmentation of MHC-correlated perfume preferences. *International Journal of Cosmetic Science, 34*(2), 161–168. http://doi.org/10.1111/j.1468-2494.2011.00696.x

Hendrie, C. A., & Brewer, G. (2012). Evidence to Suggest That Teeth Act as Human Ornament Displays Signalling Mate Quality. *PloS One, 7*(7), e42178. http://doi.org/10.1371/journal.pone.0042178

Hofman, M. A., & Hofman, M. A. (2014). Evolution of the human brain: when bigger is better. *Frontiers in Neuroanatomy, 8.* http://doi.org/10.3389/fnana.2014.00015

Holmes, B. M., & Johnson, K. R. (2009). Adult attachment and romantic partner preference: A review. *Journal of Social and Personal Relationships, 26*(6-7), 833–852. http://doi.org/10.1177/0265407509345653

Hong, L., Walz, J. M., & Sajda, P. (2014). Your eyes give you away: prestimulus changes in pupil diameter correlate with poststimulus task-related EEG dynamics. *PloS One, 9*(3), e91321. http://doi.org/10.1371/journal.pone.0091321

How to Flirt Best: The Perceived Effectiveness of Flirtation Techniques - ProQuest. (2015). How to Flirt Best: The Perceived Effectiveness of Flirtation Techniques - ProQuest. *Interpersona.*

Höfel, L., Lange, M., & Jacobsen, T. (2007). Beauty and the teeth: perception of tooth color and its influence on the overall judgment of facial attractiveness. *International Journal of* ....

Hölzel, B. K., Carmody, J., Evans, K. C., Hoge, E. A., Dusek, J. A., Morgan, L., et al. (2010). Stress reduction correlates with structural changes in the amygdala. *Social Cognitive and Affective Neuroscience*, *5*(1), 11–17. http://doi.org/10.1093/scan/nsp034

Hsu, D. T., Sanford, B. J., Meyers, K. K., Love, T. M., Hazlett, K. E., Walker, S. J., et al. (2015). It still hurts: altered endogenous opioid activity in the brain during social rejection and acceptance in major depressive disorder. *Mol Psychiatry*, *20*(2), 193–200. http://doi.org/10.1038/mp.2014.185

Hughes, S. M., & Gallup, G. G., Jr. (2003). Sex differences in morphological predictors of sexual behavior. *Evolution and Human Behavior*, *24*(3), 173–178. http://doi.org/10.1016/S1090-5138(02)00149-6

Hughes, S. M., Farley, S. D., & Rhodes, B. C. (2010). Vocal and Physiological Changes in Response to the Physical Attractiveness of Conversational Partners. *Journal of Nonverbal Behavior*, *34*(3), 155–167. http://doi.org/10.1007/s10919-010-0087-9

Huynh, H. K., Willemsen, A. T. M., & Holstege, G. (2013). Female orgasm but not male ejaculation activates the pituitary. A PET-neuro-imaging study. *NeuroImage*, *76*, 178–182. http://doi.org/10.1016/j.neuroimage.2013.03.012

Jonason, P. K., Li, N. P., Webster, G. D., & Schmitt, D. P. (2009). The dark triad: Facilitating a short-term mating strategy in men. *European Journal of Personality*, *23*(1), 5–18. http://doi.org/10.1002/per.698

Jonason, P. K., Lyons, M., & Blanchard, A. (2015). Birds of a "bad" feather flock together: The Dark Triad and mate choice. *Personality and Individual Differences*, *78*, 34–38. http://doi.org/10.1016/j.paid.2015.01.018

Jones, A. L., Kramer, R. S. S., & Ward, R. (2014). Miscalibrations in judgements of attractiveness with cosmetics. *Quarterly Journal of Experimental Psychology (2006)*, *67*(10), 2060–2068. http://doi.org/10.1080/17470218.2014.908932

Jones, B. C., Hahn, A. C., Fisher, C. I., Wang, H., Kandrik, M., Han, C., et al. (2018). No Compelling Evidence that Preferences for Facial Masculinity Track Changes in Women's Hormonal Status:. *Psychological Science*, *29*(6), 996–1005. http://doi.org/10.1177/0956797618760197

Jones, B. C., Little, A. C., Burt, D. M., & Perrett, D. I. (2016). When Facial Attractiveness is Only Skin Deep. *Perception*, *33*(5), 569–576. http://doi.org/10.1068/p3463

Kanazawa, S. (2011). Intelligence and physical attractiveness☆. *Intelligence, 39*(1), 7–14. http://doi.org/10.1016/j.intell.2010.11.003

KapogiannisDimitrios, KapogiannisDimitrios, DeshpandeGopikrishna, DeshpandeGopikrishna, KruegerFrank, KruegerFrank, et al. (n.d.). Brain Networks Shaping Religious Belief. *Brain Connectivity.*

Karim, R., & Chaudhri, P. (2012). Behavioral addictions: an overview. *Journal of Psychoactive Drugs, 44*(1), 5–17. http://doi.org/10.1080/02791072.2012.662859

Karremans, J. C., Frankenhuis, W. E., & Arons, S. (2010). Blind men prefer a low waist-to-hip ratio. *Evolution and Human Behavior, 31*(3), 182–186.

Kida, T., Kida, T., Kida, T., Nishitani, S., Nishitani, S., Nishitani, S., et al. (2013). I love my grandkid! An NIRS study of grandmaternal love in Japan. *Brain Res, 1542*, 131–137. http://doi.org/10.1016/j.brainres.2013.10.028

KIRKPATRICK, L. A., & HAZAN, C. (1994). Attachment styles and close relationships: A four-year prospective study. *Personal Relationships, 1*(2), 123–142. http://doi.org/10.1111/j.1475-6811.1994.tb00058.x

Kniffin, K. M., & Wilson, D. S. (2004). The effect of nonphysical traits on the perception of physical attractiveness. *Evolution and Human Behavior, 25*(2), 88–101. http://doi.org/10.1016/S1090-5138(04)00006-6

Kniffin, K. M., Wansink, B., Griskevicius, V., & Wilson, D. S. (2014). Beauty is in the in-group of the beholded: Intergroup differences in the perceived attractiveness of leaders. *The Leadership Quarterly, 25*(6), 1143–1153. http://doi.org/10.1016/j.leaqua.2014.09.001

Kober, H., Lacadie, C. M., Wexler, B. E., Malison, R. T., Sinha, R., & Potenza, M. N. (2016). Brain Activity During Cocaine Craving and Gambling Urges: An fMRI Study. *Neuropsychopharmacology : Official Publication of the American College of Neuropsychopharmacology, 41*(2), 628–637. http://doi.org/10.1038/npp.2015.193

Koranyi, N., Gast, A., & Rothermund, K. (2012). "Although Quite Nice, I Was Somehow Not Attracted by That Person." *Social Psychological and Personality Science, 4*(4), 403–410. http://doi.org/10.1177/1948550612467037

Korichi, R., Pelle-de-Queral, D., Gazano, G., & Aubert, A. (2008). Why women use makeup: implication of psychological traits in makeup functions. *Journal of Cosmetic Science, 59*(2), 127–137.

Korichi, R., Pelle-de-Queral, D., Gazano, G., & Aubert, A. (2011). Relation between facial morphology, personality and the functions of facial make-up in women. *International Journal of Cosmetic Science, 33*(4), 338–345. http://doi.org/10.1111/j.1468-2494.2010.00632.x

Kret, M. E., Fischer, A. H., & De Dreu, C. K. W. (2015). Pupil Mimicry Correlates With Trust in In-Group Partners With Dilating Pupils. *Psychological Science*, *26*(9), 1401–1410. http://doi.org/10.1177/0956797615588306

Kret, M. E., Roelofs, K., Stekelenburg, J. J., & de Gelder, B. (2013). Emotional signals from faces, bodies and scenes influence observers' face expressions, fixations and pupil-size. *Frontiers in Human Neuroscience*, 7, 810. http://doi.org/10.3389/fnhum.2013.00810

Kringelbach, M. L., Lehtonen, A., Squire, S., Harvey, A. G., Craske, M. G., Holliday, I. E., et al. (2008). A specific and rapid neural signature for parental instinct. *PloS One*, *3*(2), e1664. http://doi.org/10.1371/journal.pone.0001664

Kross, E., Berman, M. G., Mischel, W., Smith, E. E., & Wager, T. D. (2011). Social rejection shares somatosensory representations with physical pain. *Proceedings of the National Academy of Sciences of the United States of America*, *108*(15), 6270–6275. http://doi.org/10.1073/pnas.1102693108

Kuukasjärvi, S., Eriksson, C. J. P., Koskela, E., Mappes, T., Nissinen, K., & Rantala, M. J. (2004). Attractiveness of women's body odors over the menstrual cycle: the role of oral contraceptives and receiver sex. *Behavioral Ecology*, *15*(4), 579–584. http://doi.org/10.1093/beheco/arh050

LAMBERT, N. M., MULDER, S., & FINCHAM, F. (2014). Thin slices of infidelity: Determining whether observers can pick out cheaters from a video clip interaction and what tips them off. *Personal Relationships*, *21*(4), 612–619. http://doi.org/10.1111/pere.12052

Langeslag, S. J. E., Jansma, B. M., Franken, I. H. A., & Van Strien, J. W. (2007). Event-related potential responses to love-related facial stimuli. *Biological Psychology*, *76*(1-2), 109–115. http://doi.org/10.1016/j.biopsycho.2007.06.007

Langeslag, S. J. E., van der Veen, F. M., & Fekkes, D. (2012). Blood Levels of Serotonin Are Differentially Affected by Romantic Love in Men and Women. *Journal of Psychophysiology*, *26*(2), 92–98. http://doi.org/10.1027/0269-8803/a000071

Langlois, J. H., Kalakanis, L., Rubenstein, A. J., Larson, A., Hallam, M., & Smoot, M. (2000). Maxims or myths of beauty? A meta-analytic and theoretical review. *Psychological Bulletin*, *126*(3), 390–423. http://doi.org/10.1037/0033-2909.126.3.390

Langlois, J. H., Roggman, L. A., Casey, R. J., Ritter, J. M., & et al. (1987). Infant preferences for attractive faces: Rudiments of a stereotype? *Developmental Psychology*, *23*(3), 363–369. http://doi.org/10.1037/0012-1649.23.3.363

Lanuza, E., Lanuza, E., Novejarque, A., Novejarque, A., Martínez-Ricós, J., Martínez-Ricós, J., et al. (2008). Sexual pheromones and the evolution of the reward system of the brain: The chemosensory function of the amygdala. *Brain Research Bulletin*, *75*(2-4), 460–466. http://doi.org/10.1016/j.brainresbull.2007.10.042

LASSEK, W., & GAULIN, S. (2008). Waist-hip ratio and cognitive ability: is gluteofemoral fat a privileged store of neurodevelopmental resources? *Evolution and Human Behavior*, *29*(1), 26–34. http://doi.org/10.1016/j.evolhumbehav.2007.07.005

Lawlor, D. A., Lawlor, D. A., Taylor, M., Taylor, M., Davey Smith, G., Davey Smith, G., et al. (2004). Associations of components of adult height with coronary heart disease in postmenopausal women: the British women's heart and health study. *Heart (British Cardiac Society)*, *90*(7), 745–749. http://doi.org/10.1136/hrt.2003.019950

Lennon, S. J. (1990). Effects of Clothing Attractiveness on Perceptions. *Family and Consumer Sciences Research Journal*, *18*(4), 303–310. http://doi.org/10.1177/1077727X9001800403

Leonti, M., & Casu, L. (2018). Ethnopharmacology of Love. *Frontiers in Pharmacology*, *9*, 567. http://doi.org/10.3389/fphar.2018.00567

Lick, D. J., Cortland, C. I., & Johnson, K. L. (2015). The pupils are the windows to sexuality: pupil dilation as a visual cue to others' sexual interest. *Evolution and Human Behavior*. http://doi.org/10.1016/j.evolhumbehav.2015.09.004

Lie, H. C., Simmons, L. W., & Rhodes, G. (2010). Genetic dissimilarity, genetic diversity, and mate preferences in humans. *Evolution and Human Behavior*, *31*(1), 48–58. http://doi.org/10.1016/j.evolhumbehav.2009.07.001

Liebowitz, M. R. (1984). The Chemistry of Love. Berkley.

Lopez, Y., Le Rouzic, J., Bertaud, V., & Pérard, M. (2013). Influence of teeth on the smile and physical attractiveness. A new internet based assessing method. *Open Journal of Stomatology*, *3*, 52–57. http://doi.org/10.4236/ojst.2013.31010.

Lu, J., Li, D., & Xu, J. (2012). An event-related potential study of maternal love in mothers. *Brain Topography*, *25*(4), 399–407. http://doi.org/10.1007/s10548-012-0224-3

Luby, J. L., Barch, D. M., Belden, A., Gaffrey, M. S., Tillman, R., Babb, C., et al. (2012). Maternal support in early childhood predicts larger hippocampal volumes at school age. *Proceedings of the National Academy of Sciences of the United States of America*, *109*(8), 2854–2859. http://doi.org/10.1073/pnas.1118003109

Luevano, V., Guichard, A., & Pedersen-Pennock, A. (2015). Making tradeoffs between personality and physical appearance when choosing short-term and long-term partners.

Lundström, J. N., & Jones-Gotman, M. (2009). Romantic love modulates women"s identification of men"s body odors. *Hormones and Behavior, 55*(2), 280–284. http://doi.org/10.1016/j.yhbeh.2008.11.009

Luo, S. X., & Huang, E. J. (2016). Dopaminergic Neurons and Brain Reward Pathways: From Neurogenesis to Circuit Assembly. *The American Journal of Pathology, 186*(3), 478–488. http://doi.org/10.1016/j.ajpath.2015.09.023

Lyons, M. T., Marcinkowska, U. M., Helle, S., & McGrath, L. (2015). Mirror, mirror, on the wall, who is the most masculine of them all? The Dark Triad, masculinity, and women's mate choice. *Personality and Individual Differences, 74*, 153–158. http://doi.org/10.1016/j.paid.2014.10.020

Lyons, M., & Blanchard, A. (2016). "I could see, in the depth of his eyes, my own beauty reflected": Women's assortative preference for narcissistic, but not for Machiavellian or psychopathic male faces. *Personality and Individual Differences, 97*, 40–44. http://doi.org/10.1016/j.paid.2016.03.025

MA KELLAMS, C., WANG, M. C., & CARDIEL, H. (2017). Attractiveness and relationship longevity: Beauty is not what it is cracked up to be. *Personal Relationships, 24*(1), 146–161. http://doi.org/10.1111/pere.12173

Macdonald, K. S. (2012). Sex, receptors, and attachment: a review of individual factors influencing response to oxytocin. *Frontiers in Neuroscience, 6*, 194. http://doi.org/10.3389/fnins.2012.00194

Maestripieri, D., Henry, A., & Nickels, N. (2017). Explaining financial and prosocial biases in favor of attractive people: Interdisciplinary perspectives from economics, social psychology, and evolutionary psychology. *The Behavioral and Brain Sciences, 40*, e19. http://doi.org/10.1017/S0140525X16000340

Magon, N., & Kalra, S. (2011). The orgasmic history of oxytocin: Love, lust, and labor. *Indian Journal of Endocrinology and Metabolism, 15 Suppl 3*(7), S156–61. http://doi.org/10.4103/2230-8210.84851

Marazziti, D., & Canale, D. (2004). Hormonal changes when falling in love. *Psychoneuroendocrinology, 29*(7), 931–936. http://doi.org/10.1016/j.psyneuen.2003.08.006

Marazziti, D., Akiskal, H. S., Rossi, A., & Cassano, G. B. (1999). Alteration of the platelet serotonin transporter in romantic love. *Psychological Medicine, 29*(3), 741–745.

Marcinkowska, U. M., Hahn, A. C., Little, A. C., DeBruine, L. M., & Jones, B. C. (2019a). No evidence that women using oral contraceptives have weaker preferences for masculine characteristics in men's faces. *PloS One, 14*(1), e0210162. http://doi.org/10.1371/journal.pone.0210162

Marcinkowska, U. M., Helle, S., & Lyons, M. T. (2015). Dark traits: Sometimes hot, and sometimes not? Female preferences for Dark Triad faces depend on sociosexuality and contraceptive use. *Personality and Individual Differences, 86,* 369–373. http://doi.org/10.1016/j.paid.2015.06.030

Marcinkowska, U. M., Lyons, M. T., & Helle, S. (2016). Women"s reproductive success and the preference for Dark Triad in men"s faces. *Evolution and Human Behavior.* http://doi.org/10.1016/j.evolhumbehav.2016.01.004

Marcinkowska, U. M., Rantala, M. J., Lee, A. J., Kozlov, M. V., Aavik, T., Cai, H., et al. (2019b). Women"s preferences for men"s facial masculinity are strongest under favorable ecological conditions. *Scientific Reports, 9*(1), 3387–10. http://doi.org/10.1038/s41598-019-39350-8

Marin, M. M., Schober, R., Gingras, B., & Leder, H. (2017). Misattribution of musical arousal increases sexual attraction towards opposite-sex faces in females. *PloS One, 12*(9), e0183531. http://doi.org/10.1371/journal.pone.0183531

Mayne, B., Berry, O., Davies, C., Farley, J., & Jarman, S. (2019). A genomic predictor of lifespan in vertebrates. *Scientific Reports, 9*(1), 17866–10. http://doi.org/10.1038/s41598-019-54447-w

McCormick, N. B., & Jones, A. J. (2015). Gender Differences in Nonverbal Flirtation. *Journal of Sex Education and Therapy, 15*(4), 271–282. http://doi.org/10.1080/01614576.1989.11074969

Mehta, P. H., & Beer, J. (2010). Neural mechanisms of the testosterone-aggression relation: the role of orbitofrontal cortex. *Journal of Cognitive Neuroscience, 22*(10), 2357–2368. http://doi.org/10.1162/jocn.2009.21389

Meston, C. M., & Frohlich, P. F. (2003). Love at first fright: partner salience moderates roller-coaster-induced excitation transfer. *Archives of Sexual Behavior, 32*(6), 537–544.

Milinski, M. (2001). Evidence for MHC-correlated perfume preferences in humans. *Behavioral Ecology, 12*(2), 140–149. http://doi.org/10.1093/beheco/12.2.140

Montoya, R. M., Kershaw, C., & Prosser, J. L. (2018). A meta-analytic investigation of the relation between interpersonal attraction and enacted behavior. *Psychological Bulletin, 144*(7), 673–709. http://doi.org/10.1037/bul0000148

Moore, M. M. (2010). Human Nonverbal Courtship Behavior—A Brief Historical Review. *Journal of Sex Research, 47*(2-3), 171–180. http://doi.org/10.1080/00224490903402520

Mostafa, T., Khouly, G. E., & Hassan, A. (2012). Pheromones in sex and reproduction: Do they have a role in humans? *Journal of Advanced Research, 3*(1), 1–9. http://doi.org/10.1016/j.jare.2011.03.003

Mulhern, R., Fieldman, G., Hussey, T., Lévêque, J.-L., & Pineau, P. (2003). Do cosmetics enhance female Caucasian facial attractiveness? *International Journal of*

Cosmetic Science, 25(4), 199–205. http://doi.org/10.1046/j.1467-2494.2003.00188.x

Muñoz-Reyes, J. A., Iglesias-Julios, M., Pita, M., & Turiegano, E. (2015). Facial Features: What Women Perceive as Attractive and What Men Consider Attractive. *PloS One, 10*(7), e0132979. http://doi.org/10.1371/journal.pone.0132979

Murray, D. R., Haselton, M. G., Fales, M., & Cole, S. W. (2019). Falling in love is associated with immune system gene regulation. *Psychoneuroendocrinology, 100*, 120–126. http://doi.org/10.1016/j.psyneuen.2018.09.043

Muscarella, F., & Cunningham, M. R. (1996). The evolutionary significance and social perception of male pattern baldness and facial hair. *Ethology and Sociobiology, 17*(2), 99–117. http://doi.org/10.1016/0162-3095(95)00130-1

Nash, R., Fieldman, G., Hussey, T., Lévêque, J.-L., & Pineau, P. (2006). Cosmetics: They Influence More Than Caucasian Female Facial Attractiveness. *Journal of Applied Social Psychology, 36*(2), 493–504. http://doi.org/10.1111/j.0021-9029.2006.00016.x

Neave, N., & Shields, K. (2008). The effects of facial hair manipulation on female perceptions of attractiveness, masculinity, and dominance in male faces. *Personality and Individual Differences, 45*(5), 373–377. http://doi.org/10.1016/j.paid.2008.05.007

Nettle, D. (2002). Women's height, reproductive success and the evolution of sexual dimorphism in modern humans. *Proceedings of the Royal Society of London B: Biological Sciences, 269*(1503), 1919–1923. http://doi.org/10.1098/rspb.2002.2111

Newberg, A. B. (2014). The neuroscientific study of spiritual practices. *Frontiers in Psychology, 5.* http://doi.org/10.3389/fpsyg.2014.00215

Nisbett, R. E., social, T. W. J. O. P. A., 1977. (n.d.). The halo effect: evidence for unconscious alteration of judgments. *Psycnet.Apa.org*

Noriuchi, M., Kikuchi, Y., & Senoo, A. (2008). The functional neuroanatomy of maternal love: mother"s response to infant"s attachment behaviors. *Biological Psychiatry, 63*(4), 415–423. http://doi.org/10.1016/j.biopsych.2007.05.018

O'Connor, M.-F., Wellisch, D. K., Stanton, A. L., Eisenberger, N. I., Irwin, M. R., & Lieberman, M. D. (2008). Craving love? Enduring grief activates brain's reward center. *NeuroImage, 42*(2), 969–972. http://doi.org/10.1016/j.neuroimage.2008.04.256

O'Doherty, J., Winston, J., Critchley, H., Perrett, D., Burt, D. M., & Dolan, R. J. (2003). Beauty in a smile: the role of medial orbitofrontal cortex in facial attractiveness. *Neuropsychologia, 41*(2), 147–155.

Ogolsky, B. G., & Bowers, J. R. (2012). A meta-analytic review of relationship maintenance and its correlates. *Journal of Social and Personal Relationships, 30*(3), 343–367. http://doi.org/10.1177/0265407512463338

Orghian, D., & Hidalgo, C. A. (2020). Humans judge faces in incomplete photographs as physically more attractive. *Scientific Reports, 10*(1), 110–12. http://doi.org/10.1038/s41598-019-56437-4

O'Connor, J. J. M., Pisanski, K., Tigue, C. C., Fraccaro, P. J., & Feinberg, D. R. (2014). Perceptions of infidelity risk predict women's preferences for low male voice pitch in short-term over long-term relationship contexts. *Personality and Individual Differences, 56*, 73–77. http://doi.org/10.1016/j.paid.2013.08.029

Pascual, L., Rodrigues, P., & Gallardo-Pujol, D. (2013). How does morality work in the brain? A functional and structural perspective of moral behavior. *Frontiers in Integrative Neuroscience, 7*, 65. http://doi.org/10.3389/fnint.2013.00065

Paunonen, S. V. (2006). You are honest, therefore I like you and find you attractive. *Journal of Research in Personality, 40*(3), 237–249. http://doi.org/10.1016/j.jrp.2004.12.003

Pawlowski, B., & Jasienska, G. (2005). Women's preferences for sexual dimorphism in height depend on menstrual cycle phase and expected duration of relationship. *Biological Psychology, 70*(1), 38–43. http://doi.org/10.1016/j.biopsycho.2005.02.002

Pazhoohi, F., Hosseinchari, M., & Doyle, J. F. (2012). Iranian men's waist-to-hip ratios, shoulder-to-hip ratios, body esteem and self-efficacy. *Journal of Evolutionary Psychology, 10*(2), 61–67. http://doi.org/10.1556/JEP.10.2012.2.2

Perilloux, C., & Buss, D. M. (2008). Breaking up Romantic Relationships: Costs Experienced and Coping Strategies Deployed:. *Evolutionary Psychology, 6*(1), 147470490800600. http://doi.org/10.1177/147470490800600119

Phelps, E. A. (2004). Human emotion and memory: interactions of the amygdala and hippocampal complex. *Current Opinion in Neurobiology, 14*(2), 198–202. http://doi.org/10.1016/j.conb.2004.03.015

Platek, S. M., & Singh, D. (2010). Optimal waist-to-hip ratios in women activate neural reward centers in men. *PloS One, 5*(2), e9042. http://doi.org/10.1371/journal.pone.0009042

Porcheron, A., Mauger, E., & Russell, R. (2013). Aspects of facial contrast decrease with age and are cues for age perception. *PloS One, 8*(3), e57985. http://doi.org/10.1371/journal.pone.0057985

Porcheron, A., Mauger, E., Soppelsa, F., Liu, Y., Ge, L., Pascalis, O., et al. (2017). Facial Contrast Is a Cross-Cultural Cue for Perceiving Age. *Frontiers in Psychology, 8*, 1208. http://doi.org/10.3389/fpsyg.2017.01208

Preckel, K., Scheele, D., Kendrick, K. M., Maier, W., & Hurlemann, R. (2014). Oxytocin facilitates social approach behavior in women. *Frontiers in Behavioral Neuroscience, 8*(185), 191. http://doi.org/10.3389/fnbeh.2014.00191

Puts, D. A., & Puts, D. A. (2010). Beauty and the beast: Mechanisms of sexual selection in humans. *Evolution and Human Behavior, 31*(3), 157–175.

Quintero, G. C. (2013). Role of nucleus accumbens glutamatergic plasticity in drug addiction. *Neuropsychiatric Disease and Treatment, 9,* 1499–1512. http://doi.org/10.2147/NDT.S45963

Qureshi, C., Harris, E., & Atkinson, B. E. (2016). Relationships between age of females and attraction to the Dark Triad personality. *Personality and Individual Differences, 95,* 200–203. http://doi.org/10.1016/j.paid.2016.02.047

Rahaman, H. M. S. (2015). Romantic Relationship Length and its Perceived Quality: Mediating Role of Facebook-Related Conflict. *Europe's Journal of Psychology, 11*(3), 395–405. http://doi.org/10.5964/ejop.v11i3.932

Ranaldi, R. (2014). Dopamine and reward seeking: the role of ventral tegmental area. *Reviews in the Neurosciences, 25*(5), 621–630. http://doi.org/10.1515/revneuro-2014-0019

Renninger, L. A., Wade, T. J., & Grammer, K. (2004). Getting that female glance. *Evolution and Human Behavior, 25*(6), 416–431. http://doi.org/10.1016/j.evolhumbehav.2004.08.006

Restrepo, D., Lin, W., Salcedo, E., Yamazaki, K., & Beauchamp, G. (2006). Odortypes and MHC peptides: Complementary chemosignals of MHC haplotype? *Trends in Neurosciences, 29*(11), 604–609. http://doi.org/10.1016/j.tins.2006.08.001

Ricciardi, E., Rota, G., Sani, L., Gentili, C., Gaglianese, A., Guazzelli, M., & Pietrini, P. (2013). How the brain heals emotional wounds: the functional neuroanatomy of forgiveness. *Frontiers in Human Neuroscience, 7,* 839. http://doi.org/10.3389/fnhum.2013.00839

Ridgway, J. L., & Clayton, R. B. (2016). Instagram Unfiltered: Exploring Associations of Body Image Satisfaction, Instagram #Selfie Posting, and Negative Romantic Relationship Outcomes. *Cyberpsychology, Behavior and Social Networking, 19*(1), 2–7. http://doi.org/10.1089/cyber.2015.0433

Roberts, S. C., Owen, R. C., & Havlicek, J. (2010). Distinguishing between Perceiver and Wearer Effects in Clothing Color-Associated Attributions. *Evolutionary Psychology, 8*(3), 147470491000800. http://doi.org/10.1177/147470491000800304

Rosier, J. G., & Munz, E. A. (2015). Attachment and Relationships (1st ed., pp. 1–5). Wiley. http://doi.org/10.1002/9781118540190.wbeic163

Rotheneichner, P., Lange, S., O'Sullivan, A., Marschallinger, J., Zaunmair, P., Geretsegger, C., et al. (2014). Hippocampal neurogenesis and antidepressive therapy: shocking relations. *Neural Plasticity*, *2014*(11), 723915–14. http://doi.org/10.1155/2014/723915

Roy, M., Shohamy, D., & Wager, T. D. (2012). Ventromedial prefrontal-subcortical systems and the generation of affective meaning. *Trends in Cognitive Sciences*, *16*(3), 147–156. http://doi.org/10.1016/j.tics.2012.01.005

Russell, R. (2009). A sex difference in facial contrast and its exaggeration by cosmetics. *Perception*, *38*(8), 1211–1219.

Sacks, O., & Hirsch, J. (2008). A neurology of belief. *Ann Neurol*, *63*(2), 129–130. http://doi.org/10.1002/ana.21378

Salgado, S., & Kaplitt, M. G. (2015). The Nucleus Accumbens: A Comprehensive Review. *Stereotactic and Functional Neurosurgery*, *93*(2), 75–93. http://doi.org/10.1159/000368279

SANDROCARVALHOSANTOS, P., AUGUSTOSCHINEMANN, J., GABARDO, J., & DAGRACABICALHO, M. (2005). New evidence that the MHC influences odor perception in humans: a study with 58 Southern Brazilian students. *Hormones and Behavior*, *47*(4), 384–388. http://doi.org/10.1016/j.yhbeh.2004.11.005

Saunders, B. T., & Richard, J. M. (2011). Shedding light on the role of ventral tegmental area dopamine in reward. *The Journal of Neuroscience : the Official Journal of the Society for Neuroscience*, *31*(50), 18195–18197. http://doi.org/10.1523/JNEUROSCI.4924-11.2011

Saxton, T. K., Mackey, L. L., McCarty, K., & Neave, N. (2016). A lover or a fighter? Opposing sexual selection pressures on men's vocal pitch and facial hair. *Behavioral Ecology*, *27*(2), 512–519. http://doi.org/10.1093/beheco/arv178

Scheele, D., Striepens, N., Güntürkün, O., Deutschländer, S., Maier, W., Kendrick, K. M., & Hurlemann, R. (2012). Oxytocin modulates social distance between males and females. *The Journal of Neuroscience : the Official Journal of the Society for Neuroscience*, *32*(46), 16074–16079. http://doi.org/10.1523/JNEUROSCI.2755-12.2012

Scheele, D., Wille, A., Kendrick, K. M., Stoffel-Wagner, B., Becker, B., Güntürkün, O., et al. (2013). Oxytocin enhances brain reward system responses in men viewing the face of their female partner. *Proceedings of the National Academy of Sciences of the United States of America*, *110*(50), 20308–20313. http://doi.org/10.1073/pnas.1314190110

Schild, C., Stern, J., Penke, L., & Zettler, I. (2020). Voice Pitch – A Valid Indicator of One's Unfaithfulness in Committed Relationships? *Adaptive Human Behavior and Physiology*, *3*(6), 682–16. http://doi.org/10.1007/s40750-020-00154-0

Schjødt, U., Schjødt, U., Stødkilde-Jørgensen, H., Stødkilde-Jørgensen, H., Geertz, A. W., Geertz, A. W., et al. (2008). Rewarding prayers. *Neuroscience Letters*, *443*(3), 165–168. http://doi.org/10.1016/j.neulet.2008.07.068

Schneiderman, I., Zagoory-Sharon, O., Leckman, J. F., & Feldman, R. (2012). Oxytocin during the initial stages of romantic attachment: relations to couples' interactive reciprocity. *Psychoneuroendocrinology*, *37*(8), 1277–1285. http://doi.org/10.1016/j.psyneuen.2011.12.021

Schoenthaler, S. J., Blum, K., Braverman, E. R., Giordano, J., Thompson, B., Oscar-Berman, M., et al. (2015). NIDA-Drug Addiction Treatment Outcome Study (DATOS) Relapse as a Function of Spirituality/Religiosity. *Journal of Reward Deficiency Syndrome*, *1*(1), 36–45. http://doi.org/10.17756/jrds.2015-007

Sciara, S., & Pantaleo, G. (2017). Relationships at risk: How the perceived risk of ending a romantic relationship influences the intensity of romantic affect and relationship commitment. *Motivation and Emotion*, *51*, 1173–12. http://doi.org/10.1007/s11031-017-9650-6

Shohat-Ophir, G., Kaun, K. R., Azanchi, R., Mohammed, H., & Heberlein, U. (2012). Sexual deprivation increases ethanol intake in Drosophila. *Science*, *335*(6074), 1351–1355. http://doi.org/10.1126/science.1215932

Shoup-Knox, M. L., & Nathan Pipitone, R. (2015). Physiological changes in response to hearing female voices recorded at high fertility. *Physiology & Behavior*, *139*, 386–392. http://doi.org/10.1016/j.physbeh.2014.11.028

Singh, D. (1995). Female judgment of male attractiveness and desirability for relationships: role of waist-to-hip ratio and financial status. *Journal of Personality and Social Psychology*, *69*(6), 1089–1101.

Singh, D., Singh, D., Dixson, B. J., Dixson, B. J., Jessop, T. S., Jessop, T. S., et al. (2010). Cross-cultural consensus for waist–hip ratio and women's attractiveness. *Evolution and Human Behavior*, *31*(3), 176–181.

Skoda, K., Oswald, F., Brown, K., Hesse, C., & Pedersen, C. L. (2020). Showing Skin: Tattoo Visibility Status, Egalitarianism, and Personality are Predictors of Sexual Openness Among Women. *Sexuality & Culture*, *39*(4), 190. http://doi.org/10.1007/s12119-020-09729-1

Smith, G. D., Smith, G. D., Greenwood, R., Greenwood, R., Gunnell, D., Sweetnam, P., et al. (2001). Leg length, insulin resistance, and coronary heart disease risk: the Caerphilly Study. *Journal of Epidemiology and Community Health*, *55*(12), 867–872.

Smith, R. M. (2018). The Biology of Beauty. Greenwood.

Soller, B. (2014). Caught in a bad romance: adolescent romantic relationships and mental health. *Journal of Health and Social Behavior*, *55*(1), 56–72. http://doi.org/10.1177/0022146513520432

Song, H., Song, H., Zou, Z., Zou, Z., Kou, J., Kou, J., et al. (2015). Love-related changes in the brain: a resting-state functional magnetic resonance imaging study. *Frontiers in Human Neuroscience*, *9*(13), 59. http://doi.org/10.3389/fnhum.2015.00071

Sorokowski, P., Sorokowski, P., Pawlowski, B., & Pawlowski, B. (2007). Adaptive preferences for leg length in a potential partner. *Evolution and Human Behavior*, *29*(2), 86–91. http://doi.org/10.1016/j.evolhumbehav.2007.09.002

Stalnaker, T. A., Cooch, N. K., & Schoenbaum, G. (2015). What the orbitofrontal cortex does not do. *Nature Neuroscience*, *18*(5), 620–627. http://doi.org/10.1038/nn.3982

Stefan, J., & Gueguen, N. (2014). Effect of hair ornamentation on helping. *Psychological Reports*, *114*(2), 491–495. http://doi.org/10.2466/21.17.PR0.114k18w8

Stephen, I. D., & McKeegan, A. M. (2010). Lip colour affects perceived sex typicality and attractiveness of human faces. *Perception*, *39*(8), 1104–1110.

Stephen, I. D., Coetzee, V., & Perrett, D. I. (2011). Carotenoid and melanin pigment coloration affect perceived human health. *Evolution and Human Behavior*, *32*(3), 216–227. http://doi.org/10.1016/j.evolhumbehav.2010.09.003

Stephen, I. D., Coetzee, V., Smith, M. L., & Perrett, D. I. (2009). Skin Blood Perfusion and Oxygenation Colour Affect Perceived Human Health. *PloS One*, *4*(4), e5083. http://doi.org/10.1371/journal.pone.0005083

Sussman, S. (2010). Love Addiction: Definition, Etiology, Treatment. *Sexual Addiction & Compulsivity*, *17*(1), 31–45. http://doi.org/10.1080/10720161003604095

Sussman, S., Reynaud, M., Aubin, H.-J., & Leventhal, A. M. (n.d.). Drug Addiction, Love, and the Higher Power. *Ehp.Sagepub.com*.

Sümer, N., Dergisi, D. G. T. P., 1999. (n.d.). Yetişkin bağlanma stilleri ölçeklerinin Türk örneklemi üzerinde psikometrik değerlendirmesi ve kültürlerarası bir karşılaştırma. *Nebisumer.com*

Swami, V., & Furnham, A. (2009). Big and beautiful: attractiveness and health ratings of the female body by male "fat admirers". *Archives of Sexual Behavior*, *38*(2), 201–208. http://doi.org/10.1007/s10508-007-9200-5

Swami, V., Einon, D., & Furnham, A. (2006). The leg-to-body ratio as a human aesthetic criterion. *Body Image*, *3*(4), 317–323. http://doi.org/10.1016/j.bodyim.2006.08.003

Swami, V., Furnham, A., & JOSHI, K. (2008). The influence of skin tone, hair length, and hair colour on ratings of women's physical attractiveness, health and fertility. *Scandinavian Journal of Psychology*, *49*(5), 429–437. http://doi.org/10.1111/j.1467-9450.2008.00651.x

Takahashi, K., Mizuno, K., Sasaki, A. T., Wada, Y., Tanaka, M., Ishii, A., et al. (2015). Imaging the passionate stage of romantic love by dopamine dynamics. *Frontiers in Human Neuroscience*, *9*, 191. http://doi.org/10.3389/fnhum.2015.00191

Talamas, S. N., Mavor, K. I., & Perrett, D. I. (2016). The influence of intelligence on the endorsement of the intelligence–attractiveness halo. *Personality and Individual Differences*, *95*, 162–167. http://doi.org/10.1016/j.paid.2016.02.053

Tatarunaite, E., Playle, R., Hood, K., Shaw, W., & Richmond, S. (2005). Facial attractiveness: A longitudinal study. *American Journal of Orthodontics and Dentofacial Orthopedics*, *127*(6), 676–682. http://doi.org/10.1016/j.ajodo.2004.01.029

Thornhill, R. (2003). Major histocompatibility complex genes, symmetry, and body scent attractiveness in men and women. *Behavioral Ecology*, *14*(5), 668–678. http://doi.org/10.1093/beheco/arg043

Tiedt, H. O., Beier, K. M., Lueschow, A., Pauls, A., & Weber, J. E. (2014). A different pattern of lateralised brain activity during processing of loved faces in men and women: a MEG study. *Biological Psychology*, *103*, 255–261. http://doi.org/10.1016/j.biopsycho.2014.09.014

Tornquist, M., & Chiappe, D. (2015). Effects of Humor Production, Humor Receptivity, and Physical Attractiveness on Partner Desirability. *Evolutionary Psychology*, *13*(4), 1474704915608744. http://doi.org/10.1177/1474704915608744

Tottenham, N., Hare, T. A., Quinn, B. T., McCarry, T. W., Nurse, M., Gilhooly, T., et al. (2010). Prolonged institutional rearing is associated with atypically large amygdala volume and difficulties in emotion regulation. *Developmental Science*, *13*(1), 46–61. http://doi.org/10.1111/j.1467-7687.2009.00852.x

Tsukahara, J. S., Harrison, T. L., & Engle, R. W. (2016). The relationship between baseline pupil size and intelligence. *Cognitive Psychology*, *91*, 109–123. http://doi.org/10.1016/j.cogpsych.2016.10.001

Tsukiura, T., & Cabeza, R. (2011). Shared brain activity for aesthetic and moral judgments: implications for the Beauty-is-Good stereotype. *Social Cognitive and Affective Neuroscience*, *6*(1), 138–148. http://doi.org/10.1093/scan/nsq025

Tsukiura, T., Tsukiura, T., Cabeza, R., & Cabeza, R. (2011). Remembering beauty: roles of orbitofrontal and hippocampal regions in successful memory encoding of attractive faces. *NeuroImage*, *54*(1), 653–660. http://doi.org/10.1016/j.neuroimage.2010.07.046

Ueno, A., Ueno, A., Ito, A., Ito, A., Kawasaki, I., Kawasaki, I., et al. (2014). Neural activity associated with enhanced facial attractiveness by cosmetics use. *Neuroscience Letters*, *566*, 142–146. http://doi.org/10.1016/j.neulet.2014.02.047

Vacharkulksemsuk, T., Reit, E., Khambatta, P., Eastwick, P. W., Finkel, E. J., & Carney, D. R. (2016). Dominant, open nonverbal displays are attractive at zero-acquaintance. *Proceedings of the National Academy of Sciences*, 201508932. http://doi.org/10.1073/pnas.1508932113

Versluys, T. M. M., Foley, R. A., & Skylark, W. J. (2018). The influence of leg-to-body ratio, arm-to-body ratio and intra-limb ratio on male human attractiveness. *Royal Society Open Science*, 5(5), 171790. http://doi.org/10.1098/rsos.171790

Walker, D., & Vul, E. (2014). Hierarchical encoding makes individuals in a group seem more attractive. *Psychological Science*, 25(1), 230–235. http://doi.org/10.1177/0956797613497969

Wallis, J. D., & Kennerley, S. W. (2011). Contrasting reward signals in the orbitofrontal cortex and anterior cingulate cortex. *Annals of the New York Academy of Sciences*, 1239(1), 33–42. http://doi.org/10.1111/j.1749-6632.2011.06277.x

Wang, T., Wang, T., Mo, L., Mo, L., Mo, C., Mo, C., et al. (2014). Is moral beauty different from facial beauty? Evidence from an fMRI study. *Social Cognitive and Affective Neuroscience*, 10(6), 814–823. http://doi.org/10.1093/scan/nsu123

Zhang, Y., Kong, F., Zhong, Y., & Kou, H. (2014). Personality manipulations: Do they modulate facial attractiveness ratings? *Personality and Individual Differences*, 70, 80–84. http://doi.org/10.1016/j.paid.2014.06.033

Ziegler, A., Ziegler, A., Kentenich, H., Kentenich, H., Uchanska-Ziegler, B., & Uchanska-Ziegler, B. (2005). Female choice and the MHC. *Trends in Immunology*, 26(9), 496–502. http://doi.org/10.1016/j.it.2005.07.003

https://ncadv.org/STATISTICS (15/11/2020)

http://www.tuik.gov.tr (15/11/2020)

https://www.sfgate.com/news/article/Central-Park-Zoo-s-gay-penguins-ignite-debate-2825165.php (15/11/2020)

https://www.newscientist.com/article/dn19118-why-men-are-attracted-to-women-with-small-feet/ (15/11/2020)

Photographs: Shutterstock